D1281868

Red Tempest
The Life of a Surgeon in the Gulag

A young Jewish surgeon at the university hospital in Lwow, Eastern Poland (the present Western Ukraine), Isaac Vogelfanger joined the Red Army after Hitler attacked Russia in 1941, believing it would be the safest haven from the Nazi threat. He was assigned to a major military hospital in Northern Ural as chief surgeon, a prestigious position. But his life changed radically when he was suddenly arrested, convicted as an enemy of the Soviet Union, and sentenced to eight years in a gulag for crimes he did not commit. During the years he spent in prison camps Vogelfanger witnessed Stalin's mass death factory first hand. Many inmates died within a few weeks of arriving from hard labour, starvation, and cold.

Vogelfanger's account is full of pain and suffering, both his own and that of his fellow prisoners, but his story is suffused with love and admiration for the Russian people who risked their lives to help him from no other motives than genuine goodness. *Red Tempest* is a moving testament to the strength of the human spirit and humanity in the face of death and despair.

ISAAC J. VOGELFANGER is emeritus professor of surgery, University of Ottawa.

Red Tempest

The Life of a Surgeon in the Gulag

Isaac J. Vogelfanger

McGill-Queen's University Press
Montreal & Kingston • London • Buffalo

© McGill-Queen's University Press 1996
ISBN 0-7735-1404-X

Legal deposit third quarter 1996
Bibliothèque nationale du Québec

Printed in Canada on acid-free paper

This book has been published with the help of a grant
from the Department of Canadian Heritage,
Multiculturalism Programs.

McGill-Queen's University Press is grateful to the
Canada Council for support of its publishing program.

Canadian Cataloguing in Publication Program

Vogelfanger, Isaac J. (Isaac Joel), 1909–
Red tempest : the life of a surgeon in the Gulag
ISBN 0-7735-1404-X
1. Vogelfanger, Isaac J. (Isaac Joel), 1909–
2. Political prisoners – Soviet Union – Biography.
3. Concentration camps – Soviet Union. 4. World War,
1939–1945 – Personal narratives, Polish. 5. World War,
1939–1945 – Concentration camps – Soviet Union.
I. Title.
HV9712.5.V64A3 1996   365'.45'092   C96-900028-6

Typeset in Palatino 10.5/13
by Caractéra inc., Quebec City

To my wife, Alina

Contents

Acknowledgments

I would like to acknowledge the work of Mr Daniel Woolford on the first draft of the manuscript. I also thank Mr Tim Wynne-Jones for his assessment of this book as an important document and express thanks to Ruth Latta for assisting me with the final version.

In this book, most of the names of the prisoners are authentic. All the names of officials have been changed.

Introduction

The cracks that appeared in the social and political structure of the Soviet Union in recent years eventually resulted in the liberation of its enslaved population. For almost half a century, I have harboured the story of my experiences in NKVD prisons and Gulags in the Soviet Union during the days of Stalin's terror without sharing it publicly. I finally decided to write of these experiences for two reasons. To the best of my knowledge, until the present only some Russian and a few Polish authors have published material describing the atrocities that took place behind the Iron Curtain; no citizen of a Western democracy that respects individual freedom has provided such an account.

On a more personal note, the prolonged inner growth that I have gone through in the intervening years has freed my experiences of their original emotional intensity. Past events fall into perspective when viewed through the binoculars of the present. Pain and pleasure, suffering and elation, despair and hope – all become part of a more neutral emotional landscape in the memory of the survivor. The further we are from events, the less biased our memory becomes, thanks to the healing power of time. Events are recalled in a more dispassionate form, which may be more credible and acceptable to a reader who has not been exposed to the cruelties and vicissitudes of life without freedom.

Thus motivated, I set out to re-examine the period during which I was tossed about by world events like a leaf in the wind. I bear the marks of my struggles and like to think that they have left me, not embittered, but more understanding and forgiving. With Glasnost and Perestroika, Westerners have a renewed curiosity about the Confederation of Independent States and its people. Citizens of the democratic West can now travel behind what was once the Iron Curtain. I hope that my account will not only help Westerners better understand a cruel period of history in the former USSR but will also give them a sense of the warmth and generosity of the Russian people.

Arrest

I sat in the palm of a huge hand the size of a football field. I was tiny in comparison. Turning my eyes upwards, I saw the face of the giant to whom the hand belonged. His face was huge, its expression savage. The eyes were like large balloons, looking at me with hatred. I was terrified. At any moment the giant could squeeze me, just like that, into a tiny flat stain. The fingers of the hand holding me began to close and I was in mortal fear, expecting the end. At that moment a white bird, larger than an eagle, gently picked me up in its beak and flew away, carrying me high over land and mountains. It was an exhilarating feeling. The eagle began to circle around a beautiful valley and with great care set me down on the green grass. The bird disappeared and I noticed behind me a rocky mountain. In the distance I could see huge boulders rolling down, producing a rumble like hard knocking ...

Suddenly excited by the dream, I awoke, but the rumbling did not cease. Someone was knocking vehemently at my door. My watch read 3:00 A.M. It was still dark outside. Who could it be at this time of night? Maybe an emergency had arisen in the hospital and I was being called by mistake – as a rule the hospital would first call a younger doctor, not the chief surgeon.

I jumped out of bed and opened the door. Two young soldiers rushed in. They wore blue caps and the uniform of the NKVD, the

National Commissariat of Internal Affairs (later converted into the Commissariat of Government Security, or the KGB).

"You are under arrest," said one of the soldiers in a loud voice. "Get dressed fast and come with us."

Still half asleep, I didn't fully understand him.

"It must be a mistake. I am Igor Morovitch Vogelfanger. I am the chief surgeon at the military hospital. I've done nothing wrong. I've never even been in a court of law."

"We don't know anything about that."

"But I'm not a thief or a robber or a murderer."

"We have our orders. Just get dressed and come with us. You will find out everything there. Bring warm things and whatever you feel is important with you, because you will not return to this place."

I stopped arguing and got dressed, shaken and surprised. Why was this happening? After the initial shock, I became convinced that it must all be a mistake. What else could it be? They would check into things, clear everything up, apologize, and let me go. How could it be otherwise?

Outside it was still dark. A northern Ural wind was blowing, penetrating to the bone. It was dark in the car. After a short drive we stopped before a small building. Outside, a tiny bulb threw a faint light onto the heavy wooden door. The two soldiers guided me through the entrance and along endless corridors. They handed me over to another soldier, who signed for me as though I were a package being delivered. He was older, with a thin, benign face. Silently he shook his head from side to side in an expression of astonishment. Did he know me? Was he aware of who I was? I didn't ask. Probably none of them knew. After a while, his bewildered amazement entered my resisting consciousness, filling me with the resolve to accept, at least for the moment, the inevitable.

"Take off your belt and hand it to me. Those are regulations."

I followed his order without comment. The soldier led me through a little anteroom to my cell. It was a long, narrow space; the floor was about fifteen feet by six feet and the ceiling about fourteen feet high. At the end of the long wall was a large window protected by iron bars. Heavy metal sheets covered it from the outside, leaving only a small upper part of the window open. Perhaps that would allow some light to come into the cell during the day. All the glass in the window was broken. The only furniture in the cell was a bare wooden cot.

I sat on the cot and tried to gather my thoughts, tried to understand what had happened and why. In those early days I was still unaware of the strange things that happened to innocent people in the USSR during Stalin's terror.

I was the chief surgeon of Evacuation Hospital 2537 in Asbest, Swerdlowsk County, in Northern Ural. With 1,000 beds in my charge, I was in very good standing, returning a larger percentage of soldiers to the front than any other military hospital. I had published articles in the scientific medical journal of the district. General Lazerew, the head of the Sanitary Department of the Ural Military District, considered me one of the best military surgeons in the area. General Lazerew was a huge, bearlike man with a heart of gold. Whenever I came with a report to his office in Swerdlowsk, he would greet me with a smiling face, grab me as though I were a toy, sit me on his desk, and ask, "*Czto nowoho dietina?*" ("And what is new, my child?").

But at the time of my arrest, my position and high standing were of no help to me; the medal of a "Hero of the Soviet Union," the highest military distinction, would not have freed me from the clutches of the NKVD. Even Tupelow,* the famous and much-decorated aviation engineer, still got arrested from time to time because he did not take care but spoke his mind freely.

But in those days I was naive; all I could do was wonder why.

My thoughts were interrupted as my body started shivering in the bitter cold. With great difficulty, I pressed my lower jaw up to try to stop the chattering of my teeth; I couldn't. I curled up on the floor like a snail; it didn't help. No matter what position I assumed, I could not stop shivering. It was the fifth of February and probably minus sixty degrees Fahrenheit outside. The temperature in my cell was not much warmer. I couldn't imagine what it would be like to die enclosed in a deep freezer. It was very frightening. After a while, I started to have severe and painful

---

* Andrey Nikolayevich Tupelow (1888–1972) was first arrested in 1936 on a charge of selling secrets to the Germans. While under arrest he was put in charge of a team designing military aircraft. He was freed in 1943 and given the Stalin Prize for his work, which, among other things, led to the development of the Tu-144, the world's first supersonic passenger plane, under Tupelow's son Alexey, in the early 1960s.

cramps in my calves, then in my thighs. It dawned on me that
when the cramps reached the muscles of my chest, I would stop
breathing and that would be the end.

Maybe by will I could overcome the pain and suffering, could
endure and survive. The other alternative was to give in completely, sink out of reach of the five senses, and succumb. To do
this, I had to reach a realm of nonattachment and then I could
enter a different world, free of pain. All torment results from
attachment.

Whoever wanted me here, would he like to kill me in this way?
It would be very unsatisfactory for him. He wouldn't even have
the pleasure of seeing me suffer. If I properly understood my
thoughts, I seemed to believe that I had some chance of surviving.
With great difficulty I crawled to the door and knocked violently.
After a long while, the door was opened by the thin soldier.

"Looks like you softies aren't used to this cool air. Come over
here and warm up."

In the small anteroom a little iron stove was burning. I
crawled over and breathed the warm air. A feeling of great
delight filled my mind as my body began to come alive. But my
joy was short-lived; the guard explained that he would face
severe consequences if anybody found out what he was doing.
I was taken back to the cell, where I began to freeze again. When
the cramps in my legs became severe, I banged on the door and
the guard again allowed me to warm myself briefly at the stove.
The night passed. I did not sleep at all. Close to noon, when it
got a little warmer, I felt very sleepy, but still the cramps kept
me awake.

They had arrested me on a Friday night. I had been in this cold
place the rest of that night, all day Saturday, and all day Sunday.
By Monday morning I had begun to feel very weak. I hadn't slept
or eaten all this time, except for some *kipiatok* (hot water) that the
old soldier offered me during my periods at the stove.

On Monday morning I was called to the *natchalnik* (chief) for
interrogation. Passing through a long corridor with the guard, I
caught sight of my face in a small mirror. It was not my face. It
was a dark cyanotic color, with sunken eyes, swollen eyelids,
hollow depressed cheeks, and an elongated chin. If the face was
the mirror of the soul, I wondered, then what else had changed
in me; what else did not belong to my previous self?

The guard led me into a large room with a high ceiling. The room was very warm. I stood before a desk at which sat a man I recognized as Major Litvinov of the NKVD. I had operated on his wife a few months previously; they had brought her to the hospital one night with a gall-bladder attack. But now the major's face was severe; he informed me that from then on I was to call him "Citizen Chief," and that he would address me not as "Comrade" but as "Prisoner."

He asked why I was an enemy of the Soviet Union. Taken aback, I vehemently denied that I was, citing my good work and all the commendations I had received. He screamed at me, purple in the face. This man, whom I used to see daily in the cafeteria of the Asbest industrial plant – friendly, polite, always joking – now looked like a wild beast. Finding his behaviour insupportable, I stopped answering his questions. He reached for his gun and pointed it at me. I stood motionless, indifferent, refusing to be fazed by this human animal. It was apparently not the first time he had encountered such a reaction. He called the guard and told him to take me away.

Back in my cell, something strange happened. I was cold and shivering, but the cramps did not come. Maybe my indifference had cheated the angel of death. I was gradually losing all sense of place, but the guard would come in from time to time, asking me with a concerned sort of face to take some hot water. I accepted his kind offers gratefully. When darkness came, I fell into a strange sleep, content in the feeling that I might never wake up to this place again. It must have been late at night when the guard woke me and took me back to my interrogator.

This time he was laughing. He offered me a chair and said he was sure now that I would reveal, from the bottom of my heart, why I was an enemy of the Soviet Union. After a long silence, during which I kept my face motionless, he suddenly switched off the light and I heard two shots, one after another. Then he turned on the light again. He was holding a smoking gun. His face wild with laughing rage, he muttered hoarsely, "You see, this is my way of playing Russian roulette. You never see where to shoot in the darkness, but you may be lucky and end up just with bloody broken ribs."

My face was rigid. The session was over. A guard took me back to my cell, where I was left alone for two nights. Nothing changed in the cell, but I was slowly getting used to the cold; even the shivering disappeared. I began to feel very hungry. My only food was a piece of dark bread and a cup of hot water in the morning and evening. I started to enjoy the hot water, which warmed me up.

There followed two nights in a row of interrogation, with the same lighting effects and shooting. My *sledovatel* (interrogator) was, thank God, losing more strength than I was in these sessions. My body had started to adapt to the subhuman conditions and, deprived of all affective responses, I sustained my passive emotional attitude without conscious effort – perhaps a natural psychic defensive mechanism under such circumstances.

Two weeks passed. My beard grew long. One morning I was taken under guard to the railway station. It was sunny and cold. We travelled by rail for about three hours to a small station called Beloiarka, where we got out of the train and walked. After a while the snow got very deep, up to our knees. I was doing my best, but it was getting harder and harder to pull my legs out of the snow. I was very weak, having moved so little for so many days in the dreadful prison. The guard noticed my difficulties and helped me along.

Eventually we reached a small wooden building that was divided inside into two large rooms, like classrooms in a village school. One-third of the floor space was raised about six feet, and on this platform lay some twenty prisoners. The guard told me to take my place among them. Exhausted, I lay down. The stench from the bodies was unbelievable. We were given bread and hot water, then the guard left. A man in a dishevelled military uniform began to ask how long they had kept me, and why I had been arrested. I told him I didn't know and his face became serious.

"Oh, I see. This is political. You are probably not a Russian. We know. We've lived with it for many years. Too bad. Too bad. At least if you'd murdered someone you'd know where you stood. But now everything is possible. You see, we are at war." I did not understand what he was saying, or perhaps I didn't want to understand.

Early in the afternoon it got dark and a candle was lit on a stand at the wall, enabling the prisoners to find their way to a large barrel in the corner that served as a toilet. My eyes wandered. I was trying to learn more about this place and the people in it. It was very quiet except for the monotonous breathing and snoring of the tired, wasted convicts.

For awhile, my sight fixed on the flame of the candle, which suddenly turned into the many lights of two large silver candelabra that used to stand on the table of my parents' dining room. On the immaculate white tablecloth everything was waiting, covered, in readiness for the festivities. Around the table sat my sisters, brother, mother, and myself, the youngest, on a special soft chair next my father. A warmth filled my heart, the well-known and familiar comfort of belonging. My father blessed the family and started to thank God … Suddenly the mirage disappeared. Painfully I returned to reality, but only partly; something in my unconscious refused to accept it.

Fleeting thoughts crossed my mind: Why was I being punished? Why was I put on trial for sins I had not committed? Did I have some complaint against the Almighty, or did I question His judgment? No; He knew all and everything, and His might filled the universe. He knew where my family was at that time, and he knew why, in His great wisdom, He had separated us. And He would return me to my home, with his mighty Hand, as He promised, and did for my forefathers.

Suspended in semi-awareness, I saw anguished images shifting kaleidoscopically before me: trenches filled with scraggly, scrawny human beings; thin faces, full of suffering, deformed in an agony of prayer. There seemed no end to this apocalyptic torment. But at last I lost consciousness, falling into a dreamless sleep.

The next morning I was taken back to the railroad station and put on another train. After many hours we approached a city. The railway station was familiar – Swerdlowsk. I had often travelled from Asbest to the capital of Ural to report to General Lazerew, chief of the medical department of the Ural military, or to visit with Arkadi Timofeewitsh Lidski, a professor of surgery at the university. Lidski was a surgical consultant to the evacuation hospital in Asbest. He had become a dear friend of mine and had gradually opened his heart to me, an unusual event in Stalin's USSR.

Two guards took me to the old prison built by Tsaritsa Iekaterina (Catherine the Great) when the city was called Iekaterinburg.

I was put in a solitary cell that contained a cot, a hard stool, and a pail. It was already dark outside, although it was early afternoon. I sat on the stool, my head dropping on my chest. I wanted to sleep, but every two minutes the guard would look through the little window in the door, knocking to warn me that sleep during the day was forbidden. Eventually, well into the evening, the door was opened by another guard who announced that it was 10:00 P.M. and I could now sleep. In what seemed like no time at all I was awakened and told to follow the guard, who led me through many corridors until we came to a door. He knocked and I entered.

In the room behind the desk sat a man around thirty, with the black hair and stern oriental features of one from Uzbekistan. Telling me to sit down, he reached for a cigarette and concentrated on some papers on his table. For what must have been more than two hours he paid no attention to me, as if I didn't exist. Then he slowly raised his head, lit another cigarette, and began.

"So you are the surgeon-counterrevolutionary?"

I did not answer.

"When did you start your activities against the State?"

I remained silent.

"Aha! So you think you can make me lose my composure. Fine. I will bring you to order and teach you some manners. Stand up."

I obeyed. After another hour he again raised his head, looked at me for a while, and shouted, "On your knees!"

I remained standing.

"You son-of-a-bitch. If you don't obey my orders, we have other methods."

I looked straight into his narrow eyes and in a relaxed and quiet voice said, "I don't like your manners. Do what you want. I will only answer sensible questions. The more you shout, the more calm and silent I will be."

"Is that so? We shall see?" He barked out a command and two soldiers entered the room.

"Take this bastard to a sack."

I did not understand what this meant, but I soon found out. The guards grabbed me on either side and carried me to some lower basement through long corridors whose wet walls smelled of mildew. We stopped before a wall in which numerous small iron doors, each about two feet square, were set in three rows.

One of the guards opened a door on the second level and ordered me to take off my pants and prisoner's jacket. I stood in my shirt and underwear.

"Crawl inside. It is long enough for you," the guard shouted. I still did not want to understand what these new "accommodations" were for. The little doors in the wall reminded me of the vaults for cadavers in the Department of Forensic Medicine, except that there, you pulled out a shallow long steel pan on which the corpse rested. Here, there was no such comfort. I had to crawl into this hole in the wall. Before doing so, I asked, "What is this all about? Are you going to suffocate me?"

"No, no! Nothing like that. It's just a severe punishment. It is done to all stiff-necked inmates who are too proud to follow the regulations and obey the interrogator. These cells are called the *kamennyi meshok* (stone sacks.) Your interrogator upstairs is not a Russian; he's an Uzbek and very mean, so you'd better watch yourself. Some prisoners don't make it. Last week he had three inmates inside. The other interrogator, the Russian, never uses these cells. You'll be here for three, maybe five days. It won't be so bad because they leave you in peace and you can sleep all you want. The bad thing is, they only give you half rations and sometimes there are rats. You'll see. But don't be scared. You look like a resourceful type."

Leaving me with this advice, they closed the door of the stone sack and departed. A faint light issued through a little grid about ten by ten centimetres in the iron door. The floor and walls of the cell were wet and slimy, and it was cold; air was coming in, apparently through the iron grid, and flowing out through some ventilator that I couldn't see. Laying one arm on the stone floor, I rested my head on it and closed my eyes. What could I do to survive? What did I have to do to get out of this nightmare place as soon as possible? It was evident that I would have to do whatever the interrogator wanted, follow his orders whatever they were. I would ask the guards who brought the bread and water to inform the Uzbek of my decision. With these feverish ideas in my head, I fell asleep.

I don't know how long I slept in the stone sack – I'd had no chance to sleep during the long nights of interrogation. But I woke suddenly to something crawling rapidly over my face and body. In a split second I remembered where I was and realized that the

rats were looking for food. I couldn't see anything in the dark.
Shivering from cold, disgust, and fear, I tried to be still so as not
to provoke the rats to attack my bare face, neck, or feet. Eventually
they went away, but I continued to shiver. Carefully lifting my
head, I noticed a faint, orange light issuing through the bars of
the little window. The silence was complete. Maybe the rats hadn't
been hungry enough to attack. Or perhaps they had been
thwarted by my immobility.

I slept again until I heard the screeching hinges of the iron door.
Trying to sit up, I hit my head against the ceiling of the stone sack,
which was not more than two feet high. When the guard who had
brought me there looked inside, I did not know whether it was
night or day.

"You're lying the wrong way," he said. "We won't be able to
reach you. Come out, and put your head close to the door." I
followed his advice, crawling out of the sack and slipping back
in, feet first. The guard looked around and, seeing that nobody
was about, began to speak to me.

"You know, you are the only one in any of the twelve sacks. I
brought you some bread. I know it is very tough. There are rats
around here, but don't be afraid. I'll wait at the open door while
you eat – as soon as they smell the bread, they'll take it out of
your hands and you won't be able to cope with them. Now, eat
as much as you can. I'll keep the rest for you and if I can, I'll come
back before my replacement arrives for the second shift. He is also
a good Russian boy. I'll tell him how to treat you. We will help
you."

Even in these inhumane circumstances, you could find a kind
heart when dealing with Russian soldiers. The guards would very
often give me extra hot water, or even a cigarette. Encouraged
almost to the point of tears by their goodness, I finished my bread
and said to the guard, "Please inform my interrogator that I am
in poor shape and wish to cooperate fully and follow all his
orders." The guard promised to do what he could. Left alone
again, I felt completely resourceless. As often in moments of total
helplessness, I started to pray, appealing fervently to the Almighty
to give me enough wisdom and strength to overcome this evil
power. Then suddenly I knew I would get out of this horrible cell.
Before me was a clear vision of the furious Uzbek interrogator,
caught in the web of his own perverse cruelty. The dream I had

had just prior to my arrest, the dream that had ended in my salvation, suddenly became clear to me: I was in the jaws of a giant, the savage political system. But I would be helped and I would get free. Tears began to roll from my eyes and I fell asleep, as though I were in a very comfortable place, close to God and under his protective wing.

The same warmhearted soldier who had given me the bread the day before woke me up and told me to get out of the stone sack. I had been there two nights and one day.

"I think your interrogator was pleased when he told me that you could be released, if it is really true that you will cooperate without further tricks."

I was brought straight to his office. The Uzbek did not look at me.

"Still so calm and collected? Will you further ignore my orders?'

"No, no. I will do as you order."

His face assumed an expression of triumph. He presented me with a transcript of the interrogation, loaded with descriptions of crimes I had never committed. I signed this document with composure and with my own quiet sense of triumph; victory lay in the document I was signing, as only God and I knew.

The Uzbek grabbed another cigarette and let me stand there for over an hour. I lost consciousness and awoke eventually on the cot in my cell, to which I must have been carried. It was very quiet; daylight shone faintly through the barred window. There on the stool was my ration of dark bread and the metal mug of water. My interrogator must have kept me in his office almost all night.

The guard reminded me that, according to the regulations, sleeping in the cell during the day was forbidden, even in a sitting posture. He also told me that every day at noon I had to empty the pail into a place he showed me in the outhouse. The technique of interrogation now became clear to me. They did not allow you to sleep during the day, then they interrogated you all night long. The purpose was to demoralize you completely and force you to sign anything they wanted.

The day passed in unremarkable fashion. That night the guard gave me a document to sign, confirming the time of my interrogation, which was marked as 11:00 P.M. The rest of the night was an exact repetition of the previous one. The interrogator was smoking his cigarettes. I was ordered to remain standing at all times. When I was close to fainting I lay down on the floor, getting up again shortly afterwards. The Uzbek said nothing. Perhaps prematurely, I felt that I was winning a small part of the game. When they took me back to my cell, I was told to sign the hour of my return. It was marked as midnight, but the clock on the corridor wall indicated 4:00 A.M. I signed without resistance.

The nightly interrogations regularly followed the same agenda: standing, lying on the floor, and signing for midnight rather than 4:00 A.M. Only twice over a period of ten days was I asked if I had finally decided to confess, out of a "clear heart," all my crimes against the state. Eventually I realized that I could not win. Deprived of sleep, I was getting weaker and could not last much longer with nothing but the meagre bread ration to sustain me. I said again that I would cooperate. The nights were long and exhausting and I ended up signing things that, for all I knew, had no bearing on reality at all.

Every four or five days the prosecutor would come and, in the presence of the interrogator, ask if everything were in order – whether I had been put under pressure or forced to make statements under duress. Of course I realized that this was just a formal and meaningless procedure and that the prosecutor was as helpless as I was in the presence of a NKVD representative. But on one of my nights in the "stone sack," inspired by God and encouraged by the dream He had sent to me, I had resolved to help the prosecutor and make it possible for him to fulfil his duties. That had been a decisive night; for now, as I signed once again the admission of heinous crimes against the state that I had never committed, I thought, "Not this time, you cruel Uzbek." When the prosecutor asked the usual question whether everything was in order, I responded in a quiet but determined voice.

"Nothing is in order. Sleepless nights and starvation are the techniques used to coerce me into admitting to imaginary crimes against the state. These admissions are carefully documented and later I am forced to sign the documents."

The Uzbek almost fell off his chair. The prosecutor, his face pale, asked me if I could prove what I was saying.

"Yes," I answered stoutly. "You see, at the end of my signature the little tail of the letter R is always directed down, but on the sheets where I was forced under duress to admit to things that I have never done, I purposely made the little tail on the R go upwards as a sign of protest."

Silence filled the room and the two representatives of the law looked at each other in helpless consternation. I knew right away that it had worked. The prosecutor asked to be given all the papers for review and the Uzbek called the guard and ordered him to take me to my cell immediately.

Many days passed. According to my calendar (I made marks on the wall with a piece of wire I had found) it was already the first week of April. This meant that I had already been in prison for two months. One day, I was taken to another wing of the building and made to wait in an anteroom. There was a mirror in the room that reflected a face I did not recognize as my own. Sad eyes, sharp nose, a long black beard – a face I would not have known in a photograph. But before I could think about it, I was taken to a bath, allowed to shave, handed a new uniform, fed with nice, tasty, light bread, given coffee with milk, and guided to a large, well-furnished room. A soldier with a kind smile bade me sit down on a large, comfortable chair covered with dark green leather. For a while I looked around the spacious office with its huge desk, green leather sofas, and portrait of Stalin on the wall.

A door opened to admit a tall, impressive man in the uniform of a general of the NKVD. His face was genial and benign as he greeted me with the usual Russian welcome, "Zdraswuite," and offered me a cigarette – Severnaia Palmira, the best kind there was. I inhaled gladly, relaxing more and more in the warm and elegant atmosphere. The general assumed a comfortable posture, not behind the desk but reclining easily on the sofa, adding to the friendly informality of the meeting. Then he spoke.

"I received express orders from Moscow to come to Swerdlowsk to help out with your case here. From the start, let me apologize for the way you were treated. You see, our people don't know how to handle men like you, who are valuable to us. Even in the best levels of society one doesn't find many specialists like you. It takes buckets of money and decades of effort. But you are the product of a capitalist upbringing and your paradigm is unacceptable to us in our onward march towards communism. By sharing an image of the capitalist democratic way of life with our people, you fill them with a sense of sadness and loss; we cannot yet give them what you enjoyed in Poland. We could not warn you against

influencing people in this way or give you instructions on how
to behave. There is a war; there is no time. What is done is done,
and we have to isolate you for this decisive period while the war
lasts. We cannot allow you to destroy the patriotic feelings of our
people. We cannot yet improve their material conditions, but we
need them, heart and soul, now that they have to give their lives
for their motherland. You probably know that tens of thousands
of our best young men are being killed daily in a fight to defend
not only ourselves but the whole world, against the enemy of all
mankind. We have to accept this enormous sacrifice and you have
to accept the fact that we have to isolate you as long as the war
lasts. You are from Poland. You probably remember the quote
from your great poet Mickiewitsch: 'There is no time to save the
roses when the forests are burning.' But we are losing out by not
being able to use your talent and knowledge as a surgeon. I'm
asking you to understand and cooperate. As soon as the war is
over, you will be free to select any professorship of surgery in any
city, and we will be proud to have you."

Although not convinced by his arguments, I sensed in them a
way out of my situation. I had a choice. The alternative, not
accepting his offer, probably meant death: the odds of surviving
a confrontation with a brutal and merciless power were poor. I
thought for a while and told him that I understood. We parted,
and I never met him again.

I was transferred directly from his office to a clean, warm, bright
cell where a guard brought me a mug of real hot tea. The animal
phase of my survival ended with this first symbol of freedom.
Somewhere inside a voice accused me of treason against my true
nature. But I did not listen. Integrity, under the present circumstances, had no meaning. It was a luxury that I could not afford
in this fight to stay alive. For the time being I had found a way
to hang on; I would face the issue of integrity later.

I was awakened by the guard, who led me to a room where I
met my new interrogator. A tall, lean, greying man in his fifties,
he greeted me with a smile and explained that he saw no difficulties in my case.

"Let's get started," he told me. "You were an enemy of the
Soviet Union."

It sounded awful. In what kind of mess had I landed myself?
After a short hesitation, I realized that I had no choice in the
matter.

"Yes, I was an enemy of the Soviet Union." I echoed his words. The next question followed right away.

"Since when have you been an enemy of the Soviet Union?"

Without further thought I replied, "Since the day the Soviet army entered Western Ukraine and came into the city of Lwow, where I was living."

"That is not true, because the oppressed people of the region greeted our army as liberators, with flowers, expressing their gratitude." The Western Ukraine, to which he referred, had once been part of Poland. When Hitler and Stalin made their nonaggression pact in late August 1939, they had agreed to divide Poland between them. The USSR had taken over the eastern half of Poland.

I did not know how to answer him. "So please tell me," I asked. "When did I start to become an enemy of the Soviet Union?"

"Don't make jokes and don't try to be smart. If you really want to know, this hatred of us started when you were working at the university hospital among the Polish aristocracy, who were our worst enemies – enemies of the people. You could just as easily have worked in the Jewish hospital in Lwow, where you would have been more welcome, being Jewish."

"Yes, you are right," I answered. And so on, and so on.

After about two hours of his suggestions and my agreements, the interrogation was over for the day. I was brought back to the cell early and given some hot soup. That night I enjoyed a rare luxury, sleeping undisturbed in a clean shirt.

The interrogations lasted about two weeks. It became obvious that, in spite of the helpful hints from my interrogator, I was running out of ideas on how to invent new crimes that I had supposedly committed against the state. My man from the NKVD noticed this and found an original way to help me out of my predicament. One evening when my session was over, I returned to the cell to find that another cot had been placed by the wall. Grigori, my new cellmate, greeted me with a smile. He was well-mannered, an engineer by profession, and looked to be about my age. He had been accused of a similar crime against his motherland, a crime popularly known, I later found out as a more experienced political prisoner, as Paragraph 58 (10) of the Criminal Code of the Soviet Union. The new man seemed very friendly and we exchanged some information about our situations. I was glad the long lonely days were over.

Late next evening, when I returned from the interrogator's office, Grigori noticed from my confused expression that something was wrong. When he asked, I explained that I could not cooperate with the NKVD man because he asked me about other crimes against the state and I didn't know what to answer. I had already told him how many suits I had and how many pairs of shoes. I had told him of my house and car and many other small bourgeois crimes I had committed, but it was not enough.

A smile appeared on Grigori's face.

"Don't be afraid. Give them all the sensational material you can think of," he urged. "Tell them of crimes you never even thought about, from the tiniest to the most gigantic, from sending your secretary a dozen pairs of nylon stockings for her birthday to how you wanted to blow up the Kremlin but didn't have enough dynamite. You have to feed these bastards with so much garbage that they choke from indigestion."

In the next two sessions, my interrogator could hardly keep up with the avalanche of crimes that I confessed to him. Bewitched, his face expressed rare professional delight. In a grateful voice he announced that my interrogation was over. I did not return to my cell and never again saw Grigori. Weeks later, experienced prisoners explained to me that Grigori was an NKVD collaborator. So what? This was neither the first nor the last time I would hear such tales. But I preferred to trust rather than suspect and Grigori had actually helped me.

I was brought to a very large cell in which about thirty prisoners were lying on the floor along both sides of the room. On one short wall was a long window, barred and covered almost completely by sheets of metal except for a narrow unscreened rectangle at the top that allowed some light to enter during the day. On the other short wall was the door, and close by, in a corner, was a large barrel that served as a latrine for the inmates.

Many curious eyes turned in my direction. Two young boys, about sixteen or seventeen, guided me towards the window and introduced me to Grisha, the boss of the cell. He was a small skinny boy, with blond hair and sharp features. I later found out that he had not been elected cell boss; he had won the position by virtue of having killed many people in the past. After I had answered a few questions concerning my last few years, my professional standing in the army, and so on, he told the boys to "organize" a place for me, close to him. When they left, he handed me two white rolls with butter and a cup of tea. He advised me to get some sleep and said we would have a chat in the morning.

I opened my eyes, refreshed from an undisturbed sleep. The other prisoners were already up but, on Grisha's orders, they were very quiet. I was given some tasty sausage, white bread, and tea by one of the boss's "servants." When I asked my benefactor where such food had come from, he told me, "You don't ask in prison. That's the rule. You'll find out for yourself later on."

In a brief conversation I told him all he wanted to know about me. Born in Austria, the youngest of seven children, I had lost both my parents to typhoid within a twenty-four-hour period in 1918. Following World War II, the part of Austria where we were living changed hands, as the Ukrainians and Poles both wanted independence. Terrorist bands roamed the area, burning our house and orchard. Soon my brothers and sisters moved to Lwow, taking me with them. Only one of my sisters was married at that time, and it fell to my elder brother, a lawyer, to support not only himself but our four unmarried sisters and me. At ten, I decided that I was a man and should take responsibility for my own future and get an education. Determined not to be a burden, I ran away from home and presented myself at the gymnasium (secondary school) in Lwow. I told them that I was an orphan and had no home. After I had spent several nights on mats in the gymnasium, the headmaster arranged for me to tutor and board with a boy my age. I continued in school and eventually studied medicine, specializing in surgery.

Then Grisha shared with me the story of his life, or as much as he knew. He too was an orphan but had never known his parents and had grown up on the streets of Moscow with other orphans. These street kids – *bezprizornye* in Russian, children for whom nobody cared – survived by picking pockets and other sorts of theft. When he grew up, as Grisha told it, he had had to kill some people and had spent a good deal of his life in prisons and labour camps. He explained that survival in these places was based on the power principle.

"The difference in muscular power does not really matter. What is important is blind courage and the conviction that you are stronger in spirit. Then you are a winner. So, if necessary, strike the first blow and strike in the right place, in the eyes." He demonstrated with the extended first and second fingers of his right hand.

He told me that I would have a tough time. As a political prisoner, categorized under the Criminal Code as an "antirevolutionary agitator," the shortest sentence I could get was ten years. "There is no amnesty in political matters," he said. "If you had killed someone it would be much better for you. People in the labour camps are afraid to be friendly with politicals. Here in prison, where we're only numbers, nobody cares." But, he continued, I had one thing going for me. I was a doctor and might be all right because they would need my skills. "Here in prison they won't bother you any more. You'll just have to wait a few months for the sentence. And during this time you will be our storyteller here in the cell, because you are a learned man and know so many things. As long as I'm here, you'll be under my protection."

Slowly the weeks passed and I assumed the role of storyteller. I would usually tell stories for about three hours after breakfast and again for about two hours after the midday soup. As long as Grisha was my protector, I did not go hungry. The prisoners' rations were completely inadequate. In the morning there was a cup of hot water – every prisoner had his metal cup, usually an old tin can – and the daily ration of 400 grams of bread. The quality of the bread was poor. There was very little flour in it, just a lot of rough bran, and it was usually wet so that most of its weight was in the water. At noon there was a bluish-grey watery soup made out of a bit of rye flour and some salt. A few minutes after you drank it, it was converted directly into sweat. Sometimes they added dry fish from spoiled army reserves and, in the spring, hot nettle leaves. The soup smelled like rotten meat. In the evening, we got about two spoons of kasha, not buckwheat, but watery, unhulled ordinary wheat.

On this diet, people slowly lost their fat, then their muscles. When the diarrhoea set in they would be taken to the prison hospital. We never saw anybody return from the hospital to the cell. Some people were frightened to go to the hospital and tried to hide their conditions; often in the morning we would find one of them dead. The guards were not usually told about this, and when the morning head count took place, two prisoners would hold the cadaver upright to get his ration of bread. They would continue to do this for as long as they could stand the stench of the decomposing body.

But while Grisha was the cell boss he would not allow this to happen. It was too undignified for his code of conduct; it was the way of the cowardly, not the courageous. He himself believed, as he often explained to me, that there was no justice in this world; that the law of the strong, under different guises, was the true driving force of life, at all levels. He believed that if you could step on people and keep them under your heel, you could survive.

Some prisoners were getting food parcels from their family and friends at home. Every parcel was brought to Grisha, who, after selecting the best of it for himself, would send the rest back to the owner. He would give his prison ration to his assistants, usually young boys. Any sign of insubordination was met with a horrible beating, and nobody would defend the unhappy victim. It seemed to be an accepted law.

Late one afternoon, after I finished telling stories and before supper, I lay down to think. The cell was quiet, the silence disturbed only by the loud breathing of the prisoners. I thought about the people around me. For the first time in my life I was rubbing shoulders with criminals – thieves and murderers. Earlier, I'd only read about such people and was glad not to know any. Now, living with them, I saw that they were human beings, not all that different from ordinary, so-called honest, normal people. Despite what they had done, they could be warm and caring.

We all have a shadow side to our souls, a dark recess containing amoral, antisocial instincts. Rarely do people consider or admit that they have this darker side. They cover it up, usually by projecting – accusing others of what they themselves are guilty of or fear they might do. All objects, if there is any light at all, throw a shadow; this is a sign of their physical existence. It is the same with human nature. Our failure to acknowledge the dark side of our natures prevents us from being able to forgive and love others. But can virtue be genuine if it sets itself apart from evil?

It seemed to me that to accept and forgive the ugly, to point the finger at oneself rather than at someone else, shows saintliness. I had read Oscar Wilde's *De Profundis*, in which he notes that Christ was crucified between two thieves, like two fallen angels. Perhaps Grisha was a fallen angel. He stole when in need and to feed the poor, and he would kill to protect himself or his friends from danger.

Early one morning, Grisha was called by the guard. He approached and hugged me, and I noticed that his eyes were wet. "Fight for your life," he told me. "You are a superior human being and you have to survive. Maybe our paths will cross again. I would like that. I could learn a lot. May God protect you." He disappeared and I never saw him again. I will never forget him. Strangely, in spite of his cruelty, he was someone whom one could love.

Grisha's departure changed my life markedly. Although the prisoners still treated me with some deference and admiration, my privileges ended abruptly. Even if someone wanted to share something in his parcel with me, I declined, to avoid envy or violence. I decided to use Grisha's technique only in situations of impending personal danger.

Days were passing, and I began to starve like everyone around me. I was still telling stories and because of this, many people liked me. I was often given *machorka*, the coarse and horrible Russian tobacco in the form of very small crumbs, which we rolled in pieces of newspaper. Such a cigarette would usually be shared by several prisoners. It helped to relieve the hunger pangs. The last puffs were usually given to the young boys because the end of the cigarette burned the lips, but the boys did not mind; they suffered the most from hunger. There was always a shortage of newspaper for rolling the cigarettes. I still had in my possession an official list of the valuables confiscated at the time of my arrest. The paper on which it was written was heavier than newspaper, but it was all I had. And so, every day I had to decide which of the items on my list I would sacrifice for another cigarette. One day it was my wrist watch, the next my camera, then my diploma, and so on, until I convinced myself that there was no sense in holding onto a piece of paper that was largely meaningless in this alien and artificial existence. Here every event of my life seemed unreal, floating somewhere between fiction and lie. Anything projected beyond the immediate required a leap of trust that we had lost, and thus it remained outside reality. The past was a vanished luxury; the future was blanked out as too threatening.

Every day we were taken out for a walk in the prison yard. My eyes hurt from the sudden exposure to the brilliant sunlight in the white, snowy world outside. The row of yellow-faced prisoners was like a parade of cadaver-marionettes; our walk was slow, apathetic, dignified, and resigned. And although the sun was shining and little shimmering crystals of fresh snow whirled in the gentle breeze, we, victims of suffering, had stopped reacting to the beauty of nature. There was no talk among the prisoners, only an exchange of accepting, fleeting looks, each frightened at seeing in another, as if in a mirror, the inevitable, merciless approach of death by starvation.

We felt the lack of salt painfully in our daily rations. Not only did we long for anything salty but we also grew progressively weaker and were often close to fainting. On the other hand we lived without sugar with no difficulty. I remember one day I exchanged with another prisoner an almost full cup of sugar, which I had collected from rations for over a month, for one flat teaspoon of the crude salt. I crushed the salt with my tin mug on the concrete floor, spread it on the bread, and ate as though it were the rarest delicacy.

Most degrading and debilitating was the hunger of the afternoon, as we waited for evening with its few spoonfuls of kasha. During this time we often lapsed into a semisleep abundant with something on the borderline between daydreams and real dreams. Tables of delicious fat and brown barbecued chickens, hams and sausages disappeared as soon as they were conjured up, leaving us with the fierce disappointment of the fata morgana.

The prisoners who received food packages were lovingly observed as they consumed their food. Two or three "prisoner observers" would usually sit close to the blessed consumer, looking into his mouth. They imitated each bite, turning their tongues inside their mouths. Perfect examples of Pavlovian dogs, they would produce as much saliva as the real eater, proving the principle of a conditioned reflex. This saliva, probably accompanied by the invisible sympathetic secretion of gastric juice, could be helpful in alleviating the feeling of hunger.

The prisoners were placed in a row against the walls on the concrete floor, with their meagre belongings – in my case, a military coat rolled up to serve as a pillow. In this cell, while waiting for transport to the labour camp, you could sleep as much as you wanted. Valuable belongings such as *machorka*, a bit of sugar, or a piece of bread were hidden, for example in a rolled coat, to protect against theft while you slept.

As time passed I grew progressively emaciated and weak. One night I had diarrhoea and spent all the time on the barrel that stood in the corner of the cell. In the morning, when the body count was taken by the guard, I could not get up off the floor.

"One for the hospital," the prisoner beside me shouted to the soldier. "He's sick." The soldier ordered me to get up. My neighbour helped me to my feet, embraced me, and said, "I will pray for you, my friend."

I waited in the hospital outside the doctor's office to be examined and admitted. Every few minutes I had to get up and run to the middle of the corridor to a pail that served as a toilet. I had severe cramps but could only pass a few drops of blood and mucus. I felt completely abandoned.

Quite unexpectedly, three naked women appeared at the end of the corridor, moving in my direction. As they passed me, they covered their private parts with their hands. The extreme suffering that had distorted their once-attractive features showed in their deeply sunken eyes. Though we were all naked, it was for me a moment of extreme humiliation, invoking a devastating feeling of shame and self-contempt. I hid my face and looked at the floor, wondering about the space within the soul that still responded, despite severe physical pain, to the desecration of human dignity.

After a while, sitting on the floor, we all got used to our nakedness and started talking as though we were fully dressed in an ordinary doctor's waiting room, sharing the various small anxieties of sick people. One of the women was a former secretary of the Communist Party of a big city in Ural. The other two were officers in the medical corps of the Soviet army. None of us asked why we were here. We only knew that we did not know – that there was no reason other than Stalin's terrorist policies.

At last a lady doctor arrived and, after a few questions and answers, advised me that I would be admitted to the hospital. After more hours of waiting, an orderly appeared and took me to the prison infirmary. I was placed close to the entrance at the corner of a large hall holding about twenty beds. It is impossible to describe the bliss of finding oneself on a mattress after months of sleeping on concrete floors. As I relaxed, my thoughts carried me back to Lwow and a past that had vanished forever.

War

Lwow, known earlier as "Lemberg," was where my brothers and sisters had moved after our parents died. It had a population of some 300,000, including Poles, Ukrainians, and a sizeable Jewish community, of which we were a part. Often called "Little Vienna," this once-happy city with its opera, theatres, coffee houses, and cabarets was culturally and intellectually alive. After briefly studying in Germany, I had returned to Lwow to work. In 1939, when the city came under the control of the Soviet Union, its character changed greatly. Former government officials, members of the intelligentsia, Polish army officers, wealthy business people were arrested and sent for "Special Resettlement" in Siberia.

In Lwow, I didn't hear a great deal about the German's treatment of Poles and Jews in the part of Poland they controlled. From time to time I heard a few things from German Jews who had fled and were living in tents on the outskirts of Lwow, and from friends at the hospital. At the time, I was chief resident in the Department of Surgery of the John Casimir University Hospital. After the annexation, the surgical department became the "Ukrainian Government Surgical Institute" and my position was renamed "senior surgical worker." The title and obligations of the medical head of the department remained with my teacher, Professor Ostrowski, but the administration was transferred to a Soviet Ukrainian, Dr Oleshko.

The population that remained slowly started to adjust to the new reality, assuming different positions in the administration and in business, gradually learning to speak Russian. During the two years between 1939 and 1941 the food supply was adequate. There were many government stores or *Narkompishtcheprom*, stores of the National Commissariat of the Food Industry, where you could buy unlimited quantities of good-quality beluga caviar and "Soviet" champagne. Unfortunately the people earned very little and only in rubles. Those who still had some dollars converted them on the black market, making the most of their dwindling purchasing power. A Soviet patient of mine in the hospital, who happened to be the assistant head of all these government stores, told me a secret: "We will tire them out; they only have a limited amount of hard currency and certainly we have more merchandise than they have dollars."

Thus life gradually became very austere, materially and culturally. One day a representative of the Soviet army called a few doctors to the office of the administrator. The colonel addressed us in Russian.

"By now I trust you realize that you are Soviet citizens and therefore benefit from all the privileges of our great socialist land. By the same token, you also assume all the responsibilities that such citizenship involves. One of these is your military duty to defend our borders. You may be called upon to discharge this duty by becoming soldiers in the Red Army of the Soviet Union. Now, in peacetime, you will be given pink mobilization cards to keep. In case of war you will be obliged to register with the appropriate military unit as indicated on the mobilization card. Are there any questions?"

There were no questions.

At the time we paid no attention to the seemingly unimportant slips of paper. But in September 1941, Hitler attacked the Soviet Union. The first few days were horribly confused; the Germans were constantly bombarding the city. They came at night, directed by signals given from the roofs by Ukrainian nationalists who trusted Hitler to save them from the communists. Since well before the war, Hitler had looked forward to conquering the Slavic peoples of Eastern Europe. His hope was to provide *lebensraum*, or living space, for the Germans by setting up German colonies in the East, to be served by Slavs. His pact with the Soviet Union

had been merely a temporary measure to avoid a two-front war.
He planned first to put the British out of action but, despite his
Blitzkrieg, Britain never gave in.

By June 1940, the USSR had moved close to the Romanian
oilfields, thus posing a threat and causing Hitler to make plans
for an eastern front, Operation Barbarossa, which began 22 June
1941. The German troops advanced rapidly, with Leningrad (now
St Petersburg) under siege in September 1941 and German troops
at the outskirts of Moscow by December 1941.

One morning at the university surgical clinic I met Professor
Ostrowski. He was a tall lean man in his late fifties with an open,
confidence-inspiring face and large grey blue eyes that revealed
an engaging intelligence. He came close to me, looked around and
then told me: "Whatever you do, don't rush into this Red Army.
There is no place for you there. What cause are you going to fight
for? Stay here with us, among friends. The chaos and anarchy will
be over in a few days, the situation will clear up, and then you
will be able to make a more rational decision."

That was the last time I saw Professor Ostrowski. A few days
after my conversation with him, I was invited by a colleague of
mine, Stan, to the city hospital to consult on a surgical patient.
This hospital was accepting most of the military casualties from
the front lines. The numbers of wounded and dying were enormous. The colossal injuries that you never see in civilian life
caught me by surprise, filling me with a horror I had never
experienced before. Seeing the wounded soldiers with severed
arms and legs and open, lacerated, bleeding wounds to the chest
and abdomen made me – who was used only to peacetime surgery – suddenly all too aware of the extent of the trauma of war.
After the consultation my colleague, Dr Stan Kampelmacher,
asked, "Maybe you can tell me what to do. I have this mobilization card. I have to come to some decision. What do you think I
should do?"

"Listen, Stan," I said, "you probably didn't know it, but I have
the same card as you. People have different opinions about what
we should do. Professor Ostrowski feels that I should wait until
all this blows over. I was thinking about it and came to the
following conclusion: the Soviet resistance is weakening and the
Germans are advancing. It would be senseless, and also very
dangerous, to hide as Soviet deserters before the SS and the

German army. When they find us they will execute us on the spot. The safest place for us will be the Russian army, which is always better protected and supplied than the civilian population. I'm going tomorrow; I'd be glad if you came along. Bring a set of surgical instruments and some local anaesthetic in case one of us gets wounded."

The same day my youngest sister came to the surgical clinic, because she had found out that I intended to go east and join the Red Army.

"You can't be serious, to go so far away from our family. You never were the adventurous type. What's happened?"

"I know that you came here to warn and protect me," I told her. "But you and the rest of the family are unaware of what is going on in the part of Poland presently occupied by the Germans." I reminded her of the previous year when all the escapees from western Poland came to our door asking for alms. Once upon a time, all those people had homes; some were even wealthy. They ran away and became homeless, but they saved their lives. "Go back," I told her, "and tell the family to run away to the Soviet Union. Let them leave their possessions and go, just go. Their attachment should only be to their lives. As far as I am concerned, I am going, no question about it. Now is not the time for senti-ment, but for action. Farewell. God be with you."

Unfortunately, history proved me right. After the Germans lost the war and Poland was liberated, my sister and I were the only survivors of a family of thirty-two. My brothers, sisters, their wives, husbands, and children were all murdered by the Nazis in the concentration camps. And what of Professor Ostrowski? Eight years later in Wroclaw, upon my return from Ural, I met Dr Bross, our adjunct associate professor, and asked about him.

"It's a tragic story," he said with a sigh. "In the first few days after entering the city of Lwow the Germans executed all the university professors, among them our dear Professor Ostrowski. This was a part of a master plan to remove all the intelligentsia, supposedly the most dangerous element and capable of initiating a mutiny. The body of our professor was left in the main hall of the university. From there the families were supposed to fetch their relatives' remains for burial by their own means. From his hiding place, my friend saw Professor Ostrowski's wife pulling her husband's body downstairs, his head banging on the stone

steps. Eventually she reached the lower level, where a carriage
was waiting to take the mutilated corpse to the cemetery."

But this was much later.

Very early next morning, Stan and I reached the railway station.
The memorable inscription on the front of the huge building –
Leopolis Semper Fidelis ("Lwow always faithful") – sounded strange
and meaningless now. I never saw that city again.

The station was heavily bombarded day and night for tactical
reasons, to prevent transports to and from the East. We waited all
night in the underground corridors connecting the station with
the multiple railway tracks, watching for eastbound trains. Finally
a very long train arrived, loaded with wounded soldiers for evacuation. In broken Russian we explained to the train commandant
that we were doctors mobilized to the Soviet army and that we
wanted to reach the nearest recruiting point. He was delighted to
have us.

"Just go into any of the cars and make yourselves at home. I
believe there's some food. Don't forget to go all along the train
and look at the wounded. Some of them need medical help. We
don't have a doctor on the train." We jumped in the open door of
one of the freight cars just as a bomb, penetrating the glass roof
of the station, completely destroyed the last two cars of the train.
Without hesitation the commandant gave the order to disconnect
the two destroyed cars and get the train moving as fast as possible. This was my first lesson in sacrificing the few for the many,
and it did not yet fit into my medical ethical paradigm.

Once the train had moved a few hundred feet away from the
scene of the catastrophe, we began to notice the "contents" of our
car. A few soldiers sat on the floor, leaning against the walls, their
injured extremities immobilized in splints. In one corner a soldier
with a wounded shin was singing Russian songs and playing a
balalaika. In another corner, a heap of fresh loaves of bread filled
the air with the characteristic aroma of a bakery. In the middle of
the car was a bench that supported a whole case of fresh butter,
its wooden front panel removed for easy access.

We asked the soldiers how it was on the front. They said that
things were bad, that they were overwhelmed. The German air

force was inflicting heavy casualties upon the Soviet army. In their view, Russia would soon have to awaken from her stupor and put up a real fight. We explained that we were both surgeons, come to join their army.

"You will have lots of work," they said. At the front there had been no doctors, just stretcher bearers who applied dressings and splints. They offered us food, but Stan and I decided to go and see the wounded first. It took us about two hours to go through the whole train. We had some difficulty because those cars that were not interconnected could only be reached when the train stopped at a station. Most of the soldiers had complicated fractures of the upper or lower extremities. Some also had moderate (a few had major) injuries to the soft tissue (skin and muscles). One had a serious complication in the form of gas gangrene, caused by a particular type of bacteria, called anaerobic, that lives on damaged tissue with no access to oxygen. This infection is characterized by swelling and the accumulation of bubbles of gas in the wounded extremity, and generally by very high fever. An unpleasant smell comes from the affected extremity, and when touched the gas bubbles give off a particular sound.

The usual treatment in such cases was to make deep incisions into the muscles and pack them with gauze soaked in peroxide. But this treatment was seldom effective, and no other treatment was available except early amputation of the wounded extremity; otherwise the victim, once infected, would die within three to four days. Here on the train we had no facilities for operating and therefore the afflicted soldier was doomed. It was heartbreaking to look at the pale, emaciated face of this eighteen-year-old boy, one of the masses of victims of this cruel war.

There were no abdominal or chest traumas on the train. Apparently, such cases were left on the front to die when the army retreated, or else sent as untransportable to the nearest field hospital. Eventually we reported to the train commandant, Comrade Natchalnik, that all the wounded were all right except for one, who was beyond help because of the limitations of our situation. So as not to affect their morale, we suggested that he be separated from the other wounded soldiers. We then returned to our car, ravenous after a day and night without food, and consumed an enormous amount of fresh bread and butter before lying down to sleep. We were told the next morning that the train had been heavily bombarded as it approached Tarnopol, yet we had slept like the dead, undisturbed.

Late in the afternoon we arrived in Kiev, where we were taken in a truck to a mobilization point. There we were fed and given army uniforms. I was assigned to Autonomous Surgical Unit No. 77 and Dr Kampelmacher to a field hospital, both in the Fifth Army of the southwest front. The chief of my unit was Colonel Katarin, who, prior to the war, had been a member of the surgical university staff of the Sevastopol Medical School. He greeted us with a smile.

"Welcome to our unit. Your credentials are impressive. Let's go and meet my assistant." This was Major Andrei Jegorovitch Fili-monov. Tall and lean with a high forehead, black hair, and large, blue, friendly looking eyes, he gave the impression of being a kind and friendly intellectual. Before the war he had been an assistant surgeon at the university hospital in Saratov. The Autonomous Surgical Unit was composed altogether of eight surgeons, six operating-room nurses, six orderlies, and the commandant of the unit. We left for the front that evening, travelling in five vans complete with surgical equipment. Assigned work on the basis of field hospitals, which were placed in the areas of heaviest losses, we were usually located about thirty kilometres from the front line. The surgeons worked in three eight-hour shifts: eight hours of work, eight of rest (usually sleep).

Our first assignment was in Ovrutch, east of Kiev. The little town had apparently been evacuated in a rush. We found clothes and reserves of food in homes that had been left intact. After one night we moved further east to Ratcha, where, in a vacated school, we received the first transport of wounded soldiers. Rooms were chosen for surgery and their windows masked with blankets. Major Filimonov had the difficult job of determining which of the wounded would get surgical treatment first. He explained that according to military regulations, priority was given to those with the greatest chances of recovering and returning to the front lines.

"The job of choosing is heartbreaking," he added, "because I often have to leave to their deaths badly wounded soldiers who under normal peacetime conditions would have a good chance of recovery. That's the war, and for the time being we have to change the moral code we adopted when we took the Hippocratic oath.

Only when time and resources allow will the badly wounded be operated upon, if there is still a chance of recovery. In the meantime they are given only antishock treatment. Looking at them, I always wonder who is waiting at home for this poor doomed fellow? Maybe his wife, maybe his mother? And it makes me sick. Maybe I'll build up an armour of insensitivity; otherwise it will break me."

I followed him in silence, admiring his diagnostic skill and the speed with which he could separate the operable cases from the hopeless ones. It was hot in that enclosed space. The atmosphere was suffocating, full of the sweetish smell of decomposing blood and the groans and sobs of the wounded soldiers, who were often thirsty, sometimes very dehydrated. Two young doctors and three nurses followed us, starting intravenous drips of saline in glucose, according to Major Filimonov's orders. After the selection was completed, the chosen patients were brought to the operating rooms and the surgery began.

Abdominal injuries were usually inflicted by bomb splinters, which caused multiple smaller and larger injuries to the bowels. The surgical procedure was simple, consisting of closing the holes in the gut or making small bowel resections (cutting out part of the bowel and joining the ends together). Yet in spite of its simplicity, many wounded soldiers died the day after an abdominal operation without apparent cause. One night, however, I performed eight abdominal operations and the next day all of the patients were doing well. I was subsequently interviewed by General Kretov, chief surgeon of the Fifth Army, with the aid of a translator. He looked as if he was accustomed to speaking his mind.

"Igor Morovitch, I hope I pronounce your name accurately. Don't worry, you will learn Russian very fast – it's just another Slavic language. You probably understand a lot of what I am saying. The rest will be translated to you. Tell me, Comrade, why your operations are so successful and the results of other surgeons so poor?"

"I don't know," I said. "These operations are straightforward for any general surgeon. The best way to find out why the results are so different would be to perform autopsies on the deceased."

The general made some notes and thanked me. Within two days, three pathologists from Kiev were sent in. Autopsies were performed on all the deceased who had been operated for abdominal wounds. The findings were striking: numerous holes in the bowels of the deceased had been improperly closed, as if by physicians without training in surgery. It transpired that several doctors indeed had no surgical training but, in an effort to keep away from the front lines, had declared themselves to be surgeons. All these physicians were sent to the front lines forthwith.

The Fifth Army of the southwest front was in retreat, so that it was very difficult for field hospitals to operate. At the last moment, in would come the chief of evacuation, nervously smoking a cigarette. After walking around the tables and looking at his watch, he would suddenly call out: "Finish right away and embark." In many instances all I could do was to use clamps for temporary closure of a still-open abdomen, and within half an hour the entire hospital was on the move. We functioned like this for about two weeks before reaching a place where we could rest more. The rumour was that we would have to retreat further, but nobody knew when.

The work was very tiring, and there was hardly time for eating. After an eight-hour shift we were usually so exhausted that we preferred to lie down and sleep rather than eat. It was only when we got up that we had time and appetite for a solid breakfast. Whenever we were on duty and operating, we were given large amounts of red wine, which was brought to the field hospitals in huge barrels. In the beginning, I drank very little. One night, noticing my restraint, Major Filimonov explained that the wine was a good tonic and invigorating in this heavy work.

"Igor Morovitch, you should get used to this wine. It's an excellent way not only to feel stronger but also to help you cope with the kind of suffering you are exposed to here – you don't see this kind of thing in civilian surgery." He was so right. After a few days I was consuming large amounts of this red wine, feeling stronger and doing my work better than before.

Responding to calls from field hospitals with heavy casualties, we would move the surgical unit from place to place, preferably at night. One night we were walking from the tents of a field hospital to our vans further in the field. In spite of the darkness, we were attacked by a large number of German Messerschmidts.

"Run, don't stop, no matter what!" screamed Colonel Katarin.

The bullets from the attacking planes were like bright golden lines crossing the dark velvety sky. It was a frightening sight but also strangely beautiful. Nobody uttered a word as we headed for the vans, black silhouettes running a mortal marathon towards safety in a silence interrupted only by the swish of bullets and the gasps of the runners. We all reached the medical vans safely, by which time the planes had passed over and were far away.

With me in Surgical Unit 77 was another doctor from Lwow, Eddy Hirsh. We hadn't met before since we had worked in different hospitals. Hirsh was a real comedian; you could never tell whether he was joking or serious. He had a humorous face with a flat nose and eyes that were always smiling. Early one morning he woke me up, standing over my field bed without saying a word. His face was so funny that I automatically started to laugh. He looked at me steadily for a while.

"You are laughing. To hell with your laughter. Look at my face. The situation is tragic, horrible." I kept laughing.

"Do you think I am joking? Things are very bad and tense. I overheard Colonel Katarin talking to Major Filimonov. He got the order to send us someplace. I don't know where. They didn't say."

I stopped laughing. "So what, Eddy? We're soldiers; we don't make decisions. Here today, some place else tomorrow. What's the difference? We don't have to worry about food and shelter. And as far as danger is concerned, this is a war and we are in the middle of it already, so close to the front line. Another place can't be any worse."

Eddy looked away, perhaps thinking that I was right.

Early the next day he and I were taken by jeep to a railway station and put on a train. Planes were circling above and Eddy ran to the exit and down the steps, attempting to jump out. He was frightened that we would be bombarded.

"Eddy, don't jump! Those are Soviet planes."

"I don't believe you! You are just saying that to calm me."

After a while the planes disappeared and Eddy returned to his place. I felt sorry for him. His fear would not protect him from the inevitable.

In the morning we reached a small town where all the doctors mobilized from the Lwow district were assembled in some military buildings. I saw my old colleague, Stan Kampelmacher. He told me what he had found out from the commandant of the field hospital. Two days earlier there had been an order, No. 494, from the chief commandant of all fronts, Iosif Visarionowvicht Stalin, that all soldiers mobilized from Western Ukraine were to be transferred to the eastern hinterland. We were not considered trustworthy. Stan's chief thought that the transfer was connected with the treason committed by General Wlasov of the Fifth Army of the southwest front: part of Wlasov's army had gone over to the Germans. As we understood much later, this event, combined with the retreat of the Soviet armies, created a gap in the front that was really only stopped much later in Stalingrad.

About eight surgeons from Lwow and other places in Western Ukraine were put on a train and sent to the medical department of the Ural Military District. I was one of them. After about a week we reached the city of Swerdlowsk, the capital of Ural. It was very cold in the first days of November. As we got off the train the north wind cut our faces, which had never before been exposed to such temperatures.

Not only the icy chill but everything else felt different here. It was a feeling that went beyond the senses. It was like being ahead of time, penetrating the future, or being suspended between "not yet" and "no more." Everything seemed imbued with a peculiar harshness and cruelty. Nature itself seemed threatening, as if because of some inherent and strange difference. I had a sense of anticipation and a feeling that, here, there could be no forgiveness or second chance. No mistake would be pardoned; I would always have to be on the alert.

Around us lay the taiga, endless forests inhabited only by convicts who were sent there by the tsars to end their lives in pain and infamy. Did any trace of life survive? Was any human feeling resurrected from the sentence of abandonment? Did any heart reawaken to send love to those who would later share the same fate? Wait and see. I reminded myself that everything was possible. Even on stone, moss is growing.

We were brought by vehicles to the Ural Military District. We spent one day on the premises and were each given a post in one of the evacuation hospitals in the region.

Asbest

The Ural Mountains separate the European part of Russia from Siberia. The main city in northern Ural is Swerdlowsk, formerly called Iekaterinburg. The settlement had originally been erected by Tsaritsa Catherina for political prisoners to do *katorga* (hard labour) in the famous taiga that ran throughout Siberia. Ural is a land of short summers and long harsh winters, of white nights in the summer and short gloomy winter days. Untouched by the war that raged in European Russia and far from the front, everything was quiet.

Asbest, where I was sent, is a little town northwest of Swerdlowsk. It originated as an industrial settlement populated by employees of the Asbestos Combine. The combine was under the jurisdiction and management of the Soviet Union's Federal Ministry of Industrial and Building Materials. Not far from the railway station was the main street, which ran through the whole town. At the head of the street was a large building, the local school; across the street stood a few stores, representing the local shopping centre. Further down to the right were industrial buildings that faced the administration buildings of the enterprise. From there, a narrow road led to the Sowchoz (*Sovetskoe Choziaistwo*), the government farm that supplied the workers with produce. On both sides of the streets running from the school and down along the main road were small homes built for the employees. Among them were wider, nicer streets with large homes for the families of the management.

. The medical department of the Ural Military District had instructed me to report to the chief of Military Evacuation Hospital No. 2537, located in the local school and adjoining buildings. The chief administrator and commandant of the hospital was a young female doctor in her mid-twenties. She looked like a teenager. I couldn't believe that the management of a military hospital with over eight hundred beds had been entrusted to this girl. Bending over some documents, she kept me waiting for some time.

"So you're assigned to this hospital," she asked finally, without lifting her eyes from the papers. When I didn't answer, she raised her head and gazed at me in silence. She had large deeply set cobalt blue eyes, a small nose, high cheekbones, and short black hair setting off her fair complexion. Smiling suddenly, she said, "*Zdrastwuite*. Welcome to our hospital. I'm Klavdia Fedorovna Belaia, the chief director of the evacuation hospital. You should feel proud," she continued, tidying the papers on her desk, "because we are the largest military evacuation hospital in the Ural district. I'm certain that you were sent here by the Medical Military Command because you are highly qualified. By the way, please don't mind if I call you by your father's name; it's the accepted practice here. So, Igor Morovitch, tell me something about yourself."

I responded with difficulty, in broken Russian mixed with Polish. "It's difficult to talk about myself. Let me just say that I'll certainly try to fulfil my professional obligations."

"In that case, let's make some rounds and meet the other doctors."

Along the way, Klavdia told me that she had graduated from medicine two years earlier. She was a member of Komsomol (the Communist youth party); this added political support to her modest professional qualifications because it meant she was *blago-nadiozhny* – trustworthy. As we met the other doctors and obtained reports from some of them, I could see that this beautiful girl had administrative experience as well as determination. At our approach the doctors and nurses would stand to attention in military fashion.

Back in her office, tea was served by an orderly. Klavdia asked me to sit down.

"As you know, Igor Morovitch," she began, "we'll have to work together very closely. I want you to help me bring this hospital to a proper professional level. This is not only the largest hospital but, in addition, most of the high-ranking officers are sent to us for treatment. You are going to be our chief surgeon; I expect you to treat not only the patients but also the doctors. For the first little while, I'll help you write the reports until you're more fluent in Russian. You can live in the hospital until you find your own place, and you can eat here for the entire length of your employment. The food isn't bad. Do you have any questions?"

As I hadn't, we parted for the day. Over the next few days and nights, I went through almost all of the case histories, struggling with forms written by hand in an unfamiliar language. Written and printed letters are completely different in Russian. Most of the time, I was assisted by a female internist from Moscow, Maria Stepanovna Kurygina, who was rarely tired and always willing to help, even late into the night. Maria was a lean woman in her late forties. Short light-coloured hair framed her square face with its sad grey eyes, small snubbed nose, and protruding chin. She was hardly attractive, but she had a velvety voice and her manner was warm. Her husband, a colonel in the Secret Espionage Service of the NKVD, had been lost somewhere in Germany two years before the war. They had had no children. Her one sister, a widow in Tomsk, Siberia, was very ill with cancer. This sister's teenaged son was supported by Maria, who regularly sent money and parcels to Tomsk.

Maria helped me go through all the case histories during those long nights so that I wouldn't have to ask the hospital commandant for help with this tedious work. We often took breaks during which Maria would make tea and offer her own home-made cookies.

"Don't be impatient, Igor Morovitch. You're doing very well," she assured me, "and soon you'll be able to read and understand all the histories. Medical language is very simple." She urged me to read the great Russian novelists to increase my vocabulary. "It is my obligation to make you fluent in Russian so that you can teach our doctors as well. A horrible war is being waged; we have to conquer the forces of evil that threaten all mankind. But you'll be fine," she continued. "The other doctors admire your knowledge and experience."

I thanked her earnestly. "You're so kind and helpful, and you've sacrificed so many hours of sleep – I don't know how I can repay you."

"Don't mention it," Maria said, taking my hand and gently stroking it. "I do it for myself. But as an internist I can learn a lot from you. I find it interesting when you talk about your home and how people live in the West." I realized that she was personally interested in me. She was lonely in Asbest, and perhaps, as a visitor from the free world, I carried a certain mystique and novelty. I was also an able-bodied male and thus something of a rarity. Most of the Russian men were at the front and the few that remained had usually been excused from active service for serious health reasons. Her interest worried me. I knew that I would have to find another doctor to replace me in her affections.

Among the eight doctors on staff were three young surgeons who had not finished their training and who, for health reasons, had not been sent to the front. I grew particularly fond of Genadi Petrovitch Karpov because of his unusually polite and friendly manner. A tall, lean man in his late twenties, he had been a victim of polio and limped because of the atrophied muscles in his legs. Our first meeting had been awkward; he bumped into me and Klavdia as we were making our rounds and then apologized, saying that he was having a bad day. Klavdia introduced us and suggested that he become my pupil and assistant. From that moment on, Genadi became not only my assistant but also my Russian teacher and friend. The first thing he helped me do was to write a report for the hospital administrator outlining our task and requesting the organization of certain facilities and a supply of drugs and instruments necessary to do the work. We included information about the assignment of doctors to their patients, the separation of clean cases from infected ones, the designation of operating rooms and their personnel, and the establishment of scheduled operating days.

I carried out my responsibilities in surgery and designated the hours of consultation for the interns and neurologists. Evenings were spent teaching. One Saturday afternoon, Klavdia Fedorovna arranged a meeting in the hospital's main dining-room with the doctors and the other medical personnel. When Genadi and I entered the room with Klavdia, the other doctors were already there. Klavdia introduced me to the neurologist, Vasili Ivanovitch

Shertov, a tall, well-built man in his late fifties with a pleasant round face. His forehead receded into a shiny bald scalp surrounded by wreaths of bushy silver hair. Genadi then introduced me to two friends of his, two young surgeons named Ilya and Piotr who had been helping him care for the patients. Behind thick eyeglasses Ilya's eyes looked like dark points. This extreme short-sightedness was the reason for his release from military duty. He greeted me timidly, wisps of dark hair falling over his forehead. "We all hope to learn a lot from you," he said. Greeting me, Piotr could hardly catch his breath. He suffered from severe asthma and had difficulty breathing when he was tense or suddenly faced with a stressful situation.

"It's very nice to meet all of you," I told the young doctors. "The four of us must care for all the surgical patients in this huge hospital. The workload is enormous, but as long as we understand each other, there won't be any problems. To gain experience in military surgery is a rare opportunity, one we would not normally have."

I quoted the Russian saying *Tishe iedesh dalshe budesh*, which means the more slowly you work, the further you will get, or "slow and sure wins the race." I promised not to create undue stress but warned that we would have to put in long hours to get through the work that awaited us. I asked them to meet with me the following day to organize our schedule.

Accordingly, at 3:00 P.M. the next afternoon, the young doctors were awaiting me in my office. When we were all seated, I got my notes and addressed them.

"Dear friends, I have examined all the patients and gone through their case histories. We can expect an enormous amount of work over the next few weeks. Although you know these patients, you may not be aware that about eighty percent of them require some form of surgical intervention to make them fit for military duty." I told them the observations I had made after examining the patients the previous day. All the surgical patients were experiencing late-war trauma complications such as osteomyelitis, a chronic inflammation of the bone and marrow. These infections were the usual complications of comminuted bone fractures from gunshots. As well, there were patients who still had foreign objects such as bullets and metal fragments lodged in areas that were difficult to get at, such as their lungs and livers.

Their symptoms were caused by the impaired functioning of their vital organs. Some were infected by pus draining through the fistulas. All of these patients had been hospitalized for quite a while. They had been fed and had their dressings changed, but that was the extent of their care because there had been no competent surgeon to treat them actively.

"From now on," I told them, "we'll have to work two shifts a day in the operating rooms to catch up. The only way to do justice to the name 'evacuation hospital' is to train you guys in surgery so that you can help me cure these chronically wounded soldiers as fast as possible." The young doctors listened attentively, assuring me that they would work as long and as hard as need be.

Amongst the doctors sent to Ural were a few sanitary orderlies who could work in hospitals. Vadim Zamrovitch Zelikin, who had been sent with me to Asbest, was one of them. All day, this young fellow in his early twenties stayed close to me; he tried to be helpful and sat like a well-trained dog at the feet of his master. He was, it seemed, the kind of person who felt he would benefit by being useful to those whom he believd to have power and influence.

"Igor Morovitch," he said to me one day when I was still living in the hospital, "as I'm fluent in Russian, I was looking around, and I've found a place for us to live with a very nice Russian family."

"Who told you, Vadim, that I need quarters," I asked him, "and why should you live with me?"

"I was told that there is nobody to look after you. I also learned all about your likes and dislikes. I explained everything to the hospital's personnel superintendent; he has told me to take up my duties with you."

I was amazed by the way this young man could arrange things for himself. I didn't object right away but put off, for the time being, any decision concerning his usefulness.

The next morning Vadim told me that my belongings were already in the new place that he had rented for us. The house was nice and clean and close to the hospital. We had two good-sized rooms. The owner was a middle-aged woman with two children; her husband was on the western front. She kept the place in immaculate condition and served us hot milk in the mornings.

Vadim pressed my uniform, and took my laundry to the hospital to be cleaned. All in all, he behaved satisfactorily; nevertheless, there was something peculiar about him that I couldn't define, something that made me uncomfortable. I couldn't pinpoint the source of my unease but felt intuitively that I would eventually have to move out and live alone.

We began to work very long hours in the hospital. Within two weeks we had two functioning operating rooms. In one room, with Genadi's assistance, I operated on the more pressing and complex cases; in the other, my two new trainees, Ilya and Piotr, completed the simpler procedures. The surgical-assistance personnel, such as nurses and orderlies, were trained and assigned to each operating room. For the severely ill and post-operative patients, we made rounds during the day and late in the evening. All three surgeons were instructed to make proper operation reports. Within a month we were able to discharge a few patients who were now fit to return to the front. Each day after lunch, we had an hour-long question-and-answer period. Twice a week after evening rounds, two hours were spent teaching.

Klavdia Fedorovna was very pleased. She followed our progress and didn't hide her recognition of the high standards of our treatment of the patients and training of the doctors. She also mentioned that, after receiving her last report, General Lazarew, head of the medical department of the Ural Military District, had said that he wanted to meet me. At the end of February she asked me to join her on a trip to Swerdlowsk to see the general.

On the train Klavdia was in a good mood, glad of a day's respite from the demands of her post. Deep in thought, she glowed in the lazy afternoon sun, a far-away look in her eyes. She told me about her difficult childhood, growing up with a severe factory-worker father, struggling to fulfil her dream of being a doctor. Just three years earlier, she had married Grisha, a truck driver in the Asbestos Combine. He was bright, honest, and good both to her and to her mother, who lived with them. Although I didn't understand why Klavdia was telling me her life story, I sensed that she was searching for somebody with whom she could share matters that she couldn't discuss with her husband. The time passed quickly and before we knew it, we had reached Swerdlowsk.

We went first to the medical department of the Ural Military District, where General Lazarew greeted us cordially. He was an imposing man, tall and built like a prizefighter. With his large blue eyes and charming smile, he wore a satisfied and happy expression.

"*Zdrastwuite dorogoi* [greetings], dear Igor Morovitch," he said. "I know all about what's going on at your hospital and couldn't be more pleased. I think that when you're done catching up, I'll have to send you to all the evacuation hospitals in the region to organize the way you did in Asbest. In the meantime, every week I'll send a surgeon from one of the other hospitals to spend some time with you and observe your organizational style. In this month's medical-department order, which is sent to all area units, you will receive *blagodarnost* [special thanks] for returning the largest number of soldiers to the front." He invited us to sit down for tea with brandy and some small cookies. When eventually we rose to leave, he opened his desk drawer and handed us an envelope. "Here are two tickets for tonight's performance at the opera house. Go and relax and have some fun this evening; you both deserve it for doing such good work."

That night the Bolshoi Ballet presented *Swan Lake*, featuring the well-known young ballerina Plisetskaia, a pupil of the famous Pavlova. It was a great treat for me after the long weeks of hard work and stress. During the intermission, Klavdia Fedorovna introduced me to her former professors, the surgeon Arkadi Timofeevitch Lidski and the neurologist Lev Aronovitch Shefer. Both were professors at the Swerdlowsk University medical faculty, and both served as consultants in the Ural Military District.

After the performance we went to the Red Army House* where, after a late snack, we were shown our rooms for the night. By noon the next day we were back in Asbest. Klavdia took me to her home, where her mother treated us to lunch. Later, these invitations came more frequently, especially for Sunday dinner. I became friendly with her husband Grisha, who liked my company, particularly when I told stories about travelling and life in the West.

With time it became apparent that Klavdia liked me as more than just a good friend. Yet she never made it obvious that she was interested in an amorous affair. Often it was difficult for me to understand her behaviour. Our relationship became tense, then

---

* A social centre for the military where guest rooms were assigned.

cool and reserved, at times even hostile. One afternoon she said, "Igor Morovitch, I feel that we must talk about some problems very soon."

"Of course, any time." I assumed that we were discussing hospital matters as usual. "Let's step into your office."

"No, no," she insisted, "not right now – not in my office. A friend of mine has allowed me to have this talk in her home; it will be very discreet. I've arranged it for this afternoon. We have to be there in about an hour, so let's leave now." It was a lovely sunny afternoon, not very cold. Klavdia was very talkative and seemed to be in a great mood. When we reached the house, she asked me to wait and then follow her in a few minutes. Inside, in a tidy room, we sat down.

"You don't have to be very smart to notice," she began, avoiding my gaze, "that I regard you not as my chief surgeon but more as a man I could love." She went on to say that, if possible, she would try to arrange for one of us to be transferred. A brief fling would not cure her feelings towards me: she did not believe in affairs. Besides, she was four months' pregnant. "I'm sure you have noticed the inconsistencies in my behaviour towards you," she added. "I beg you to tolerate these ups and downs and try to understand me. I know you're not in love with me. If you will only bear with me, I may get over these feelings in time."

This unexpected turn of events left me speechless, but after a few minutes of tense silence I tried to frame a response, speaking as one doctor to another. "You may not know it, but you are very precious to me. Thanks to you, I don't feel so alone here, being so far away from my family; you're very dear to me, like a beloved sister. Let us remain the wonderful friends that we are and see whether or not your feelings go away."

When I stopped talking, Klavdia got up and embraced me warmly, kissing me on both cheeks. "Thank you, Igor. Maybe you're right; maybe I love you but don't know in what way. Please let me love you the way my heart tells me to." With that, we parted and returned to our respective homes.

My social life in Asbest was quite pleasant. I spent time mainly with a few families with whom I could talk about the intellectual and spiritual life in this communist-controlled state. A young female internist working in our hospital, Natalie Davidovitch Straus, once invited me over for dinner. She was married to a young engineer from the *Nadvolzhanskaia Germanska Respublika* (the German Republic on the Volga River). When the Second World War began, the entire population of the republic, a few million people, had been transferred in the old-fashioned way, as in the time of the tsars, to different places in the Ural and Siberia as *spets peresilentsy* (special settlers). These people were given substandard living quarters and had to report every week to the local NKVD official. They weren't allowed to move from place to place; in extreme cases, they needed a special *propuska* (passport).

With such a passport, Natalie followed her husband, Helmut. As a doctor and employee of the military hospital, she was given a better home; however, her husband had to report weekly to the authorities. Helmut was employed by the Asbestos Combine but in a fairly low position with less responsibility than he was qualified to carry. Natalie was an attractive young lady in her late twenties with long dark curly hair, a pretty face, and large brown eyes. Helmut was tall, lean, blond, and blue eyed. Both were well read and intelligent. They had met during their studies in Kiev, where they later married.

That evening at dinner there were only Helmut, Natalie, her mother, and myself. The meal was very modest. Afterwards, sitting in the other room, Helmut produced a bottle of brandy, Staraia Leningradzkaia Starka, which he had kept hidden from the good old days.

"You know, Igor Morovitch," he began, "we don't see any people here; they're afraid to have any contact with us. I'm considered to be a German – an enemy – and treated like a prisoner. I don't dare talk to anybody; my words would be misinterpreted and brought to the attention of the NKVD. This is a difficult situation for us, and I regret that Natalie suffers because of it. But what can we do? You're probably the only one I can talk to without being afraid."

"Being a foreigner from Poland, I can't really speak for the Russians," I told him, "but I imagine they are afraid of a fifth column, especially as the German army is approaching Stalingrad. And the Nazis' racial policies don't make the Slavs feel much sympathy for anything German. They must trust Natalia, though, since they put her to work in this military hospital. Your situation is probably better than that of other Germans here."

The women didn't participate in this conversation. The atmosphere was becoming heavy as I was certainly not on the side of the Germans. After an uncomfortable silence, I made my excuses, saying that I still had a few patients to see after their operations. I felt sorry for Natalie. I wondered why I had taken such a reserved or, rather, pro-Russian position. Maybe between the two, I still preferred the Russians to Germans as people.

Several new activities began to occupy my time. I sent two papers – "The Technique of Removal of Foreign Bodies" and "A New Technique of Block Anaesthesia" – to the journal *Materialy Nauchnych Rabot Uralskoho Vojennowo Okruga* ("Materials of Scientific Works of the Ural Military District"). Both were accepted and published in 1942. Genadi was a tremendous help, editing and making excellent anatomical drawings. I was also a consultant to the local civilian hospital, which suffered from the shortage of surgeons, and ran its surgical out-patient clinic once a week.

One day, the hospital superintendent found me a new place to stay, a pleasant house on a nice street. The owner, a widow, occupied only one room and kept the place in immaculate condition. Vadim stayed back in the old place, so I was able to enjoy my privacy. Utterly exhausted after weeks of strenuous work and with low immunity, I got a bad sore throat. Genadi visited me daily; when my fever came down, he started to bring lots of books, encouraging me to read. I passed the days reading Russian classics and deepening my knowledge of that most beautiful and rich Slavic language. The thoughts and feelings of the Russians seemed exotic to me, so warm in comparison to sober Westerners like myself. Dostoyevsky's insight into the deepest recesses of the human soul dwarfed the works of psychology and psychiatry I had once studied. Pushkin's brilliant poetry, his untranslatable, subtle, and weightless metaphors of love and irony, make him the greatest Slavic poet that ever lived. At times, these flights to the dreamland of poetry were strangely juxtaposed like a *memento mori* with the frightening reality of a world becoming more and more monstrous and inhuman, thanks to Hitler and Stalin. These two evil geniuses were drawing humankind deeper and deeper into suffering, cruelty, and death.

There is no spring in the Ural. The first days of summer arrived suddenly, bringing long days whose bright hours lasted beyond midnight. The snow was gone, and the first green leaves were the harbinger of a pregnant nature. In man, this is a time of renewed energy and creativity, a time to solve mysteries and reach for new heights, a time of longing for romantic adventures – the call of nature for renewal.

Unexpectedly, my emotional equilibrium came to an end. My practical plans for improving the quality of our medical services in the hospital were completely lost when certain strange happenings changed my life. The first was my meeting with Natalia Petrovna.

My main responsibilities were at the Asbest military evacuation hospital; however, in view of the shortage of surgeons (most of whom were in military service) I consulted in the local civilian hospital, and ran the surgical out-patient clinic once a week as well.

One balmy afternoon in mid-March, I was at the out-patient clinic at the local hospital. As the sun set in the mountains, I was just finishing my notes when a voice said, "Doctor?"

"The hours are over. Who are you to be coming so late?" I said, without looking up. But the voice had been soft and hypnotic. I lifted my head and saw a beautiful woman standing at the door. Golden hair framing a creamy complexion, big blue eyes, high cheekbones – it is difficult to do justice to Natalia Petrovna in mere words. Controlling myself with an effort, I asked, "How may I help you?"

"My name is Natalia Petrovna and I've sprained my ankle. I am the wife of the minister of Industrial and Building Materials of the Soviet Union. We have been evacuated, along with other ministers' families, from Moscow to Asbest. I got a late call from my husband in Moscow concerning some important matters. That's why I'm late. Please forgive me." Mesmerized by her, I didn't even follow her explanation. She showed me her ankle. "It's swollen and it hurts when I put my weight on it." I examined her foot. "Stay in bed for a few days and put compresses on it," I advised. "Please come to the next clinic."

"I know where you live," she said. "It's on the same street where we're living. If I'm supposed to be in bed, would you be so kind as to visit me at my home? You could check my progress and tell me when I can start to walk again."

I went to their house in the early evening two days later. I was greeted politely by her sister-in-law, Maria Ivanovna, who guided me to the living-room and invited me to take a seat. Soon a tall man in his sixties with a genuine smile entered the room and introduced himself as Natalia Petrovna's husband. He thanked me for coming to their house. He was just home for a day before leaving on a long and difficult mission. "We heard from the Ural Military District that you're one of our outstanding surgeons," he said, "so I know Natalia will get excellent care. Now, before I leave, let's have a drink."

Natalia Petrovna was in her bedroom, lying down with a compress on her ankle. Since the swelling was down, I told her that she could get up for short periods, taking care not to put too much weight on the injured foot. As a doctor attending the family of a state minister, I tried to behave as disinterestedly as possible. Even a touch of the most platonic infatuation could play havoc with our lives. We both knew we were attracted to each other, as if a force greater than ourselves had engaged us in a mortal game.

"I believe, Doctor, that you're satisfied with my progress, but I would still like to be under your care until I recover completely and start to walk again without pain."

"Yes, of course, I'll be with you as long as you wish." Our conversation, flowing through the open door to her husband and sister-in-law, seemed casual enough but had a double meaning. I left Natalia Petrovna's house feeling elated. Outside it was one of those enchanting nights in the Ural Mountains, the green stars dancing in the midnight blue sky and the frosty, invigorating air filling my lungs. The snow crunched happily under my feet as embraced the nearest tree in an ecstatic harmony with nature. I felt as if I had received a wonderful gift.

Days passed. I worked as hard as possible to escape my relentless daydreams. At one time, a silvery voice stopped me in one of the hospital corridors. "What is going on with you these days, Igor Morovitch? You're short-tempered and unapproachable." It was Klavdia, the director. Her voice was soft and melodic, like birdsong, a characteristic of the voices of Russian women.

"It's nothing to worry about," I said. After her confession, how could I tell her I was infatuated with Natalia Petrovna? I didn't want to cause her unnecessary pain and hoped that time would solve the problem. Maybe she'd find out later on her own.

Time crawled. I came home late from work. My sleepless nights were filled with provocative fantasies of Natalia Petrovna and myself. Weeks later I started, with some effort, to bring myself to order, scolding myself for my weaknes of character. More time passed. No longer did I lose myself in unproductive fantasies and musings. I got back into the usual routine and social life of the town. One evening I was invited for dinner at Vasili Ivanovitch Shertov's home. He was the neurologist in our hospital, mobilized as a civilian on contract from his former position as a professor at Leningrad University. His wife, Xenia Petrovna, was the head nurse in the operating rooms. They had three lovely teenagers, all of whom played musical instruments. Vasili was an example of a Russian intellectual with a beautiful soul.

Because of my titles and high position, I got large supplies of rare foods from the military, as well as vegetables from the Asbest government farm. Since I was single and ate in the hospital or at the cafeteria for the Asbest Combine's selected staff, I sent all my unwanted food to Vasili Ivanovitch's family to complement their meagre food rations. That night Vasili filled two glasses with a nice red wine, and we sat in the living-room while his wife Xenia prepared something for us to eat.

"You must feel very lonely here amongst strangers in this small place in the northern Ural, so far away from your home and family," Vasili commented.

"It's not as bad as you think. I feel very comfortable with your people. The Russians are so warmhearted and sincere. As they say, *dusha na rozpashonku* [the unfettered soul]."

"Probably they are, or rather were."

"Why do you use the past tense?" I asked.

"Oh, you know." Vasili spoke in a near whisper, instinctively glancing around. "During these strange times, the best features of the Russian soul are lost in an ocean of mistrust, even between members of a family. I tell you this in confidence. To me, you're different. You still have a sense of decency and understanding of personal freedom. Here we live in a police state. Everybody is afraid of his own shadow. You'll find out for yourself. Don't trust anybody unless you are quite certain that you will not be deceived."

"You're not the first to warn me," I replied. "Everybody here is afraid. Is there nothing but fear?" Again Vasily looked around.

"You see, Igor Morovitch, this socialist revolution was the noble but misguided product of idealists. They never really grasped that it goes against human nature to expect people to relinquish and renounce private property and to accept the principle 'From each according to his ability, to each according to his needs.'"

"So you're saying that it was beautiful in theory but a failure in practice?"

"Well, just look at what has happened. Remember the famine in the Ukraine, which Stalin used as a means to forcibly introduce farm collectivization. Many people died of starvation."

"I know," I said. "Yet there is something good in this system. There is no envy. You don't accumulate a fortune, but neither does anyone around you. In the capitalist system, inequality creates a lot of bad blood."

"But the noble intentions have gone wrong," my friend insisted. "We pay dearly for our attempt at equality. You have to watch yourself all the time. You're always surrounded by informers; you can't trust your friends or even, in many cases, your own children. It's tragic; it's a complete loss of basic human freedom. I wouldn't exchange freedom for the questionable pleasure of being free of envy." At that moment the door opened and Xenia called us for dinner.

Later, Vasili's daughter played the piano for us like a virtuoso. The subtle sounds, full of longing, of a Chopin piano concerto were like a prayer rising to heaven and praising God for the gift of romantic passion. Vasili and I sat in soft chairs, hypnotized by the flow of the celestial music and enjoying the last sips of the old Caucasian wine he had kept for special occasions like this. Wrapped in this warm and peaceful atmosphere, we forgot for a moment the reality that we inhabited.

Around midnight I left their home, walking quickly under a sky brightly illuminated by the moon. Heedless of direction or distance, I reached home and went to bed right away, falling into a sound sleep.

Was I dreaming, or was somebody really knocking on my window? I couldn't tell. Initially, the knocking was very gentle; then it became louder. Finally I realized that I wasn't dreaming. Who could it be at this time of night? I wasn't expecting anybody; and anyhow, why couldn't they use the door? Wary of intruders, I got up and lifted the curtain on the other window very slightly so that I wouldn't directly face the uninvited visitor. What I saw filled me with fear but also with a deep sense of gratification, as if I had been transported to a fairy-tale land: hiding her face in her brown beaver coat, a white woollen cap pulled down over her head, Natalia Petrovna stood outside, her eyes urgent and afraid lest no one respond to her knocking. I ran to the other window and knocked on the glass to let her know that I was there. When I opened the door, she threw herself into my arms. We stood thus for a long time, full of wonder and longing. In the moonlit room shadows from the naked trees outside moved against the walls. The only sound was the scud of snowflakes against the windowpanes. I was afraid of trespassing, even in this state of bliss; I didn't want to ruin the tranquillity we had achieved.

We found ourselves in bed; I felt no fear and wouldn't have minded dying at that moment in Natalia's embrace. Gradually, the blizzard subsided and a velvety silence embraced us both as we fell into a deep sleep. When I opened my eyes again, it was still dark and Natalia was gone.

For the next few days I was completely absorbed by my thoughts. I performed my regular tasks in an almost absent-minded fashion. I did all the required work; I got up on time; I attended administrative meetings and did my duty in the operating room and at the bedsides of the post-operative cases. However, I functioned like an automaton; my mind, my consciousness, was somewhere else, far away from the trivialities of daily life. Who would have imagined that love would make its appearance in such troubled times and in such a depressing place? And how would I handle this compelling attraction?

I knew I was playing with fire, but to resist temptation was to deny myself an area of warmth in a cold and forbidding environment. My brief marriage in Poland had broken up. Natalia Petrovna had offered herself to me. It did not seem fair that I should be obliged to turn from love when it was offered. I was devastated with desire for her and believed I could spend my life with her, if only that were possible. In spite of my mature age, I had never been as much in love with anyone. I saw her in every cloud in the sky, every needle on the pines, and every snowflake on the ground. She made my life meaningful. I forgot the pain of the recent past and felt hope and joy – except in brief moments of lucidity when I saw the potential dangers. She was a married woman, the wife of a high government official. I was an unimportant guest in a strange country that had a totalitarian government. Surely this was a recipe for disaster.

My inner conflict lasted a month. Gradually I realized that I was deeply involved and couldn't will away my feelings. I decided to let Natalia Petrovna make the next move. I had to arrive at some decision to get out of a stupor that would affect my work. Natalia, meanwhile, seemed to be keeping to herself. Like me, she was trying to decide what to do, but I began to believe that she didn't want to see me any more. Although the thought was practically unbearable, I decided not to attempt to meet her and upset her life. Painful as this decision was, I believed that in taking it I had settled the matter once and for all. But I was wrong.

The days became very short, and winter achieved its full splendour. In the sunny, frosty mornings the air was dense and dry; crystalline snowflakes decorated the pines. It was almost the end of December when I realized that I had received an invitation from Klavdia Fedorovna for the approaching New Year's Eve party at her home. This was the first sign of my return to real life: I started to absorb what people said to me. I was staying late every night at the hospital to make up for my time on Cloud Nine. I had fallen behind in my case histories and other paperwork and was surprised that nobody had noticed.

Late one evening on my way home, I was wondering what to bring Klavdia Fedorovna for the New Year. I didn't know the local customs and decided to ask my friend Vasili Ivanovitch, the neurologist. As I walked to and from his house, bright stars danced in the black sky. I was so exhausted by my weeks of unrequited love that, once home, I crawled into bed and fell asleep fully dressed. Sometime later I heard a knocking on my window and I jumped up, still half asleep. Looking through the window, I could hardly believe my eyes. There stood the stranger in the fur hat wearing a woollen shawl around her face. I quickly opened the door. Natalia Petrovna embraced me violently before she even entered. I didn't dare interrupt the silence that ensued.

"This is the third time I've come knocking at your window!" She sobbed as she spoke. "Where were you? I thought I'd die if I didn't see you tonight." It took her a while to recover; then she told me about what had been happening with her during the time

since we had last seen each other. She had gone through exactly
what I had – the same feelings, fears, and hesitation – before
making her final decision. We had both come to the conclusion
that we should rely on fate and live in the only way bearable for
us. We would be true to ourselves, no matter what we had to face.
That resolution brought a sense of inner freedom. Without trying
to make our bond known, we nevertheless felt ready, in case
events betrayed us, to stand up in defence of our union.

Natalia Petrovna mentioned that her husband was returning in
a few days from Moscow to spend Christmas at home. We
wouldn't see each other for a while, but she intended to invite me
for lunch on New Year's Day. We parted early the next morning.

Klavdia's house was filled to overflowing on New Year's Eve.
Many of the guests were hospital staff, or friends of Klavdia's from
Swerdlowsk. The mood was very festive. Although there were no
traditional features such as the Christmas tree or other Western
customs on display, the unique Russian lovingkindness, the *dusha
na rozpashonku* [unchained soul] permeated the atmosphere.
Despite limitations in the quantity and quality of food available
in those difficult times, the number, variety, and taste of the dishes
we were served was astonishing. Furthermore, we were offered
endless supplies of vodka and other drinks. Longing for joy and
delight, people mingled, made small talk, and tried to forget the
bad times. Male and female singers performed Russian romances
accompanied by the melancholy music of the balalaika. As we
listened to these melodies, we looked at the flickering flames in
the fireplace, thinking of loved ones who were cut off from us by
the war, wishing we could share with them the magic of this gathering, sorry that we could not wish them *Wstretcha Novoho Goda*
(Happy New Year).

"Igor Morovitch, we have to leave right away." Klavdia Fedorovna spoke quietly but firmly, awakening me from my romantic
reverie. "Something terrible has happened at the hospital."

What we found upon our arrival was frightening. In the corridors and rooms of Building No. 3 patients were vomiting in their
beds and on the floors; some of them lay prostrate in pools of
watery, pinkish grey fluid. Although I had never seen anything
like it, the thing that came to mind was a sudden outbreak of

Asiatic cholera. However, there was no time to ponder the diagnosis. Immediately, I had Klavdia Fedorovna call all the doctors and started a quick fluid-replacement treatment. In about three or four hours, all the sick patients were on intravenous fluid drips; some received mild sedatives, and samples of vomit were taken for laboratory investigations. Naturally, the commandant notified the NKVD; they came in and took reports from all the doctors. Their frightening presence was normal to the Russian doctors, who lived in a police state where calamities and catastrophes were always blamed on the enemies of the revolution. There are no such things as bacteria or unavoidable mishaps: everything is the fault of somebody, some enemy of the revolution.

We spent the entire night in the hospital, after which Klavdia took me back to her home for some breakfast. It was an especially cold morning. By that time all the guests had gone; only Klavdia's mother awaited us with hot tea and Russian blintzes. Deep in thought, Klavdia suddenly made a short, sad prophecy:

"I don't know how, but all this will end very badly; our lives will never be the same again."

The first half of January was dark. Heavy clouds brought lots of snow, and there were times when I thought the sun would never return. The roads and passes were like tunnels with walls of packed snow ten to twelve feet high. Often there were blizzards accompanied by violent winds that eventually subsided, leaving a world shrouded in white. A painter would need only three shades to capture the landscape: white, grey, and black. To me, this monochrome effect mirrored the depressing melancholy that permeated my soul as it wandered somewhere between hopelessness and dreams of a happier past. With all my strength, I tried to overcome this mood with daydreams about being with Natalia Petrovna. I completely forgot Klavdia's ominous prediction and went on with my life as usual.

These days I was often a guest at Natalia Petrovna's home in the evenings. Maria Ivanovna usually greeted me cordially, never revealing whether she knew about her sister-in-law and me. If she did know, it didn't affect her warmth towards me. We would have supper; then Natalia would come back with me to my place a bit further down the street. Later, I would walk her home.

Sometimes there were other guests at Natalia Petrovna's, usually friends from Moscow. I met writers and musicians, and even the famous chess player Botvinik. "The Soviet Union has so many chess masters," I remarked to him. "It's a tradition. What are the qualities required to be a chess master?"

"It's difficult to say. Basically, it's an inner resource, the ability to assess realistically the near and distant future and act accordingly."

"What do you mean by 'act accordingly?'"

"To have stamina and courage," he replied, "without hiding it behind a mask."

"I can see that a lot of psychology is involved."

"Oh yes," he agreed. "You must be able to define your opponent from the very first encounter, picking up information from his face, body language, voice, and so on. The eyes are the most important; they are the mirror of the soul. Sometimes in them you can read fear, desperation, even panic. The eyes are important because a smart opponent usually keeps silent. But if you can provoke him to speak, then you open a new source of information. You pick up on shades of feeling from his voice and, accordingly, decide whether to defend your position or attack." Listening to Botvinik, it was clear to me that chess was an allegory of life.

Sometimes Natalia invited the wives of the *narodni* commissars (cabinet ministers) of the coal and forest industries. Their conversations usually centred around the lack of cultural entertainment in this small place, on the latest news from the fronts, and on the work their husbands were doing in Moscow. They would ask me about life in the West, what the stores looked like, whether you could buy whatever you wanted, and so on. Often these ladies invited Natalia Petrovna, Maria, and me to their homes for dinner or small dancing soirées or for afternoon tea parties. With this social activity there was no time for depressing thoughts. Natalia and I were very much in love, and her tenderness was indescribable. Strangely enough, she didn't hide her feelings around other people. Intoxicated by the pleasant atmosphere, I actually believed that our happiness would last.

Monotonous grey days passed in the hospital. Doctors and nurses alike avoided the usual small talk and gossip in the corridors. Everybody worked in a kind of cocoon, confining themselves to a few formalities during hospital rounds or the necessary orders at bedsides and in operating rooms. An ominous silence prevailed in an institution that, not long ago, had been filled with excited conversation in small gatherings at tea breaks and bursting with a vitality that was both stimulating and necessary for efficient work. It seemed that everybody was aware of some impending doom – everybody but me.

On my way to the hospital each morning, I would drop in at Klavdia's house; she liked to have breakfast with me. Her mother prepared the food with love, as one could tell by the taste of the warm *piroshki* and the excellent hot tea.

"You know, Igor Morovitch," her mother said one day, "I am so scared for Klavdia. I know very well what's going on within her. We may have two separate hearts, but they are like one; she doesn't have to say anything because I'll already know. I'm so worried. With her demanding job, and her involvement with you … I pray daily and trust that God will help us all in the end."

"I can see how worried Klavdia is," I said, "but maybe I don't fully realize the full extent of the impending problems."

"Yes, yes, maybe it's better for you not to know; it saves you anxiety over an uncertain future."

Klavdia tried to hide her feelings for me. Her affection was sincere but occasionally tinged with jealousy. Sometimes she would ask, "And how is Natalia Petrovna doing these days?" To this I only responded with a serious look, as if to say, "You're married, you're pregnant, so it has to be like this." I liked Klavdia very much because she was bright, honest, and devoted, but my feelings towards her were more like those of a brother towards his sister. It was totally different, however, in Klavdia's heart. As I understood later, she had decided to wait so that she could be close to me, hoping for a brighter future. But after the catastrophe in the hospital, she found her daydreams changing: she could see only dark clouds ahead.

One morning on my way to work, Klavdia and a girlfriend of hers, also a physician, were walking close by, and I overheard part of their conversation. "You know, I feel that Igor Morovitch should suddenly disappear, not come to work and leave Asbest completely," said Klavdia, without lowering her voice. "Then he could go far away and try to find work as a surgeon, without telling anyone where he comes from. He can claim that he lost his

memory on the front when a bomb exploded. We are in a state of
war and nobody will try to check his identity. He will be safe."
Her girlfriend walked on in silence, probably not wanting to
comment and get involved. After a while Klavdia came up to me
and repeated her warning.

"Igor Morovitch, I was thinking and thinking, and I've come to
the conclusion that maybe it would be better for you to go somewhere far away. As you know, the Soviet Union is so enormous
that you can get lost and start a new life. I've decided that with
the help of my friends, we can help arrange some documents for
you. What do you think?"

I was flabbergasted. "I don't understand. Do you think that I'm
involved in some way with what happened at the hospital? You
know very well that the lab report from Swerdlowsk indicated
that, without any doubt, the food poisoning resulted from the
meat filling in the pancakes being left out all day before New
Year's Eve."

"I know," she answered, "but the Soviet reality is such that
somebody has to be blamed. The poisoned soldiers are angry and
they're asking, 'Is this the reward we get for fighting for the
fatherland?' The authorities can't assume the responsibility of
negligence; there is no such thing, even though everyone knows
that an inexperienced cook was put in Building No. 3 by the
Pompolit (assistant for political matters in the hospital). His sister
was a mining engineer, and yet he put her in charge of the food
in Building No. 3. The authorities can't be blamed even for this
criminal appointment – because they never make mistakes. The
counter-revolutionaries, on the other hand, are always found
guilty. But how else can we calm the poor victimized soldiers in
the hospital? The reality is that everybody is aware of the Party
teachings: 'Be alert, the enemy is hiding and ready to attack.' And
who is better suited for the role of scapegoat than you, Igor
Morovitch, brought up in the bourgeois system, the natural enemy
of the revolution?"

I was unaware that for some time already, secret investigations
had been conducted in the offices of the NKVD, and that all hospital employees were called in for questioning. As I found out
later, the majority of questions posed during those hearings concerned me, my past, and my activities. But at the time, knowing
nothing of this, I felt Klavdia's fears were irrational. Unaware of

the consequences, used to proceedings held in a democratic court of law, I completely disregarded her plan. It seemed like something out of a thriller movie. "I'm not going anywhere," I insisted. "I know I have nothing to do with this hospital affair, and I'm sure everything will be all right. Don't worry, Klavdia Fedorovna, I appreciate your concern, but you have to be realistic."

We walked on in silence. Klavdia maintained this silence in the days and weeks that followed. I didn't understand why at the time. Only later did I realize that, as a Party member, she had really gone out on a limb trying to warn me. It would be inexcusable if her warnings to me ever became generally known.

Suddenly, on the fifth of February, I was arrested in my home. I never saw Klavdia or Natalia again. While I was in the Asbest prison, a guard told me that a lady had brought me a parcel, but it was confiscated by the investigator's office.

And so eventually I found myself in the prison infirmary. In my sleep, I had drifted back into the recent past, unaware of my surroundings. Now, awake once again, I was thankful for the comfort of the hospital mattress instead of the cold concrete floor of the prison. The hospital windows were not covered with metal sheets.

The Prison Infirmary

Soon after I awoke, the male orderly came in with breakfast. With a large ladle he emptied kasha into deep tin plates. We received no other food, just kasha three times a day. Nobody, but nobody, could digest this hard, unhulled, and badly cooked wheat grain. The only effect it had was to cause intractable pain as it passed through the prisoners' atrophied bowels, aggravating our persistent diarrhoea. Many prisoners left their plates untouched; those who wanted to avoid the pain did not eat this food.

One or two prisoners died every day, I was told, on our hall alone. Once they were removed, their beds were immediately filled by new arrivals who little suspected that their lives would probably end in this efficient death factory. This frightening information put me on the alert, and I tried to find some way of preventing the inevitable outcome of my stay in the infirmary. I exercised all my powers of inventiveness to solve the impossible riddle and find a way of escape.

I had a dream while in the infirmary: I was standing with my father on a cliff. Before us, as far as the eye could see, lay a beautiful green valley filled with wild flowers. At the far end on the horizon there was a cottage. My father indicated this little house with his right hand, and told me that from now on there would be no more uphill climbing, only a pleasant walk through the meadow to the home that awaited me.

When I awoke dark clouds covered the sky; it looked like snow. I was still thinking about my dream and could not decide on its meaning. Was it just wish fulfilment, the longing for a lost warmth? Or had fate decreed that I would one day find a home, my home, again? I told myself that it was a good omen and began to focus on my situation. Sometimes, precarious circumstances force a departure from linear thinking and allow the emergence of imaginative ideas.

A nurse came in with a few bottles of medicine. Though middle aged and robust, her face had an almost childlike openness, a rare phenomenon in these surroundings. I knew right away that she could be persuaded to help me save my life. I had an idea I wanted to try, my only chance, although I did not know whether it would work. The nurse gave us each ten drops of "Tinctura Opii," or opium, to stop the diarrhoea – hardly enough to have any effect. As with other parts of the body, the muscular layer of the bowel as well as the inner mucosal lining disappears as a result of starvation, and cannot retain or absorb any food. At this stage of emaciation, only intravenous feeding with special liquid food containing lots of protein and vitamins can possibly stop the progress of an otherwise fatal condition. If I reached this advanced stage I would have no hope of recovery. I would have to try to stop the diarrhoea for a few days to gain time and get discharged from the hospital. Later, maybe, I could get something more digestible to eat and thus save myself from death.

I had already learned under desperate circumstances to divide any plan into stages just to get a reprieve, gain time, and postpone the inevitable. In such a way I could carry my shaky existence a step further into new territories, new dimensions of fate, new possibilities. I took a deep breath, and when the nurse approached my bed I looked her straight in the eye. My face probably expressed some of those feelings that emerge only in moments of despair: begging a stranger to save your life is only a request for mercy, after all, unless it also jeopardizes the stranger's safety.

"Listen," I began, "I am a doctor. I want to see my family again. Please help. You know what's going on here." I stopped. She looked around to see if anybody could hear us. Then: "What do you want? I can't help. I have no means, you know that."

"I know, but I have an idea. You give each patient a few drops of opium but it doesn't help. All these patients will die, and you can only watch helplessly. Don't you want to save at least one human life? That way, you will help me and I will help you. You will try to save my life and that will help you to save your soul. Do you believe in the soul?" She again looked around and in a frightened voice answered: "My grandmother prays to God every day and she has told me a lot about souls. There are the happy souls in Heaven, and those that burn in Hell. I promised her to be careful and not speak about this with anybody, only with those who give a sign that they believe in God."

"I see that you are a believer. You know that souls never die."

"But tell me, how can I help you? I myself am helpless, yet I have to watch all this death around me."

"I will tell you. I am a doctor and I just want to get out of this place. If I can stop the diarrhoea for a few days, they'll discharge me and then maybe some new opportunity will come up. Just give me the whole of this small bottle and I'll drink it in one gulp." I warned her that I might pass out or fall asleep, as if in a coma, but that it was the only way to stop the permanent running of my bowels. "If they see that I'm dry, they'll discharge me. Just watch over me when I am unconscious, and if they think I'm already dead, show them that I still have a heartbeat."

Finally she handed me the bottle, which without any hesitation I emptied in one gulp. I did not notice the nurse leaving the hall, so intensely did I separate myself from the environment, cutting off all my senses. I began to feel I was in a completely private and separate place, away from the other beds in the room and the moans and groans of the dying all around me. Then the light was gone and I lost consciousness.

I don't know how long I was out. When I opened my eyes the woman doctor who had admitted me to this place stood over me, poking her finger at my chest. "Good thing you've opened your eyes. You were deeply asleep for a whole day; we thought we might lose you. But your heart was beating and your bed was dry – no more diarrhoea. Maybe it's because you haven't eaten anything all this time."

My throat was parched and I couldn't speak. I gestured to show that I wanted to drink. They gave me some water and I asked for more. Then, with some difficulty, I started to remember my talk with the nurse before I lost consciousness. I became aware that the plan I had initiated with her was working. I looked around but she was not with the doctor, as she usually was on their weekly visits. I became concerned that maybe something had happened to her. I knew that I had no time to do anything but try to impress upon the doctor that I didn't know why I had fallen asleep. I whispered hoarsely, "Maybe I was getting very weak and just fell asleep. Maybe I was going to die but for some reason woke up instead. I am very hungry. Can I get some milk?" At this she simply laughed and left the hall. I slowly drank some water. It got dark outside, and the people moving about in the room threw long shadows on the walls. I slept again.

Somebody was shaking me. "I was so afraid that I'd killed you with this medicine." The nurse was leaning over me. "When I got home I told my grandmother what I'd done, and she assured me that I did the right thing. For the last two days I've been praying for your life. Yesterday, when the doctor was by your bed, I was standing at the door; I was so happy that you woke up. When I went home I told my granny that God had heard my prayers and that you had woken up. Here, I brought you some good soup. Eat it quickly, so that nobody can see." She hurried out, her face showing fear and joy like a successful conspirator – which is what she was, considering that she lived under a regime that made any religious practice, any expression of belief in God, a criminal offence.

When the woman doctor arrived on her morning rounds, she approached my bed and gave me a strange look and announced: "You are going back to your prison cell because the diarrhoea has stopped. That has also been confirmed by the report of the order-lies." Her odd behaviour struck me. I realized that she was not used to discharging patients; hers generally died. My unexpected recovery must have left an unsolved riddle in her mind. A transfer from the prison cells to this so-called hospital was not intended to cure sick inmates, merely to bring them to a place to die.

My plan for survival had so far succeeded. I was out of the infirmary. I had no idea what fate had in store for me, but I hoped that somehow I could get out of prison and go somewhere where I could use my skills and survive.

Back in my prison cell, something did occur. Fate offered me a chance on a silver platter. In the morning two soldiers entered and loudly read out the names of four prisoners, mine among them. "Take all your belongings," they ordered, "and come with us." We went to the prison office where, after some waiting, the guards took some documents and ordered us again to follow them. At that moment the nurse came into the office, approached the commanding officer, and said something to him. He nodded of his head and she came to me, holding out a little bundle. "You forgot this in the hospital," she said, her face hiding some secret and imploring me not to give the secret away. I took the bundle and watched her depart, wondering at this tiny island of goodness in an ocean of indifference and malice.

The guards took us to the railway station, where we were loaded into a wagon with many other prisoners who were arriving from other places. I was already used to being crowded in with emaciated people dressed in malodorous rags and fighting for space and survival. Thanks to my military uniform and the lectures I had received from Grisha, I knew how to get along in such conditions, and even to get ahead. Now, a space was made for me by one of the windows.

The Gulag, the entire prison system, comprised many separate regions or lagers, of which the Sevurallag (Northern Ural Lager) was one. Each lager was divided into sections or departments (*otdelenie*), which in turn were divided into several compounds, or "lager points." We were going north; the rumour was that we were heading for one of these points.

Through the window of the moving train I could see the open world that had been hidden from me for six months by the metal-sheeted windows of the prison. I opened the bundle that the nurse had given me. Inside there were crispy light pieces of toasted white bread. Again I was deeply moved to have found someone who was willing to endanger her own life to save a stranger, without any expectation of a reward. She had done this just for the sake of doing a good deed and for the glory of God, in whom she and her old grandmother so fervently believed.

It was a sunny day in the early summer. Within a few hours the train entered a deep forest of tall pine trees. The underbrush was moist and green, the air fresh and cool – this was the famous taiga. Very soon we reached our destination, the lager point of Voronka. We were taken off the train and ordered to lie on the grass in front of the fence of the point. One of the guards was left to watch us, while the other entered to report and transfer our documents. We were ordered to remain on the ground.

It had been a very long time since I had rested directly upon the earth. I turned my head towards the grass and looked. It was quite a discovery after prolonged months on the concrete floor of the prison cell – a whole world of ants and other insects, some crawling, some moving fast, working, carrying dry blades of grass larger than themselves. All these little insects were free, doing what they wanted. That was more than could be said of millions of human beings who were caught up in the war or living in this totalitarian state. I began to wonder about the smartest animal in God's kingdom. Was high intellect self-defeating? Reflecting upon the deranged schemes of Hitler and Stalin, it almost seemed so.

The sun was setting behind the line of pines when my name was called. Together with a few other prisoners I was taken inside the fence.

Voronka

The compound of the Sevurallag was called Voronka. It was a square area of about ten acres fenced with heavy wooden planks about ten feet tall, with barbed wire running on top. On each corner above the fence a roofed turret hid a guard with a machine gun. Inside were wooden barracks for the inmates and for the administration, as well as a bath-house, a kitchen building, and an outpatient's medical building.

I was brought straight to the little medical shack and introduced to Anton Grigorevitch, who ran the place. He was a strong-looking fellow of over six feet, with an open and pleasant face. Anton was a Latvian *feldsher* (a lower-level physician akin to a paramedic) who knew only practical treatments but no theory. *Feldshers* were trained in large numbers in Russia, which had enormous territories that required at least rudimentary medical service. Depending on their talents and application, some *feldshers* gained substantial experience over the years and could diagnose and treat many diseases. They could also do minor surgery and handle complicated deliveries. The feldsher's existence is portrayed in masterly fashion in the writings of Anton Pavlovitch Chekhov, who was himself a doctor.

Anton prepared a little supper for us. He served a soup that was far better than any I had tasted in all the months in prison. He then told me to eat as much bread as I wished from the loaf that he placed on the table. In view of the strict rationing, I was amazed and overwhelmed by the possibility of having as much bread as I wanted, but I had learned from Grisha not to ask any questions. The meal ended with a cup of good tea. All the time I was answering Anton's questions about my past and my credentials. I noticed, along with his curiosity, a growing deference and respect for me. I was returning to a world that needed my knowledge and experience and was pleased to get my first fee, paid in the form of a generous amount of bread.

After supper a few prisoners with small lacerations came in for help and I handled them all while Anton was clearing the table and preparing my place for the night. It was a bunk bed in a small room adjacent to the main reception area. Anton offered me the lower bunk, explaining that it was no problem for him to climb up. As in the prison hospital, I delighted in a bed with linen. And the window was not barred, so I could admire the night sky. The moon seemed to be smiling on me as I went to sleep. But in the middle of the night, I was awakened by a terrible itching all over my body. Frightened, I jumped out of my bunk, waking Anton, who asked in a scared voice: "What happened, Igor Morovitch?"

"I don't know. I am very itchy."

"Oh, that's nothing, just bed bugs," he assured me, sounding relieved. "You can't get rid of them no matter how many times you take these wooden bunks apart and put them in boiling water. You clean your place, you think you've got rid of them, but no. They come out from some other place that wasn't cleaned. The *natchalnik* (chief) pays no attention to it. What does he care if people get bitten? At first nobody can sleep but then you get tired and you get used to it. As they say here, '*Iak nie priwyknesh to zdochniesh*' (If you don't get used to it you will perish). Who cares? People are expendable," he continued, in full swing, "especially these enemies of the Soviet Union. So what is left but to accept it and live with it? I tried everything, like putting the bunk in the middle of the room instead of against the wall, and then placing pails of water around the bunk. But they are smarter that we are, these bloodthirsty rascals. They climb onto the ceiling and then parachute down on you, the poor victim. I came to the conclusion that the best thing to do is live with them and pay no attention. I don't know, maybe I'm stupid, but with this armistice approach they seem to bite you less. Maybe it's silly, maybe you just stop feeling, maybe you get used to them, or maybe they treat you like a friend, with gentility."

"I am very tired," I pleaded. "How will I fall asleep tonight?"

"OK, wait a moment. I have a remedy – some vodka. It's not so good; the farmers around here call it *samogonka* (home-brew). It shakes you a bit when you swallow it, but your mood soon improves, as if it were the finest brandy." In the darkness I swallowed some stuff from the bottle that Anton handed me. The initial impact was terrible, the sensation of burning so strong that instinctively, as if hit on the head, I fell back, literally shaking, as Anton had said. Then the burning became more bearable until just a bitter hot taste remained. But it worked; I lay down and didn't even know when I passed out.

Next morning I got up well rested. After a mind-boggling breakfast of plenty of bread and scrambled eggs, we started the morning reception. Anton looked after most of the sick inmates. The commonest complaints were swollen legs with cracked skin from which serum was oozing – signs of malnutrition. I tried to explain to Anton that it was no use painting the skin with iodine. The other major complaint was diarrhoea, also the result of lack of food, especially proteins. Again, I tried to explain that the castor oil Anton prescribed in these cases would only make matters worse. He listened attentively.

A patient came with the back of his neck swollen and red, with multiple pus-filled carbuncles. I told Anton that this case could not be treated with iodine and that we would have to operate, first putting the patient to sleep. He brought me a bottle of ether and a few surgical instruments, which I told him to sterilize. With the patient in an ether narcosis, I made four deep parallel longitudinal incisions through the swollen mass and filled the gaping wounds with vaseline gauze. I had the patient put into the sick room adjacent to the ambulatorium, which had three beds. Two days later we changed the dressing. The swelling, redness, and pain were gone and within eight days the wounds were almost healed. This case was the origin of my fame. Anton was delighted that he had finally found himself a teacher.

Each night upon retiring, I would find a whole loaf of bread on the night table at my bedside. Anton did not know where it came from, nor to whom it belonged. Since nobody claimed this bread, Anton and I started to eat it. A few days later, when I unexpectedly entered the bedroom looking for something I had forgotten, I found a prisoner putting another loaf of bread on the night table. The captive turned around, obviously dumbfounded and bewildered. After a moment, seeing my look of surprise, he explained: "I am the *chleborez* (bread cutter). I cut the bread portions for all the prisoners in this lager point. When you cut twelve hundred portions it is easy to save a loaf every second day. I found out that you, Doctor, had just arrived from the prison and I know that everybody from there arrives hungry, so I took the liberty of feeding you a little bit. I wanted to do it incognito but unfortunately I got caught. I am unlucky. I also got caught when working in Kiev, where I was the manager of one of the big stores of *Narkompishtcheprom* (National Commissariat for the Food Industry). I wanted to help a few hungry families with small children, and so I ended up here. But please, Doctor, don't be embarrassed, you need more food. The prisoners here need you very badly and I have to keep you healthy."

I thanked this kind man, advising him to be very careful and not expose himself to danger. He left very moved, with tears in his eyes.

The man who brought me the bread did me another service, too: he brought me up to date on what was going on in the world. It was July 1943, and General von Mannstein was launching a summer attack against the Soviets to the south. The Soviet troops were stretched over a massive front that bulged westward around Kursk. On 5 July, the Germans, using their Tiger and Panther tanks, struck at the Soviet army. Hitler committed more than a thousand airplanes against the Red Army's concentration of troops, artillery, and tanks. The encounter was one of the largest battles ever fought. Over three thousand tanks were engaged on the grasslands. By 12 July, the advantage swung to the Russians. Mannstein lost seventy thousand men and was forced to withdraw. This, in retrospect, was the turning point of the war for Russia. Such news was encouraging. With an Allied victory might come my freedom. In the meantime, I continued to be conscientious in my work.

A few days later Anton presented a patient who was suffering from intractable pain and a tongue so swollen that he could not close his mouth. The prisoner sleeping next to him in the barracks explained that he did not eat and hardly drank and had cried the last two nights. I examined the patient. It was a rare case of what is called Angina Ludovici, a huge pus-filled abscess under the tongue. Without any anaesthetic I plunged the knife under his tongue and a stream of foul-smelling pus escaped from the cavity. I hardly had time to put away the knife and gloves before the sick man, after all those sleepless nights, began to snore. A few days later he had fully recovered.

This second case confirmed the rumour that the inmates had finally got themselves a real doctor. Anton was in an exalted state. But unfortunately the happy mood did not last long. After less than a month an order came from headquarters to transfer me to a new place, the lager point Kasalmanka, a short trip from Voronka by train. This prison compound also had a hospital. With about sixty beds, it served the needs of other points in the vicinity. Apparently, the new post had been given to me once it was learned that I had some experience as a surgeon.

Kasalmanka

The present eradicates the past. You cannot afford the luxury of remembering yesterday when today mobilizes all your resources for the effort to survive. Already, the prison infirmary and Voronka had become distant memories, no more substantial than a dream.

After a supper consisting of soup and a bread ration, I retired to my new room for the night. The next morning, two nurses introduced themselves to me, Nina Vasilevna, the senior nurse, and Barbara Petrovna. Together with the hospital orderly, Stepan Iefimovitch, we started our rounds. There were four large rooms occupied by inmates suffering from various diseases, mostly complications due to malnutrition coupled with industrial trauma. The main industry of the Sevurallag was forest exploitation; the trauma was associated with injuries caused by falling trees and large branches, and also from negligent and unskilled use of saws and hatchets. Another room with about ten beds had been isolated for cases of terminal open tuberculosis.

Treatment and documentation were poor at the hospital. The food rations were markedly inadequate and very few drugs were available. Surgical cases such as fractures and major injuries to soft tissues were badly handled and neglected. Seldom, as I later discovered, were patients discharged to return to work. Having been admitted with advanced signs of malnutrition, the majority would die in the hospital. The nurses were not responsible for

this sad state of affairs; however, working helplessly like autom-
atons, they gradually became indifferent in this death factory.

After a few days, I realized that I could not do much to increase
the supply of food and drugs; all I could do was secure a separate
room for surgery and, with the available means, attempt a more
rational method of treatment.

One day, after our rounds were completed, Nina Vasilevna
volunteered some information about herself. Before her imprisonment, she had been head nurse in a hospital in Tbilisi, Georgia.
She had also been a member of the Communist Party. Dissatisfied
with something the local Party chapter had done, she had dared
to criticize publicly its handling of the matter and had returned
her membership card to the local Party secretary. One week later,
she was arrested and sentenced to fifteen years in the Gulag.

Nina Vasilevna was a beautiful, proud lady in her late twenties
who never complained. One afternoon, she invited me for tea in
the room that she shared with the other nurse. Aware that I had
previously been a citizen of a free and democratic country, Nina
told me the entire story of her family life, her school years, and
her time in Komsomol, the youth wing of the Party, when she
dreamt about a better world for the working class. Becoming
excited, she raised her voice: "We Georgians are a very proud and
independent people. No Georgian can really be a devoted Communist once he becomes aware of the falsehood and the abuses
of the Party. The whole Party philosophy is alien to human nature.
What they really preach is: 'Be happy or I'll shoot you.' We
Georgians are good people. You can always trust and rely on a
Georgian. The only degenerate in our nation was this horrible
Dzugashvili [Stalin] and his few companions, who were mostly
non-Georgians except for Beria, the boss of the NKVD."

Gazing into space, her face displayed a mixture of pain and lost
hope. It was an expression that I was to see quite often, an
expression shared by people who were no longer here but for a
moment had shifted their consciousness far back to better days
when life was still bearable. Living in the past preserved the soul
when the body had no other choice than to suffer.

For a few moments, I followed her into the never-never land of
our former lives. Then the door opened and a loud voice interrupted our silent communion.

"Where is the new doctor? Has he arrived yet?" There stood Catherine Osipovna, a visiting nurse who acted as supervisor or controller for the authorities. She was in her early thirties, tall and attractive, with large black eyes. Over her white nurse's uniform she wore a military coat with the emblem of the NKVD on the collar. When she saw that we were in a reverie, she spoke politely. "I am sorry. I did not know that you were in conference."

"No, not at all. It is very good that you came to visit us," Nina assured the nurse. "Please join us for tea and meet our new doctor." Although she refused to sit down with us, Catherine took off her coat and started to warm her frozen back at the oven. Shortly, Nina left the room, to allow for an official visit.

Catherine said she was pleased I had been sent there, and that she hoped I could bring some semblance of proper order to the hospital. She explained that she couldn't supply more food and medicine, and that I would have to make do and try to be inventive. She promised to do all she could to help. I assured her that I would do my best, appreciative of her sincerity and honesty. Over lunch – a slice of bread and a bowl of bluish-grey hot water that passed as soup – Catherine told me that she had graduated from the school of nursing in Perm and had worked in a hospital there for almost a year. After joining the Party, she was sent to the medical supervising corps of the NKVD. Following a month of political indoctrination into the Gulag system, she was appointed to the starting post of junior supervisor in the Sevurallag.

As we talked, it began to get dark. The days were shortening and winter was almost upon us. With a knock on the door, Nina reappeared carrying a lighted kerosene lamp. She told Catherine that a bed had been prepared for her in Barbara Petrovna's room. Shortly afterwards I left them and retired to my room, where the orderly, Stepan Iefimovitch, was making my bed. As I sat down, I noticed that both my legs were red and swollen. The tight shiny skin was cracked in many places, oozing a pinkish yellow fluid. Malnutrition.

"I am hungry, Stepan," I said. "Do you have any bread?"

He turned from the bed and looked at my legs. "Bread is no problem," he said. "Here is a loaf. Those legs of yours, however, will not heal without milk." Milk is an excellent source of protein. Though he probably didn't know that malnutrition results from a lack of this essential, he knew from personal experience and observation that milk would help my legs.

"I have some milk in my cabin," he continued, "but it won't be enough. Normally, I exchange it for bread with the farmer's wife. At one time I was getting three quarts for one loaf of bread, but now she's only giving me two quarts for a loaf."

He left the room and returned shortly with a full can of milk. I sipped the milk slowly; it tasted like ambrosia. This unusual, almost ecstatic sensation probably results from the body's receiving some specific food that it requires. I had last drunk milk like this almost a year earlier in Asbest. "We can't count on having milk regularly," Stepan warned me. "I can't let the farmer's wife know that we really need more milk or she'll drive a hard bargain and ask for more bread, and my supply of bread from the *chleborez* is limited."

I slept well that night and woke to the warm rays of the sun shining through the window, whose panes were patterned with shimmering crystals. Stepan entered with a can of milk and a loaf of bread.

"Sorry for not knocking, but I didn't want anybody to see me bringing this to you."

"Why have you done this? I can't repay you in any way." With a furtive backward glance Stepan replied, "In old Russia, there's a saying: 'Don't have a hundred rubles. Just have a hundred friends.' This saying holds true, even in these trying times. You never know what tomorrow will bring, and the greater the friend, the greater the hope." In his combination of youth and practical wisdom Stepan reminded me a lot of Grisha from the prison cell. His past was similar to that of many young boys I would later meet in the camps, and he had a maturity rarely found, even among adults, in those who have not been forced to grow up fast. I admired him.

I arrived at the hospital office later that morning to find that Catherine had left very early. I spent most of the day on rounds with the two nurses, trying to familiarize myself with the patients. Most of them were chronic cases. Their complications were mainly caused by traumas inflicted while cutting trees in the forest. A large number of them were the victims of negligence, suffering from inadequate medical attention and prolonged starvation in hospital. Lying in the vicinity of open-tuberculosis cases in a room where the average rate of survival was not more than six to eight weeks, the outcome for many of these patients was death.

We dined that evening in Nina's room, where she shared some hidden treasures such as a piece of dry sausage and a bottle of Georgian wine she had received from her mother in Tbilisi. I had brought the bread and milk. I resolved to talk shop with her as soon as possible to see how we could improve the situation in the hospital. Meanwile, Nina and Barbara began the very next morning to reorganize patients in different rooms according to their ailments, and to prepare the primitive operating room, while I attempted to bring some order to the medical documentation.

At noon, Stepan announced the arrivals of Olga Pavlovna, who had been sent from headquarters ostensibly to inspect the hospital. She looked no older than twenty, a blonde girl of medium height with a loud, high-pitched voice that filled the room. Since she was formal rather than friendly, I decided to act calm and businesslike. When she told me that she had graduated from medical school in Swerdlowsk the year before, I showed no interest in her curriculum vitae. She fired off a series of questions from a sheet of paper, mechanically jotting down my answers. Now and then she interrupted me to ask, with an innocent air, challenging and provocative questions that were quite unrelated to business. I took my time, ignored her provocations, and responded very carefully. I knew where she was heading and determined that she wouldn't get anywhere; not with me.

When she noticed my scepticism towards her dubious medical interests, she awkwardly tried to speak of the weather instead. At this moment, Stepan knocked, entered, and handed me a letter. This unexpected interruption gave her a chance to cover up her clumsy attempt to spy on me. She suggested that we take a break so I could read my letter in peace.

"No, thank you, Olga," I said. "I would much rather finish our medical discussion. Please keep your questions to medical matters." She knew that I knew that she had been trying to trip me up and get me to disclose something incriminating. I later learned that unmasking an informer was dangerous, spelling major difficulties for those poorly chosen by the NKVD.

Olga got up from her chair. "I am very tired, Doctor," she said in an uncertain voice, "and I have another place to visit today, so I'll leave now. Perhaps I'll see you next week." Obviously she lacked experience as a spy. I neither saw nor heard of Olga Pav-lovna again throughout the next seven years in the Sevurallag.

Alone in the room, I hastily opened the letter. It was from the so-called Court, and went as follows: "After thorough investiga-tion of your case and your voluntary admission that you are an enemy of the Soviet Union, you are hereby sentenced by the Court in accordance to paragraph 58 (10) of the Criminal Code to eight years of imprisonment and labour in the Sevurallag of the NKVD." The signature was illegible.

Eight years! The span of time frightened me. It seemed immense. I doubted whether I would ever return to my previous life. For a long time I stood dazed. But finally a whisper of inner wisdom urged me not to despair. Life is lived in bits and pieces; days come and go, some good, some bad. We have to take what comes. Often, things that seem bad when they occur turn out to have saved us from worse catastrophes. Millions were dying in the war, but the decrees of Providence are unknown, and we must accept them with humility. I left my room. Outside the atmosphere was pure and dry, hazy in the full light of the midday sun. The air was so dense you could hang an axe on it. The intense rays of the sun restored my peace, and with lightness in my heart, I set off in search of people.

I went to the hospital pharmacy, a large room with neat cabinets and shelves filled with bottles and jars. The pharmacy was run by Boris Davidovitch Shimkin, a man in his fifties with a pleasant, confident face. I introduced myself and, over tea, Boris began to tell me how he had come to this place.

He had been a deputy minister of the Soviet Union's pharma-ceutical industry. Millions had been arrested after the assassina-tion of Kirov;* he was one of them. During his two-week-long interrogation in the famous Lubianka (the main NKVD prison in Moscow), they used all possible methods to try and find out

---

* Sergei Kirov had been general secretary of the Leningrad Communist Party, a
  position of considerable influence. Touted as the man most likely to succeed –
  or oust – Stalin, he was assassinated on Stalin's orders in December 1934. Stalin
  used his popular rival's death as an excuse to strike at his other enemies
  through mass arrests and terror, implying that others, not he, were responsible
  for the crime.

which British agents had recruited him to become a spy for the capitalist enemy. In order to save his health and his life – he had endured incessant beatings – he decided to "admit his guilt," but he didn't know a single English name. "Frantically, I tried to invent a name," he told me, "but without success. After spending many days in pain, Providence came to my aid and I suddenly remembered something: once, while ordering suppository-making machines from some Ukrainian pharmaceutical import-ers, I had noticed the name of the manufacturer on one of the batches from Britain, 'Brown & Co.' It was written on the base in gold letters."

"I was so relieved. When the investigators called for me the next morning, I told them that I had decided to divulge the names of the agents who had recruited me into the British intelligence service. With a straight face, I revealed that their names were Brown and Co. The next day my interrogation was over. I was sentenced to a reduced term of only fifteen years because from the sincerity of my heart I had admitted my crime against the state." More than half his term was over, he said, but he didn't expect ever to be a free man again. He knew of a doctor in Stupino, a surgeon from the *Kremlinskaia Bolnica* (the Kremlin hospital), who had been arrested when he was and who got twenty-five years because he didn't admit his guilt. "Dr Deminski had a tough time in prison," Boris told me. "Maybe you'll have a chance to meet him sometime. When your term is over, they always invent some new crime to keep you in here. Why they take so much delight in keeping people away from their families and the outside world, I really don't know."

Boris's story frightened me. I noticed, too, that he gave his account without emotion. Perhaps he had repeated it to so many people that he himself was now dead to its impact. But I thought the problem ran deeper. All ability within him to be human, to be affected by the sadness and humour of life, had been killed. His sense of right and wrong, of compassion for the suffering of others, had been brutally violated when his soul was turned inside out. Afterwards, nothing was the same. Light and dark, hot and cold, even extremes of pain: nothing any longer moved him to a normal response.

This soulless storytelling troubled me. Boris had experienced things that would tear an ordinary man apart. Depression was not his problem; he slept well and responded to hunger. One could best describe Boris as a man whose soul had been cut out, an automaton responding to life by reflex only. During my later years in the Gulag, I met a lot of people like Boris. I wondered whether they would ever be normal again, or whether they would be just so many more cases of "soul extirpation," a permanent mutilation of the inner being.

Boris had finished his story. To break the painful silence that ensued, I said, "Boris Davidovitch, I hope that as an experienced pharmacist you have a medicinal drink for us." Mechanically Boris turned around and poured some red liquid from a small bottle on one of his shelves into a measuring glass, which he handed to me.

"This is a special drink made of pure alcohol and the red berries that grow here in the taiga. Try it, it's good. I don't drink, but I keep it for the few NKVD officers who drop by for a visit to the hospital." I tasted the drink; it was excellent. For a long time I sat, thinking about how I could help Boris, how I might inject a bit of life into him. As I left the room, Boris said, "Come again, often. Even when we don't speak, somehow the air around me, the atmosphere, feels different. Maybe it's just your presence; I don't know."

As we got up, our eyes met, and I saw in his a glimmer of healing love.

The long hospital corridor was lit only by a few candles. A tall emaciated figure stood in the entrance to my room. The person apologized in a subdued voice for bothering me so late at night. Apparently, he had seen me enter the pharmacy and waited all afternoon until I returned to my room so that nobody would see him.

"My name is Jasha and I am a very sick man in the TB room. I'm only twenty-two, but I know I will die tonight. I have here a final letter to my mother, but I have no way of sending it from the Gulag hospital. For the love of God, will you be so kind as to send this letter for me? Here's the money for the postage." In the flickering light of the candle, I faced the pale, gaunt boy. His large eyes begged me not to refuse his last request.

"I promise in the name of God to send this letter," I answered. Large tears rolled down his cheeks as he turned around and disappeared into the darkness. I knew that I could do nothing for Jasha; I could not reverse his imminent end. There were many like him. Without food or medicine, without the means to fulfil my basic duty as a physician to heal and relieve pain, all I could do was feel a deep sadness that weakened my spirit as a lifesaver and bringer of help.

For a while that night I couldn't fall asleep; I wished I had had more of Boris's drink in the pharmacy. At that moment, I wanted to be totally drunk. I wanted not to exist. The wind moaned through the windows, sounding a lament for those who died in pain and were forgotten in loneliness. After hours of distress I fell into a restless sleep, then woke in a cold sweat in the interminable darkness. There was no more wind, only a mortal silence that penetrated to the soul. I tried to read by the light of the kerosene lamp but could not understand a word.

Finally, resting in a chair, I lit a cigarette and punished myself with images of bestial human cruelty. I reflected upon political systems that were intended to save the poor from oppression by the rich but instead represented the most heinous negation of humanity, creating great suffering, inventing mass death factories in which innocent victims ended their lives in agony and degradation. I was still deep in melancholy when Stepan entered my room at dawn.

"What's happened, Doctor?" he queried, noticing my tired, unshaved face. I told him about meeting Jasha the night before and about his request.

"I'm sorry, Doctor. Jasha died this morning at 5:00 A.M. I tried to feed him as much as I could, but he was very sick. He was a good boy. I knew him because he was from a *kolkhoz* [collective farm] in the Ukraine close to my birthplace." Stepan told me that, two years earlier, Jasha had been mobilized into the Red Army. Wounded in Stalingrad, he got the highest military distinction, "Hero of the Soviet Union." He was then transferred to Revda, one of the northern Ural evacuation hospitals. One day, he told an anti-Soviet joke to his comrades. He was arrested and sentenced to fifteen years of labour in the Sevurallag. Because the wound on his thigh was continually oozing pus, he was transferred to the hospital in Kasalmanka. Here he contracted tuberculosis, and his health deteriorated very quickly.

I gazed at Stepan, utterly immobilized. A bitter thought mocked my sadness: in the end, Jasha won the game – he died owing his fatherland thirteen years of imprisonment. I pulled out the letter he had given me and handed it to Stepan.

"We both owe it to Jasha to ensure that this letter reaches his mother. I'm sure you understand." Stepan's cheeks were wet with tears as he made the sign of a cross over his heart.

"Yes, I promise to send the letter, even if I pay dearly for it; otherwise I won't be able to pray." He swiftly departed, leaving on the table some bread and milk, which I didn't touch. I dressed, washed, and left my room to call Nina Vasilevna for the rounds.

Around noon, Catherine arrived at the hospital and handed me Jasha's death certificate to sign. The cause of death was already filled in: "weakness of the heart muscle." When I hesitated, she explained that this was the only permissible cause of death to write on any death certificate.

That afternoon, a warm wind from the south brought in some moist air. The masses of snow bending the pine branches were melting in the retreating sun, loosing golden droplets on the immense white surface of the taiga, which was crossed by the elongated blue shadows of the evergreens. It had a soothing effect, this soft watercolour landscape, painted by the merciful hand of the Almighty, healing wounds in the souls of men – wounds inflicted by other men. All afternoon I walked on the narrow wooden path around the hospital inside the high fence of barbed wire. I would look from time to time at the watchtowers in the corners of the encampment where soldiers carrying submachine guns were protecting the stability of Stalin's criminal regime. Protecting it from whom? From the sick, starving mass of citizens who were fated to die but who, although imprisoned, had freedom in their hearts and love of God.

Time, filled by monotonous activity and the limited possibilities of this cramped space, seemed to pass faster than usual. During the last few months of winter, I had operated on a few compound fractures caused by industrial trauma in the forest, performed four appendectomies on inmates, and removed the gall-bladders of two farmers' wives who lived in *kolhoses* close to Kasalmanka.

The sudden transition to summer brought a few visitors from headquarters. One such guest was Iakov Mironovitch, the head of the whole *otdelenie*. He explained how much the *natchalstvo* (administration) appreciated my good work; they were aware that my possibilities were limited in Kasalmanka; and while he could not confirm the rumour, he said that I was to be transferred very shortly to Sossva, the seat of the NKVD command of the entire Sevurallag region. Although the doctor there was supposedly very experienced, he was not as good a surgeon as they would have liked to have.

Iakov Mironovitch was a tall, heavy-set man in his late forties. His large dark brown eyes expressed, in spite of their twinkle, a strange sadness. He looked to me like a successful businessman who nevertheless was not suited to his profession. His high forehead and the whole architecture of his countenance suggested an intelligence that was wasted on the job he was assigned to. Who knows, he may once have occupied a high position in the establishment; if so, he must have been deemed "untrustworthy" and transferred to a lesser post. Such mild punishment was standard policy among the ever-vigilant government agencies. During my later years in the Gulag I came across many cases of the kind.

After dinner that evening, we spent some time in my room. It appeared that Iakov was testing to see how far he could trust me. He then shifted the topic to literature and promised to send me some Russian classics. A few days later, Stepan brought to my room several books and a very short note from Iakov Mironovitch: "I hope you will enjoy these." They were works by Tolstoy, Dostoyevsky, Turgenev, and Pushkin.

Because the summer days were very long in Ural, one could easily read until midnight, and I did so during my free time after work. Russian literature is completely different when read in the original. No Western language, no other Slavic tongues like Polish or Ukrainian, can give the reader the same feeling as the Russian original. The soft, full feeling of the *dusha na rozpashonku*, the unleashed Russian soul, comes fully alive only in the silky tenderness of this most expressive Slavic language. When Tolstoy describes Natasha's love in *War and Peace* or the tragic storm in

Anna's soul before her suicide in *Anna Karenina*; when Dostoyevsky presents the inner dialogues of his heroes, especially that between Ivan and the Grand Inquisitor in *The Brothers Karamazov*: the Russian language alone reflects the real psychodynamics of the Russian soul and its immense capacity for suffering. The romantic, lyrical cry of Lermontov can only reach your heart in the original Russian tongue.

I was enchanted, often reading the same book twice to discover new treasures. It was a good time for me: I was able to forget my miserable surroundings and become lost, at least for a short while, in the imagery of great literature. The novels were conducive to daydreams and the birth of hope for a better tomorrow.

Sossva I

At the end of the summer, the order was delivered to Kasalmanka for my immediate transfer to Sossva. Located north of Swerd- lowsk, Sossva was the headquarters of the Sevurallag, or North- ern Ural Lager. The total number of inmates in the Sevurallag was about one million, although it increased markedly in times of war or when domestic unrest threatened, and when there were sudden personnel changes in the ruling echelons of the Party. The num- bers would also increase (they never decreased) when the secret police were at their most active, camouflaging the drastic actions of a government bent on evil.

I heard extraordinary stories from the prisoners. In those uncer- tain times when waves of mass incarceration were common, even those who occupied small, unimportant posts used to take to work each day a small bag containing a toothbrush and some food in case they were arrested and, as was usually the case, not allowed to return home. This was the Soviet reality; people were not ashamed to be led as prisoners through the main streets of the city where they had lived all their lives. On the contrary: it was just a normal fact of existence. They would look around to see if they could attract attention and be seen by a friend or relative. Only thus would their family come to know they had been arrested. There was little difference between those who were still free and those who no longer were. It used to be said that the

Soviet population was composed of three categories: those already imprisoned, those who would be imprisoned in the future, and those who had been imprisoned in the past (the smallest group, since political prisoners were rarely released but generally died in the Gulag).

The administration of the Sevurallag, like any other concentration camp, was made up of the usual triad. The real administration consisted of the people who ran the enterprise. Then there was the NKVD, the people who spied on all living souls in the prison, administrative personnel and inmates alike, and incarcerated their victims in a prison-within-a-prison. For this purpose they recruited spies among all free lager personnel as well as among prisoners, the latter selling their souls for an extra slice of bread. Therefore experienced inmates would be very careful not to talk unless they knew very well whom they could trust. But even with the greatest care you could never be completely certain, and some people paid dearly for misjudging. It was the art of the NKVD to recruit those who were least likely to be suspected. They made cautious arrangements to meet with their spies and usually took their reports in written form. After being in the lager a long time people developed a sixth sense in recognizing these dangerous outcasts.

Lastly, there were the Pompolit workers, the members of the Communist Party who were responsible for the political indoctrination and supervision of the other two groups, and who tried to streamline all agenda in the spirit of the Party. Of the three, the NKVD was the most potent and feared in the Gulag.

The different branches of the administration were ensconced in different buildings in the small town of Sossva, which was an NKVD settlement whose inhabitants all served in some capacity as employees of the Sevurallag. Apart from these buildings and a few houses for free citizens, there was the inmates' compound, as well as a hospital serving the entire Sossva district, which comprised many compounds (or "lager points") in the vicinity.

After many hours on the narrow railway I was taken directly to the hospital within the encampment. An orderly led me down the hall to my room, which was small but clean, with an iron bed in the corner. We went from there to the dining-room, where the other doctor and the nurses ate their meals. When I arrived, there was only one person at the table, a corpulent, bald man with a round shiny face and smiling brown eyes.

"I am Dr Michail Antonovitch Kurovitch. Call me Misha." He spoke in a soft tenor voice, his expression relaxed and cheerful. His whole appearance was pleasant and inviting. He explained that, as a gynaecologist, there wasn't much for him to do here in his area of specialization. He did what he could, writing case histories and progress notes and helping out in the pharmacy and in the laboratory.

Misha liked to talk. I sat and listened, eating my soup and ration of bread. He was originally from Yugoslavia. He did not tell me exactly why he was arrested, something other prisoners never failed to do, presenting their stories like introduction cards. Otherwise, he gave his account dramatically and excitedly, with an evident hostility towards the regime. He looked warmhearted. From my first attempt to find the inner person behind the benign face, I started to feel empathy for this husky man who seemed so innocent and naive in the midst of a hostile reality. Perhaps it was the absence of anger or malice that enabled him to preserve his psychic energies, which other prisoners wasted in helpless fury.

It was getting late. The room was warm and stuffy. I got up, thanking Misha for the stories he was still telling me, and announced my desire for bed. Misha led me to the door and reminded me that tomorrow morning I would take over the patients from Doctor Kadzejev, who was temporarily in charge.

Outside in the crisp air, I sought the Pole Star in a luminous sky. Suddenly, I beheld a spectacle of unusual beauty, one I had never seen before: against a background of bright pink mauve, fantastically bizarre patterns composed of lines and shapes of deep violet, magenta, and green were undulating in an intense dance of changing forms of things unknown. This was the aurora borealis – the Northern Lights. They were like a heavenly image of the Almighty, unique paintings of abstract beauty expressive of His might. It was as if He were saying: "This is the signature of My presence, which is eternal."

My awareness of time had vanished. That my imprisoned body had such free access to the wonder of nature broke the chains of slavery; this freedom, which God bestowed, was something no human being could take from me. Tears wet my face as impulsive words sprang involuntarily from my lips: "Blessed be He for ever and ever."

The bright sun penetrated the windows as I opened my eyes after a short sleep. I sat at the table, slowly sipping my coffee and glancing at a book. A baritone voice interrupted me.

"*Zdrastwuite.* I am Dr Kadzejev. Please call me Bashat Asiatovitch." When I lifted my head I saw a man of extraordinary radiance. Bashat was tall and well-built, in his early forties. His face was tanned olive; he had very large glowing dark green eyes and a smile that showed two rows of pearly white teeth. Silver grey wavy hair crowned his impressive head. He was wearing a *rubashka* (a white Russian shirt), his grey pants tucked into shiny black Caucasian boots. He greeted me with an outstretched hand and an overpowering smile. I shook his hand warmly and poured him a cup of coffee as he sat down. His introductory story was short and incomplete; as I found out later, he was a very secretive man.

"Finally, somebody from the real West. I am delighted. You know, I am from the Karatchajevska Republic [part of Georgia at the foot of the Elbrus Mountains], where I was minister of Health. During the last wave of arrests I was incarcerated and sentenced to fifteen years. It is good that they sent me here and not to Kalyma." Kalyma was the northernmost place of imprisonment. The highest bureaucrats and professional politicians were sent there when out of favour, never to return alive.

"Never mind what was the cause in my case. I don't like to talk about it, it is too painful. I'm a surgeon of average calibre, especially now that I'm out of touch with the newest methods after so many years in administrative posts. Sossva offers little medical work with the inmates; that is left to the less experienced doctors. People like us are brought here mostly to serve the officers of the NKVD and their families, and if you're good they often forget that you're a prisoner. You have to behave properly. Don't talk too much to people you don't know, free or imprisoned. It is strange how depraved human nature can become when dead tired from hunger and suffering. Be especially careful when dealing with the bosses' wives. Don't get involved; it becomes very dangerous. You will see it yourself, you're an intelligent man and once you have been here for a while, you will pass through the kindergarten and understand the reality."

He did rounds with me that morning and I met all the medical personnel – another male doctor besides Misha, and a few nurses. Later, as we sat in the office, the door opened and a woman entered. Bashat got up and greeted her in a very friendly manner.

"*Zdrastwuite*, Sara Abramovna. Come and meet our new surgeon. Igor Morovitch, this is Dr Sara Abramovna Resnik. She is a bacteriologist who runs our laboratory and the wife of David Aronovitch Resnik, the second in charge of the Sevurallag below the boss, Colonel Dolochov." Sara looked around, slightly embarrassed at this formal introduction, and put her overnight bag on a chair. She was a small lady in her early forties with dark, dark hair and a pale round face. Her black-brown eyes seemed full of fear and cautious curiosity. She was not beautiful but her features presented an interesting appearance, as if suffering had sculpted an expression of beauty with the chisel of long-lasting pain.

"Glad to meet you, Igor Morovitch, albeit under such sad circumstances. But what can we do, there's a war. We don't belong here either." Bashat soon left the room and Sara offered me coffee. For quite a while she talked about herself, constantly filling our cups with the hot liquid. She was born and raised in Kiev, of a very poor family. Her parents were killed during a pogrom in a small town in Ukraine, but she was saved and ran away to her uncle, who was at that time a Party organizer in Leningrad. She told me about her studies there and her graduation from the medical faculty, about her work as a young doctor in the Far North where she met David, who was at the time a capable and promising young Party member. She told me about his rapid advance through the Party ranks, followed by his entry into the Central Committee in Leningrad, and his eventual promotion to a very high position in the Leningrad Communist Party as one of the deputy secretaries under Comrade Kirov, who was general secretary of the Leningrad Party.

Because of his great talents and accomplishments, David Aronovitch Resnik was spared imprisonment or worse during the Kirov purges. But he was appointed to serve in a minor capacity as the deputy chief of the Sevurallag. For this loss in prestige he paid with his health, having suffered ever since from high blood pressure. Colonel Dolochov, the chief of the Sevurallag and a very nice fellow, appreciated having such a talented deputy; David turned in an excellent performance and had twice exceeded the five-year plan.

When her husband was transferred to this inferior post Sara had resigned from her position as assistant chief of Bacteriology at the Leningrad medical school. She had tried valiantly to find some application for her professional talents here and had very capably organized a small laboratory in the hospital, working mostly on a research project supported in part by the medical faculty of the University of Swerdlowsk. I asked whether she had heard anything about her family. Her face grew sad as she told me about the pogroms by the German occupying forces in Kiev. A large part of the Jewish population had been lined up alongside trenches filled with lime and then machine-gunned into their mass graves. Wondering what had become of my own family, it was easy to imagine the worst. I felt helpless and desperate.

The day was almost gone and the first lights from other buildings at the lager announced the early winter evening. Hurrying into her coat, Sara announced that she was late in preparing supper for David and apologized for bothering me with her stories. But when I got up I saw a look of gratitude on her face.

The next morning an orderly came and told me I had a guest. To my pleasant surprise it was Iakov Mironovitch, the fellow who had given me the Russian classics to read in Kasalmanka. He greeted me cheerfully and gave me more books, saying that it was incredible how fast I got through the first lot, which Nina Vasilevna had returned for me with a note saying that I had enjoyed reading the authors in the orginal. "This time I have some more contemporary authors for you: Aleksei Tolstoi, Gorki and Sholochov."

We spent about an hour having breakfast and talking about books. Far from the intellectual circles of Leningrad where he was surrounded by the cream of Russian writers, artists, and musicians, Iakov was searching desperately for someone to whom he could open his heart on cultural and spiritual matters. At the time I did not know if I could fill this role, even in part. My vocabulary was not yet sufficient to express those subtle feelings so beautifully and untranslatably evoked in Slavic words. I also felt then that I did not learn and sense things the way Russians do. When I tried to explain this to Iakov he assured me that I was on the right track and that I was worth the time he gave me. Iakov was my first real friend; his personality was a refreshing change from the misery of everyday life. He seemed pleased at my appreciation of the Russian classics as they were written.

"You know, Igor," he said, "I regret that we met so late in our lives and in circumstances so different from our previous ones." He sighed. "It's such a gorgeous day. Will you join me for a trip into the forest? I have to go and see how the work is progressing." A gracious sleigh with a pair of beautiful horses waited outside the hospital building. We covered ourselves with heavy furs, and the *iamshcik* (driver) urged the horses into a fast gallop. After a while we entered a narrow taiga road, which we followed for almost an hour. From a distance we could already hear saws, axes, and the earth-shaking sounds of falling trees. We stopped at a cleared area almost an acre in size. At the edge of the clearing, groups of inmates were busy at work. The huge fallen pines, some of them completely buried in snow, had to be stripped of their branches. Then the trunks had to be cut into short logs and the latter staked together into high cubes. Every inmate had to produce six cubic metres of cut wood daily in order to get his ration of four hundred grams of low-quality bread. Those prisoners who could not fulfil the quota received less bread in proportion to the amount of their production. Inmates who before their imprisonment had been farmers or manual laborers, for example, and used to physical work were generally able, after some initial strain, to produce the required amount. White-collar workers or professionals, on the other hand, could rarely accomplish this task and as a rule would slowly lose their strength along with all residual fat and muscle and enter into a state that, in the lagers, was known as *dochodiaga*. The word comes from the Russian word *dochodith*, which means "to come close to." What these people were coming close to was death. Those who were most prone to quick emaciation were big tall people; the skimpy lager rations were not enough to satisfy their bodies' need for larger amounts of food. These husky fellows were the first to succumb to malnutrition and often died within forty to sixty days of starting work in the taiga.

The inmates working in the forest were clothed in old quilted pants, dirty and torn, and short jackets called *fufaikas*. On their feet they wore *klapchee*, shoes woven out of soft tree bark, inside which their feet were wrapped in old rags or pieces of cloth. This primitive footwear was always wet so that many inmates got frostbite and eventually lost toes and sometimes whole feet.

Thickset, squat, and muscular inmates used to physical work would endure. They would often produce more than the official quota and therefore were given more and better food as a reward. They were favoured with better clothing and footwear, as well as sharp new saws and axes, and even had assistant prisoners assigned to them. Such people were called *Stachanovec*, meaning "outstanding workers of the Soviet Union" (the name came from one efficient worker named Stachanov). These inmates were the aristocrats, the élite, examples of how real Soviet people could work. At best, one in five hundred measured up; these few were usually young men already used to hard physical labour. But the thin crust of outstanding *Stachanovecs* could hardly camouflage the mass of starving *dochodiagas* slowly approaching their end, cut off forever from the loved ones from whom they had been taken by brute force.

Iakov was talking to the foreman and guards and making some notes in his book. I started to walk into the forest to get away from this horrible scene that was like something out of Dante's *Inferno*. I entered deeper and deeper into the taiga until I could no longer hear the sounds of saws and falling trees. The snow was deep and crunchy, and the tall pines reached high into the brilliant blue sky. The air was still and dry. The noisy, suffering world disappeared, and my soul opened towards an encounter with the rare and supernatural. There was an immense silence, and in it, the answers to all questions.

In the darkest and most hopeless moments, when nothing is left except prayer, I have witnessed miracles that the sharpest logic could not dismiss as mere coincidence. For example, when I was in an apparently helpless situation at the time of my arrest, I had had the inspiration by which I was able to outwit my interrogator. Again, when I was close to death in the prison infirmary, God sent me help in the form of the nurse who saved my life. Through prayer, under the guidance of a superior power, seemingly unrelated events can work together unexpectedly to produce miraculous solutions, beyond logic or chance, to the most intractable problems.

As I stood in the forest, a warming feeling of unlimited trust and belief entered my heart, and I was not lonely. Within my being I experienced a rare intimacy with God, the One only approachable through prayer. Tears of happiness rolled down my cheeks. Driven involuntarily by an inner power, I said in a loud voice: "Hear, my people. Our God is the only One." At that moment I knew that no other human foot had ever stepped on this soil and nobody had pronounced the name of the Almighty here. An immense silence reigned. I was mesmerized, unable to depart from this now-consecrated place that had assumed the sanctity of a temple. But I had to return to my friend Iakov; he was waiting for me, his face expressing concern.

"I hope you didn't think I'd tried to escape," I said.

"No, not for a moment did I suspect that," he said, his worried expression softening. "I was just worried that you'd lost your way. Many inmates, though they leave their footprints in the snow, get lost in the taiga and much later are found dead."

On the way back Iakov did not talk at all. I wondered if he had somehow intuited my experience in the forest. He was sensitive and could respect the need for silence after so unusual an experience. At that time I knew little about his own faith and did not ask. Maybe it was just that his finely tuned Russian soul, which lived so often in the world of pure feeling, sensed that in rare moments, when some secret mood discloses itself on the face of a friend, an empathic silence is the greatest sign of true friendship.

The next morning at the hospital a nurse told me that Dr Itkin, the medical supervisor of the hospital, was expecting me for breakfast. I went down to the main office, where a short fellow in his late thirties sat at the table. Bald, round faced, and red cheeked, there was something tragicomic in the doctor's countenance, despite his serious posture.

Nate Leserovitch Itkin told me he had come to see how I found my new place. "In such a short time, I have already heard good things about you," he said. "I myself had one year of surgical training in Moscow, interrupted by the war. Then I was wounded and they transferred me here. Maybe I can be of some assistance to you." As a medical colleague, he addressed me as an equal; socially, however, we were strangers. I was a political prisoner; any social contact that he, as a free man, might have with me could mean trouble for him.

I told him about a man I had seen the day before, one of the guards, who was suffering from a duodenal ulcer. I believed he would benefit if we could operate on him. I had gone through the inventory in the operating room and found an adequate supply of instruments, but we had no intravenous fluids. "If you could get some for the first two days after the operation then we can prepare him and go ahead. You and Dr Kadzejev could assist me."

"I know a place where they store lots of IV fluids," he said. "I will get a supply for the hospital here. I will leave tonight and let you know when I can come and bring the material myself."

Itkin had hardly finished speaking when the door opened and a young lady entered the room. She was a typical Russian beauty: tall, fair, with golden hair braided back into a long tail, brilliant large blue eyes, high cheekbones and red lips. She looked like an illustration from a book of Russian fairytales.

"*Zdrastwuite*, Nate Leserovitch. I came here because you asked me to see you in connection with the general meeting of the medical staff of the Sevurallag." Itkin looked slightly embarrassed, as if he didn't know how to behave. He gazed at the newcomer with an expression of worship. After a moment of confusion he seemed to realize he was behaving awkwardly and spoke in a quavering voice: "May I introduce Dr Tatiana Osipovna, my administrative assistant. She will stay for dinner tonight." Tatiana looked around, surprised at seeing a new face in the office.

"This is our new surgeon, Igor Morovitch."

Our eyes met in a mute encounter, a *déjà vu* of bygone days that had never existed. Something inevitable had just happened in each of us. I acknowledged her presence with a slight bow. Her sweet voice broke the awkward silence. "Welcome to Sossva, Igor Morovitch. We have already heard a lot about our new surgeon. I hope you will like this place." Clearly, my accomplishments as a surgeon worked to my advantage; although a prisoner, I was being welcomed into a position of privilege.

The ensuing conversation between Itkin and Tatiana about administrative matters got very boring and I asked to be excused to start my daily chores. At that moment, Itkin stood up and announced that he had to go and complete some important field work. He asked if I could take Tatiana Osipovna with me on my rounds so that she could stay and have supper with us when he got back. He omitted to ask Tatiana how she felt about it; she was his assistant, and she treated it as an order.

Tatiana and I saw some patients with Misha Kurovitch. Misha was very entertaining, at ease in the presence of women – a must in his profession as a gynaecologist. Tatiana liked his easygoing way; slowly she began to open up and became more alive and involved. When the rounds were almost at an end, Misha was called to the ambulatorium to help an injured prisoner brought in from the taiga. Tatiana asked if she could have a private word with me, in order to ask my advice about a medical problem. I guided her to an examining room, where we would not be disturbed.

About two months previously she had experienced a sharp pain in her right lower abdomen. She had a fever and lost her appetite. Since then she had felt unwell but, lacking confidence in the local doctors, had kept her condition to herself. I examined her and found a mass in the right lower quadrant of her abdomen, a chronic abscess resulting from a perforated acute appendicitis. I put her on large doses of sulphur drugs (antibiotics were not available at that time) and advised her to go on a diet and, if possible, to rest at home. I promised to look after her until she was ready for an operation and said that if the administration allowed me to, I would come to her home regularly to check on her progress.

In the evening Itkin came back, and after supper he and Tatiana Osipovna left. Later on that night, I went for a walk with Misha. He pointed at the velvety sky. "Igor Morovitch, do you see that formation of stars? It is called Orion. It is universally regarded as the heavens' most magnificent constellation. Orion is easily identified by the three equally bright stars in his belt. To win the hand of his lover, Orion, a great hunter, was ordered by her father to rid the land of dangerous beasts; here you see he confronts Taurus the bull."

Misha made me look at Orion. "I love this constellation; whenever I look at the night sky it possesses some magic beauty that calms my soul. You know, Igor, wherever you may be, even years from now when you won't know where I am or what became of me, when you look at Orion you will remember me." His statement was prophetic. I have no idea what happened to Misha, or where he is, or even whether he is still alive. But even now, many decades afterwards, whenever I see Orion at night I always remember him.

A week passed uneventfully. Then, one grey, despondent afternoon, I got an urgent call from Itkin to be ready for a trip to a patient's home. I was taken to the residence of Andrei Petrovitch Kuragin, the NKVD head of the entire Sevurallag. In the little hall I was greeted by a tall lean man in his late thirties with an ascetic face and inquisitive, penetrating grey eyes. He tried to assume a welcoming expression, but it could not mask the underlying cruelty of his face.

"Please come in, Doctor. Your colleagues will inform you about the matter. It is my wife; she began to give birth, but there are some complications that I don't understand." He led us to the bedroom. His wife was in her late thirties, very pleasant looking though pale and drawn. Despite her evident fear and pain, she still had enough kindness to thank me for coming. "You must have been sent by Providence. I am a mother of five; don't let me die." Two other women were there, one a civilian doctor from the neighbouring town and the other a midwife who accompanied her. Both of them looked afraid when Anna Nikitovna Kuragin pronounced the word Providence. Kuragin was silent.

The doctor and the midwife told me that Anna Nikitovna had already been in labour for a few hours and had begun to bleed about an hour earlier. They were not certain what it was. Her previous deliveries had been quite straightforward, although it seemed that with the second pregnancy, years ago in Moscow, she had had some complications. Assessing the general confusion and sensing danger, I asked everyone to leave the room and examined the patient. It became clear that this was a case of *placenta previa centralis*, a complication that occurs when the placenta is attached to the uterus in front of the child, preventing a normal passage through the birth canal. The condition required an immediate Caesarean section to save the child and stop the patient from bleeding to death.

I quickly returned to the other room and explained my findings, stressing that she had to be taken to the hospital operating room immediately. I asked to be put in touch with Dr Kurovitch and soon had Misha on the line. I told him about the case, asking him to have the operating room ready and get himself and the nurse scrubbed.

Kuragin drew me aside. "If something happens to my wife, I wouldn't like to be in your skin," he said menacingly. This was too much. Here I was, mobilized into service to save a life. After all that I had been through in the last months, his attitude was the last straw. I looked at him with contempt.

"You think you can help your wife by frightening me? Okay, go ahead! Will you make two prisoners out of me? I have no time now to tell you what I think of you."

Half an hour later I was at the operating table. The Caesarian was uneventful, and Kuragin's sixth son was born. I left for my room and asked that nobody, especially Kuragin, should disturb me. I whispered to Misha to get some alcohol for me from the pharmacy. I did not stir from my room the rest of the evening. Misha, using a secret knock so that I would know who it was, came later to tell me that the patient was doing well. I asked him to stay by her beside all night. I myself, exhausted from the strain of operating under threat, went to bed. I slept badly and dreamed I was being chased by wild dogs that finally caught me. When I woke sweating from this nightmare, the first rays of the sun were filtering in through my window. I washed, shaved, dressed, and left to see my patient before breakfast. In the corridor, on a bench facing my door, sat Kuragin. He rose abruptly and approached me with a hesitant step.

"Excuse me, Igor Morovitch. Just a few words. Yesterday I behaved most improperly. It was just because of the stress of the moment. I certainly didn't mean to offend you. I am a very sensitive man. You will experience my gratitude, no matter what, as long as you are here. Please forgive me." His tired face expressed regret and repentance. Without softening, I said: "It's okay. I have already forgotten the incident. Last night I also was not myself, but when fighting for the life of my patients, I have no fear. It's part of the oath of Hippocrates, and so I will behave to the end of my days. Now please let me go and see your wife." I departed, showing no fear. I was glad that even as an inmate I could be a real doctor, proud in the fulfillment of my duties.

Anna Nikitovna was in very good condition in spite of her blood loss, and her eyes expressed infinite gratitude. As I was leaving, she grabbed my hand and kissed it. Misha was so happy with her post-operative progress that he could not hold himself back. "Igor Morovitch, I am proud of you. Now you are a celebrity." A few days later Anna Nikitovna and her baby left the hospital.

Early one morning, Itkin came into my room and announced excitedly: "Igor Morovitch, I have loads of sterile saline and glucose solutions for the post-operative period. When will you operate on the poor fellow?" He was referring to the guard with a duodenal ulcer. I had almost forgotten about it.

"Any time. If you stay tonight we can do him tomorrow." The patient was in his mid-forties and had been suffering from a chronic duodenal ulcer for nearly six years. I examined him in Itkin's presence and found him fit for the procedure. Early next morning, with Itkin and Kadzejev assisting and Misha as anaesthetist, we did a subtotal gastrectomy, removing about seventy-five percent of the patient's stomach. The procedure went smoothly.

"I have seen Professor Lidski doing this procedure in Swerdlowsk where I was an intern," Itkin remarked, "but you are faster and more relaxed. You do a major abdominal operation as if it were nothing." I explained that I had learned the procedure from my teacher, Professor Ostrowski, who had himself been a student of Professor Rydygier, the inventor of the procedure. It still bears his name in two modifications, Rydygier I and II.

It was one of those unforgettable sunny winter days whose brightness filled one's entire being with energy. No job was too daunting or difficult to undertake; the lack of basic materials, facilities, and drugs could not interfere with my ability to run the hospital and treat the patients as I would have done in the old days in comfortable surroundings with the latest facilities. Entering the hospital in this dynamic mood, I noticed Sara Abramovna Resnik through the open door of the laboratory. She was sitting at her desk, head down, deep in thought. I was moved, aware ever since we'd met that she was quite unhappy and depressed.

"Good morning, Sara Abramovna. How are you?" She turned in my direction and her expression immediately changed, as though she had had a small win on the lottery.

"Oh, it's good to see you, Igor Morovitch. I am so glad to hear about the excellent work you are doing in Sossva. David told me that, although he hasn't met you yet, he is already quite proud of you. Poor David, he suffers so much from his headaches. Nothing helps, the tablets are good for nothing. Maybe you could see him, maybe you could do something about his high blood pressure. If it were not for the war, we would send him to Leningrad for treatment."

"Whenever you say the word, I will see him." Sara Abramovna suggested that I come that evening and, when I agreed, insisted that I share their supper.

It took about an hour to reach the Resnik's house. I set off under a full moon whose brightness eclipsed the starlight and whitened the sky. The snow, shaped by the wind into abstract geometrical sculptures, gave off a sparkling silvery reflection. It was very cold, and an icy polar wind seemed to slice the very skin off my face. I was dressed warmly – in double underwear, quilted cotton pants and jacket, and a three-quarter-length sheepskin coat. On my feet were thick felt boots called *valanki*. I pulled the flaps down on my fur cap, leaving only my eyes, mouth, and nose exposed. My eyelashes and nostrils were covered with icicles from my breath. But one got used to these polar nights, and the brisk walk over empty snow-covered surfaces was exhilarating.

David Aronovitch Resnik was a tall man in his late forties, with a large, balding head, a high forehead, and penetrating brown eyes. His nose was pronounced, his lips fleshy and moist. He tried to look serious and official, but his warmth and goodness were unmistakable. The discrepancy between his visible kindheartedness and the severity demanded by his previous posting was probably one of the factors that had led him to his present degrading position.

"*Zdrastwuite*, Igor Morovitch. Welcome to our home. Here you are not a prisoner and I am not a boss. Let's forget all that for a while. Sara has told me wonderful things about you." Sara Abramovna came in from the kitchen, bringing a delicious smell of food the like of which my nostrils had not enjoyed for a long time. We ate superb chicken soup, roast chicken, and a fine dessert made from dried exotic fruits with whipped cream, and we drank excellent Russian tea. Afterwards David and I withdrew to the living-room where, at his request, I told him the story of my life. He listened with interest and assured me that my imprisonment would end as soon as the war was over. When Sara had finished her chores she joined us.

Later, I gave David an examination to check on his state of health. His blood pressure was 240 over 160, a very high level. I explained that we didn't yet know the cause of his condition, which is called "essential hypertension" (elevated blood pressure without any known cause), but that we definitely suspected in such case that psychic factors were acting in combination with a specific genetic background. There were no appropriate drugs to treat the ailment at that time, but a salt-free diet was advisable, and temporary benefit could be obtained from bloodletting. I took 300 cc of blood, stressing that we would have to repeat the procedure from time to time. It was late at night when I left.

The next few days passed uneventfully. I did my routine chores and ate the same food every day. Little news reached me from the outside world. I only knew that the war raged on. We knew that in Leningrad, which was still under siege, large numbers of people and especially children were dying of starvation, and that many thousands of soldiers were being killed every day in the siege of Stalingrad. It looked as though the angel of death would never rest. No news at all came out of the German-occupied territory where I had left my family.

A feeling of purposelessness permeated my being. I could not understand why God exposed us to such suffering in a world created by His will and in accordance with His design. It seemed as if we did not meet His expectations in exercising the little bit of free will that He, in His infinite wisdom, had invested in humankind. Or was even this too much? But then He created us in the image of angels, not so different from His own nature, and without freedom of choice man would be an automaton, bringing no joy to the Great Creator. Like a machine, man would not err but neither would he be able to create anew or discover by trial and error. No, no, humankind was the best that the Great One, the only One could do, and from time to time He had no other choice than to remind us, by making us suffer, that we deviate and are in error. So be His will for ever and ever. My faith was not only preserved but growing in strength with each philosophical challenge from my Creator.

It was a dull, grey morning in the middle of February. The sky was covered by low leaden clouds; a bitter howling wind brought all the fury of the North Pole to Sossva. The blizzard that had started the day before had stopped. The wind subsided, the air was immobile, and a milky white fog reduced visibility to zero. One could find one's way only by means of spatial orientation. It was difficult to breathe and each exhalation was accompanied by a rasping sound. Spit froze in midair. One had to decide what direction one wanted to go in and then run; it was too cold to walk. Warming up the hospital rooms was impossible even with all the stoves constantly burning. The inmates were not taken into the forest but stayed inside the barracks. They would not have lasted an hour in that cold. We were all dressed in our warmest clothes. The hospital staff was despondent.

Misha came into my room, hiding a small bottle under his coat. "Here, Igor Morovitch," he greeted me, "this is a little drop of ninety-six-proof alcohol, sent to you by our pharmacist. You have to keep warm. And it is good for the morale." We each took a few gulps from the bottle, sitting immobilized in silence, not believing that the weather-tantrum outside would ever stop. Suddenly the door was opened abruptly and a nurse entered the room, accompanied by a half-frozen prisoner still covered with snow.

"Igor Morovitch! Something terrible happened in Barrack No. 3," said the nurse, hardly catching her breath. "A prisoner wanted to kill himself with a knife. I was there but I couldn't see everything. Please hurry."

Barrack No. 3 was the smallest on the hospital territory, containing only fourteen beds. Nonpolitical prisoners were kept here, in most cases young people arrested because they did not want to work and could not show a place of employment. In those days, in the Soviet Union, it was a crime not to work. When such people were caught by the authorities they were declared to be of the *socialno opastni element* (socially dangerous element), or SOE, and usually sentenced for a short period of about five years. Among them one would occasionally find a thief or, more rarely, one or two inmates sentenced for murder (again, for not more than five or six years). These nonpolitical prisoners were sentenced under the *Bytowaja Statia* (Criminal Code of Law), which dealt with "minor" crimes like robbery and murder that, according to the Soviet socialist reality, posed less danger to the state than political crimes. On the other hand, the political prisoners, such as those who talked too much or did not know what they could or could not say (usually called *boltoons* or chatterers) were given sentences of between ten and twenty years; they were seemingly more threatening to the paranoiac government. They were sent to the Gulags in Ural, Siberia, or Kazakhstan. The real political adversaries – most of whom occupied high government posts – were sent to the northernmost lager called Kalyma, where conditions were the worst. In the camps where we were imprisoned, the story was that from Kalyma nobody ever returned alive.

We ran quickly to Barrack No. 3, holding our breath. It was impossible to inhale the frozen air. Much colder than ice, it burned like a liquefied gas. In the anteroom of the barrack stood a few barrels filled with an opalescent liquid obtained from soaking pine needles in water. This bitter-tasting fluid was used as a weak solution of Vitamin C, the only (albeit not very efficient) weapon against scurvy.

We entered the large room, where hospital beds were arranged along both long walls. Between the two rows, leaning towards the wall, sat a young fellow in a pool of blood. He held both hands on his belly, which was covered with a blood-soaked shirt. All the other inmates were in their beds, frightened to come close. It was explained to us that the fellow, whose name was Sasha, had ordered everybody to stay away from him, except for one teenager holding a glass of water, which Sasha sipped at from time to time. Stopping Misha and the nurse in the middle of the room, I myself moved a little closer.

Sasha was around eighteen or twenty years old, very thin, his light blond hair uncut. His face was lean and ascetic and his features drawn, probably as a result of severe dehydration and blood loss. His huge grey eyes were sunken and fixed. His face showed a determination not to divulge his torment. I knew that any false move in my approach would be so much wasted effort. I decided to stay still for a while to gain time, allowing him to react to our presence, which he certainly noticed once he came to terms with his surroundings. It took a long while, but I resolved to be patient. Eventually, without looking at us, he spoke in a very weak, strained voice.

"Why am I not allowed to die in peace?" It was an impersonal statement; I decided to wait still longer until he recognized and acknowledged our presence. In a matter as personal as attempted suicide, any conventional effort to save a life by enforcing my will would be bound to fail. Subtlety was the only way to awaken his will to live.

It was tough to wait because the young fellow was losing a lot of blood and his condition was worsening. Unable to see his wound and not knowing how it had been inflicted, I couldn't establish the nature of the trauma or have much idea about the prognosis. But I had to gamble. To take him by force would spell disaster because any struggle to resist could easily kill him. I had almost begun to pray (a tested method when all else fails) when the man turned his head towards me, his eyes expressing a fervent request, inviting empathy for a human being so lost in suffering.

"Don't you understand that at least I should be freely allowed to depart from this horrible world? Please, please, I beg you, leave me alone."

I had been waiting for the moment when he would recognize my presence and look at me. At that instant I knew I could respond.

"Allow me to come closer so that you don't have to strain your voice. I will do whatever you ask."

"Okay, come closer." I moved very close to him and sat on the floor, soaking my pants and white gown in the pool of blood.

"I am the chief surgeon in this hospital. I understand human suffering and will fully comply with your wishes. Just tell me if there is anything I can do for you before you go. Would you like to send a letter to somebody? Would you like to tell someone goodbye?"

"I don't have anybody. Nobody loves me."

"How about your parents, brothers, sisters, friends?"

"I am only sorry that I will not be able to see my mother. I was not the best son but she always loved me. But it is too late now. I don't even have the strength to write two words, I've lost so much blood."

"It is not too late," I answered. "I will give you my blood, which is group O, good for anybody. Just to make you a bit stronger, to write the letter to your mother, and then you can do whatever you want."

"Don't tell me tales! You just want to trick me."

"Why would I not tell the truth to a man who feels that life is not worth living, who made the crucial decision to leave this horrible world? Why don't you believe me? Going along with this one and only wish of yours to say goodbye to your mother will give me such a good feeling, to fulfil the last wish of a dying man."

His tired face relaxed visibly. "I really don't know, but if you think so, you look like a decent fellow. I trust you. Go ahead."

I gave my orders in seconds. Within five minutes the young man was on the operating table. Misha gave him a shallow anaesthetic and after taking 500 cc of my blood he said: "I won't take any more blood from you. I know it is not enough, but you have to operate. Let the nurse carry on with the anaesthesia. I know somebody with type O blood. You just go ahead and see what is inside his belly." There was a deep transverse cut across the muscles of the abdomen, and I did not want to remove the huge blood clot before I was scrubbed. We waited for his blood pressure to rise while the transfusion and glucose saline were running fast. After about half an hour Misha returned with two bottles of O-type blood and took over the anaesthesia.

When Sasha's blood pressure was ninety over seventy I began to examine the inside of his belly. The cut was quite deep, going through the left lobe of the liver and part of the large bowel. We applied sutures on the liver and closed the gap in the bowel, cleaned all the abdominal cavity with saline, and closed the cut in the belly muscles and skin. When we had finished the procedure the patient's blood pressure was a hundred and ten over seventy; we had won the battle. Physically and emotionally exhausted, I asked Misha to watch the patient and left the operating room.

I rested a whole day and night, getting reports that all was well except for a fever that Sasha was running. I advised Misha to put him on sulphur drugs and ordered him a few ampoules of Prontosil, the first form of red penicillin we had obtained. Two weeks later Sasha was ready to be discharged from the postsurgical room to Barrack No. 3.

The month of March brought slightly longer days but winter was still in its full splendour, sunny, frosty days mingling with blizzards that lifted the snow almost up to the windowsills.

Tatiana Osipovna lived about two miles from the hospital. On her last visit I had advised her to go on a diet and rest as much as she could. She got a two-month sick leave from Dr Itkin. From time to time I would examine Tatiana at her home to see how her abdominal mass was receding in order to decide when she would be ready for the operation. Although a prisoner, I had the privilege of moving freely within the limits of Sossva, a status referred to as *bezkonvoine* (without guard). The privilege was extended to me largely so that I could attend patients who were free citizens living outside the encampment. But of course I used it for other purposes too. The guards in the entrance tower who oversaw all comings and goings did not question my movements, knowing that I was in favour with the administration.

During my visits I had learned a little of Tatiana's past. Hers was a strange story. Her father was an economist in a Kolkhoz, a state farm in the Dniepropetrosvsk district. The eldest of four children, she had dreamed since childhood of becoming a violinist. She adored music. When she was twelve, her mother bought an old instrument for her from a neighbour. Once a week, her father would drive her to a music teacher in the city for lessons. Tatiana studied every night so that she could complete high school and still have time to practise music. During these nights, numerous male friends would visit her father, spending long hours discussing various topics and taking notes. Tatiana did not know what this was about but knew it was a secret, because her mother forbade her to talk about it or tell anyone about her father's nightly guests.

One night, after Tatiana had graduated from high school, some NKVD soldiers came to the house and arrested her father. She never saw him again. The family did not know where he was imprisoned, or indeed if he were still alive.

Tatiana left home and went to Moscow to study medicine, but she was not accepted at the university. No reason was given. She did not return home, but started working as a waitress in a factory cafeteria. There she met Andrei, a high official in the Party cadre. Young and handsome, he fell in love with her and soon they were married. Andrei worked it so that some of her personal file disappeared and a year later she was accepted to study medicine in Moscow. Andrei joined the army. Tatiana graduated from medical school but the "lost" part of her personal file was found, and she was sent as a doctor to serve in the Sevurallag. Andrei was deprived of his status as a political commissar in the Red Army and was sent as a soldier to Stalingrad, where he was

killed in his second month of duty. Here in Sossva, Tatiana would
sit in her little house after work, playing the violin and getting
used to a world without Andrei.

One Sunday afternoon, I wanted to see Tatiana Osipovna again.
My last examination had already indicated an almost complete
disappearance of her abdominal mass. At the time I had explained
how well she was recovering and that it was now up to her to
decide whether she wanted to be operated on. I wanted to find
out what she had decided, but that was an excuse; I was lonely
and I just wanted to see her. I had sensed on previous encounters
that she was attracted to me; for my part, I always felt more alive
in her presence.

She lived by herself, though a young village girl came in to do
some cleaning and cooking for her. After knocking on the door, I
entered the room that served as a living area. I could already hear
her voice.

"I knew you would come today. I knew for sure, because I
needed you so much. You don't know how often I have to invent
and imagine your presence. But now you are really here." This
greeting came even before I had taken off my outdoor clothing. I
hugged her.

"I brought you here by the power of my will," she continued.
"This morning Kadzejev told me about your work on the fellow
who tried to kill himself. All of Sossva, including Colonel Dolochov, knows that you gave your own blood to this prisoner. Come,
I have some good food and a bottle of wine from home." The
warm atmosphere was almost seductive. The room was only half
lit by the kerosene lamp. I sat in a shadow while Tatiana played
Beethoven's "Kreutzer Sonata" on her violin. The music permeated my body and filled my whole being with a sense of splendour.

Tatiana was completely lost in her technical mastery. She was
driven by pure feeling, in superb control of the mesmerizing
sounds. I never expected to hear, in this God-forsaken spot, music
that could move me so deeply. I was so delighted with this feast
that I embraced Tatiana in my gratitude.

With a change of mood she began to play the soul-melting
songs known as the Russian romances. I sipped the fine aromatic
wine, compelled by the melodies. Eventually Tatiana stopped.

Now we listened to the northern wind howling against the window panes. Grey reality threatened to destroy the magic. In our urgent need for human closeness we stood up and embraced for a long, long time. It was still dark when I left Tatiana's home, my mind totally blank. When I reached the hospital I crept into my room unnoticed.

Sossva II

The days were still dark but not so cold. Torn grey clouds were constantly driven eastward by the fury of the March winds. In such weather Misha Kurovitch would usually come to my room and we would talk. This afternoon I was in need of his company and especially glad when his smiling face appeared around my door. In these rare moments we would reach beyond the intellect and grope towards the essence of existence.

We would discuss how, when pain strikes, we seek healing; how, when life becomes too painful, we start to ask about our mission, the purpose of our being here. There is no panacea that grants a life free of pain, but one seeks some answer – an idea behind the pattern, a meaning behind the suffering – and tries to understand why man, the most intelligent of creatures, is driven to inflict fear and terror.

We always tried to reach beyond the world of the five senses towards a deeper wisdom, to understand the realm of nonattachment in which we could see the world in an entirely different light. After all, misery and anguish are the inevitable result of our tenacious love of life. We sought the key to mastering the world and our own existence, instead of being a slave to both. We understood the uselessness of reason and intellect against the enlightenment of experience and intuition.

Misha and I experienced the joy of spiritual closeness. We shared a sense that it was premature to ask why darkness and ignorance prevailed. There could be no answer. On the borderline of despair and despondency, only prayer helps. The potency of this remedy will forever remain a mystery.

We were dragged abruptly back to the mundane by a guard who entered the room without knocking. Turning to me, he announced: "I am ordered by the chief of the NKVD, Comrade Kuragin, to bring you to him right away." Misha and I looked at each other. A chill ran up my spine, and Misha's face paled with fear. These sudden calls only ever spelled disaster. On no matter what pretext they always found a way to incarcerate whomever they pleased. Even within the Sevurallag there was a prison. The informer-spies of the NKVD would enter into political conversations with naive and unsuspecting prisoners, who, after enduring interrogations and beatings in the dark cells of the local camp prison, would be transported to the Far North to other lagers where the work and suffering were much worse.

I stood up. "Don't worry, Misha. Somehow I will let you know what happens. If I am not back tonight, please tell Dr Sara Abramovna where I am in the morning." Outside at the gate, a *troika* with three white horses stood waiting – the personal coach of Kuragin. The guard changed his tone and very politely advised me to take the back seat. He covered me with heavy fur blankets. I could not grasp what was happening, but I began to suspect that the purpose of this evening trip was not, after all, to bring me unexpected hardship. You don't send such a luxury coach for a prisoner and tell the guard to be polite. This was probably a call to a sick member of his family. In a short time we stopped before a large, nice-looking house. Now I was certain that it was for professional reasons that I had been brought.

The guard knocked at the door and let me into the house. The smell of rare and fancy food reached me on the warm air. In the anteroom stood Kuragin, looking relaxed and benign. He invited me kindly to enter the living-room, where Anna Nikitovna, his wife, greeted me with a smile. "It is so good to see you in our home," she said. "I have wanted for a long time to have you to dinner, but my husband was always busy and so I had to wait. I will never forget that you saved my little son's life and my own with your great skill as a master surgeon. Who could tell that your unfortunate fate would bring blessing and life to us here in Ural? Under these circumstances we will never be able to repay you." Andrei Petrovitch's expression, so different from our first meeting, echoed her sentiments.

"*Zdrastwuite.*" He stretched out his hand to me.

"I am a prisoner," I said. "I'm not allowed to shake your hand or call you *Tovarishtch* [comrade]."

"*Ne bud'te durakom,*" he returned. "Don't be a fool. It's only when people can see us that I have to be formal, otherwise you are not only my comrade but a dear friend. This may surprise you, but at any time I could find myself in the same position you are in, a prisoner, and maybe far worse off because they expect much more of me. I think you understand our reality by now. Only Stalin can be sure that he won't be arrested. Everyone else, even if they don't say so, live always in mortal fear. All our people either were or are or will at some point be prisoners. If you think that I'm not permanently under observation and surrounded by spies, you are mistaken. I have more experience in this matter and even with all the precautions I take I am never certain. But don't be afraid; all the shutters are down, and nobody can see us." He grabbed my outstretched hand in a firm grip. On the table were three small glasses of vodka. We each took one and drank; Kuragin pronounced the toast, "*Na zdorovie,*" to good health.

Supper lasted almost three hours. We were served delicious Russian dishes prepared with great mastery and care by Anna Nikitovna. Wine and southern fruit were in plentiful supply. The conversation revolved around the war and the uncertain fate of the nation after the enormous losses during the siege of Stalingrad. This war was called *otechestwennaia woina,* the war for the fatherland, in an appeal to the Russian people's attachment to the land of their forefathers. Not a word was said about the land of socialism or communism. Even the distinctions of the officers and the medals for bravery carried the names of the famous generals of the tsar.

Kuragin was interested in the quality of life and the customs in capitalist countries. Not out of fear (because I was beginning to trust him) but rather sympathy, I tried not to make too much of the good life and civic freedoms in the West, to spare him the pain of having lost the liberties we enjoyed. The evening passed quickly and I almost forgot that I was a prisoner. At about 2:00 A.M. Kuragin got up and put into my pocket a pack of the best cigarettes. "It is time for you to return to the hospital," he said. "Please don't think that I have repaid my debt to you. You will hear from me a lot in the future." He himself drove me back to the hospital in his *troika*.

It was late when Misha's gentle knocking woke me the next morning. The day had started in the hospital quite a while ago. Misha was overjoyed to see me safe in bed again after yesterday's nocturnal journey.

"Thank God you are back, my friend. I hardly slept all night for wondering how we would manage here without you. I nearly panicked, not knowing if you would return at all. I peeked into your room in the morning and was glad to see you, but I know you must have got back very late and I did not want to wake you. I did the work and the rounds, and decided to let you sleep all day and night and wake you up only tomorrow. But unfortunately a messenger came from Colonel Dolochov and I had to disturb you. But you've slept for hours; it is already late afternoon." Misha would never ask where, why, or when unless I volunteered to tell him. So this time he contented himself with only the most necessary information. I dressed quickly, swallowed some coffee, and was on my way to headquarters.

Colonel Dolochov was extremely friendly and greeted me as usual with a happy face and cordial smile. As we sat down he assured me that he was satisfied with my work in the hospital. He handed me a cigarette and – reluctantly, it seemed – explained why he wanted to see me.

"As you probably know," he began, "we are going deeper into the taiga to prepare the clearing of the forest and construction of the road into the new territories that are full of excellent timber. For this work we delegated our best man, Ulianov Vasili Pavlovitch, and he has done some very good work out there. He took the best workers from here and has already completed his task. There are about four hundred inmates there. They were able to build all the barracks. So it is now a regular new compound."

Dolochov explained that Ulianov had his family with him, his wife and children, two girls and a boy. The boy, the eldest, had got sick the day before.

"About two hours ago I got a panicky call from Ulianov that the boy is having difficulty breathing. I promised to send help. It is about thirty miles away. In good weather you should make it in about three hours. I'll give you my coach and my best coachman, Sergei. He knows the way. Keep the edge of the huge plain to your left and the forest on your right. The road is good. About halfway you will pass a village on your left, about fourteen miles from here. Then turn right, along the new narrow road cut out in the forest. It will take you straight to the new point. Good luck." He told me to take whatever I needed from the hospital and gave me some authorization papers, along with a small parcel for Ulianov. "On your return," he ordered, "please report to me."

Outside the colonel's office, the coach with three magnificent horses was waiting. Sergei greeted me with a smile. I got all the necessary instruments and medications from the hospital and we took to the road. It was already getting dark. There was very little snow and the starless sky hung very low over the immense white plain before us. We passed the darkened silhouettes of the hospital barracks and the few houses on the outskirts of Sossva. Gradually the road became more difficult, while the bells on the horses were drowned out by the howling wind. A stream of arctic air slipped under the collar of my fur coat, making my spine shiver.

It was getting colder. Dry snow began to fall, driven by a strong wind coming from the left across the open plain. Sergei loosed the reins and the black horses picked up their pace. The snow and wind grew in intensity until we could hardly see. I started to wonder whether we should return and wait until morning. But the sick boy was having trouble breathing; I was almost sure it was diphtheria and that I would have to put a tube into his windpipe. I had to get there soon.

The blizzard grew stronger and stronger and the snow bit into our faces. The fury of the storm completely stifled any sound of the galloping horses. But to the left a silver light pierced the horizon, illuminating the endless plain, while the moon appeared between ragged clouds just long enough for us to see that we were following the edge of the forest on the right.

I was sure that it was past midnight but did not know how far we were from our destination. The wind shifted us towards the plain in the mad dance of the furious blizzard. The sleigh creaked ominously. Sergei did not know were he was going and let the reins go, counting on the instinct of the horses. I began to feel drowsy and was afraid to fall into a deep sleep. Only the faint sound of the bells told me I was still conscious.

The wind was changing direction, blowing now in front of us, now from the right or the left. It was horribly cold. I was concerned that the horses might drop from exhaustion after so many hours. Instinctively, they seemed to know that stopping in this bitter cold, at the mercy of the furious wind, meant certain death. Suddenly a tiny light appeared in the far distance, coming closer and closer. This must be the village Colonel Dolochov had mentioned.

We stopped at one of the houses and Sergei helped me down from the coach. A face, still half asleep, appeared in the doorway.

"*Zdrastwuite*. Come in, please." On entering we were soothed by the warmth of the room. Our host lighted a kerosene lamp and invited us to sit down. By the clock hanging on the wall it was almost six in the morning. We explained to the man that we were on an urgent mission and that we would stay only for a while to rest. Expressing surprise that on such a night we had made it alive all the way from Sossva, he persuaded us to wait until daylight and lie down for a couple of hours. His wife came with *tchai* (hot tea) and hot baked potatoes from the oven. We started with a few shots of vodka that the pharmacist had given us for the road, then tea and the wonderful potatoes. Our hosts insisted that I take their bed, while they and Sergei went slept on the floor, which they covered with furs. I fell asleep at once and it seemed only a minute later when Sergei woke me up.

It was past nine. We got up quickly and found the horses outside well rested. Our hosts cried when we left; it was difficult to understand their emotions at having to say goodbye to guests with whom they had spent so short a time. There was a saying among those who lived in the middle of nowhere: "*Gost w dom Bogh w dom*" – A guest at home, God at home.

On the right the sky was a heavy dark magenta with long reddish orange stripes that grew brighter every minute; above us the sky was bluish and on the left light weightless clouds were moving fast. The snow, deep and uneven, had been sculpted into mounds by the wind, which, while calmer, still stubbornly carried the fine dusty snow. We got under way.

Soon we noticed the opening in the forest where the new road had been cut. The forest was dense all around and the wind almost gone. In about two hours we saw from a distance the barracks of the new compound. At the end a small narrow road led to the Ulianovs' house. Vasili Pavlovitch was at the door, his face showing deep concern.

"I was talking to Colonel Dolochov and he told me you had left yesterday," he said, ushering us inside. "I did not know that you would get through this blizzard. Please come in. I don't think little Vania has a chance. Such a dear boy!" Inside, Mrs Ulianov was sitting on the bed, her eyes swollen with tears. Vania was about eleven. His face was cyanotic, his breathing very loud, screechy and laboured. I knew I had to act immediately. Dispensing with a full examination – it was unimportant whether it was just a croup or diphtheria – I opened his trachea (windpipe) and intro-duced the tube, fastening it around his neck. As usual in such cases, the result was striking. With the help of the tube, the boy's breathing at once assumed a more normal sound, and his colour improved within a minute.

This result made an unbelievable impression on Vania's parents, who had lost all hope that the boy would recover. To them it was as if a miracle had happened. I felt awkward, like a magician impressing the public with a new trick. I tried to explain that this was the most elementary procedure, that any doctor could do it, but to no avail. They would forever look upon me a miracle worker, an angel who gave them back their dying son. When Vania swallowed his first mouthfuls of warm milk, his parents did not know how to thank me and their attempts were cut off by deep sobs. I said that we would take the boy back with us and that Mrs Ulianov could come too. There was a little bit of vodka left, and we drank to the good health of Vania. I had phoned Colonel Dolochov, who was pleased with my report, and told him that we would take the boy to the hospital for further observation and treatment. After a bite to eat, we were on our way; we had been at their home only about two hours. Outside it was not as cold, the wind having almost completely subsided. Before evening we reached the outskirts of Sossva.

Sara Abramovna and Misha were waiting for me in the office. They hugged me and told me how worried they had been for my safety in the blizzard: we had all heard of people who had perished in such weather. We had lunch together, then I excused myself, again leaving everything to Misha, and went to my room to rest.

It was almost noon when I woke up next day. I dressed quickly and went to make my report to Colonel Dolochov about the trip. In the waiting room I found Kuragin, there to see the colonel on business. He was pleased to see me. Directing me to a corner sofa, he looked around to make sure nobody could hear us.

"Igor Morovitch, there is something I have to tell you," he began. "We have a new man sent to us from Moscow, Major Efimov. He is going to call you, saying that he suffers from high blood pressure, but his malady is just an excuse. In fact he is going to propose that you act as an informer for us. I know how you will react to this, but it will be difficult for you to refuse. I was thinking about how to advise you. When he calls and presents his idea to you, say something like this: 'I would be glad to help the Soviet people in their struggle against the fascist regime in Germany, but somehow your own people have made such cooperation impossible. Whenever Colonel Kuragin comes to our lager-point hospital he always walks arm-in-arm with me, and everybody in the camp is very suspicious and convinced that I am already working for you. As a result the inmates are very careful and never talk to me especially about political matters.' You will see, when you tell him this story," Kuragin assured me, "he will immediately change the subject and never return to it." Kuragin was then called in to the colonel's office and I hardly had time to thank him. On his way out again he smiled at me, waving his hand and saying goodbye.

I made my report to Colonel Dolochov, adding that the boy's health was improving and that we would remove his trachea tube in a few days. As I was leaving, the colonel told me that some new clothing had arrived for the officers. He handed me a card to give to the manager of the stores, who would give me anything I liked. I thanked him, feeling awkward. I was already dressed not like a prisoner but like the higher officers of the NKVD, and it seemed wrong to take advantage of the colonel's gesture.

It was late in the afternoon and I did not want to rush back to the hospital. I decided to drop in on Tatiana Osipovna. Tatiana had been very depressed. We had not seen each other for quite a while and it did not look as though my visits would increase. First of all, even with my privileges, I still couldn't forget that I was a prisoner. I had to assume that my movements were carefully observed and discussed. I also had to remember that Itkin was in love with Tatiana. Being a free man, an officer, and superior to Tatiana, he could create some very nasty problems for us if he chose to. The fact that she hated him and that his attempts to gain her sympathy came to nothing made no difference.

The other important reason was Sara Abramovna, whom I had suspected for some time of harbouring tender feelings for me. Sometimes she was forgetful, not realizing that as a married woman she was playing with fire. All these matters grew in my consciousness, forcing me to think hard about what to do. I didn't think there was any point in giving Tatiana my reasons for avoiding her, however much she deserved an explanation. She didn't seem able to separate her rational thinking from her emotions. Most likely, despite the danger, she would not hesitate to follow instinct rather than reason.

I decided not to let her see for the moment that I considered our situation hopeless. It was a sad state of affairs; I liked Tatiana very much and knew that I could easily feel more. But in addition to concerns for my own fate, I was aware that, as a free citizen, she risked much in getting involved with me, particularly with her unfavourable political past. Since I was already a prisoner, the danger to me was much less.

The spy system was perverse, destroying the most beautiful human feelings for the sake of a phobic tyranny that aimed, supposedly, at making mankind happy. How many lives had already been destroyed in this way, how many families torn apart? How many people had already disappeared without trace while the government professed ignorance of their fate, even offering rewards for finding them?

Tatiana looked more beautiful than ever. Her golden hair sparkled in the setting sun. Although her cornflower eyes glistened with sadness, she tried to assume a look of perfect calm. I wondered whether she could see into the future, or perhaps read my thoughts. It was as if we were both hiding something we did not have the courage to disclose. In that warm room we felt an overwhelming attachment to the present moment, an urgent wish to postpone the cruel uncertainty of tomorrow. Tatiana came close to me.

"*Dushenka*, it is not right to be in this mood. Time is an invention of the mind. 'Now' is what matters." These were the last words spoken in the room for a long time. We savoured the time we had together, hungry for each other's bodies. Much later, on my way back to the hospital, it took a long time for the cold to return me to reality.

I was in my office the next morning looking at plans for additional operating rooms, when Misha came in.

"Igor Morovitch, Sasha is after me all the time, asking me to arrange an appointment with you. He is here. I cannot delay any more; he is very insistent. You remember him, he is the fellow who wanted to commit suicide and opened his belly with a knife."

"Please let him in." Very shyly, his head down, Sasha entered the room. He stood there in silence until Misha left and then looked at me. After a while he spoke.

"See what you have done. I have no reason to be alive but I don't have the courage to try and take my life again. I can't go on like this any longer. It is unbearable." The torment was clear on his face. I waited. "You have to give me some quick-acting poison if you believe in God as you said you did," he resumed. "I'm asking you first since you tricked me. I have no father. Maybe he exists but I've never met him. Maybe he doesn't have the guts to tell me he is my father. Maybe he doesn't even know I exist. Maybe my mother never had the guts to tell him I was born. Or maybe she didn't know him well enough to tell him. My whole existence is one big joke. Mother is far away and I never really knew whether she cared at all. Don't you understand that everybody has to have somebody in life? Somebody to love and live for?"

Sasha stopped suddenly. There was an immense sadness in his eyes, though he did not cry. He was beyond affection, deeply immersed in a quiet despair. His depression had gone far and I had no idea how to bring him back.

For a moment I began to doubt whether saving his life had been a "good deed" after all, suffering as deeply as he did. It was now much more important to save his soul. But where to begin? How to stem the tidal wave of his despair? He came to me, I thought. He is asking for my help. It has to come from me, if I am the only thread he is holding onto. What can I do for him? Maybe I can do something just by existing, just by allowing him to be close to me. Maybe he could work in the hospital, maybe Misha could train him to become a nurses' aide.

"Listen, Sasha," I said aloud. "You will work here in the hospital and help others. You will be close to me and I'll think of a way to get you something even better if you behave. You won't be alone. I love you and Dr Misha loves you. Now go and do what he tells you." For a moment there was a tiny change in the expression of his eyes, a small flicker of hope. Or maybe it was only what I wanted to see, in my desire to overcome his helplessness.

The rest of the afternoon was grey and sad, until the moon came out and embraced the world in its silver light. I went out walking, inhaling the frosty air and observing my shadow on the snow. I changed my pace, trying to run away from my shadow, but I knew I could not. I felt the burden of my conscience. It is part of our destiny to live out our own myth, including all the criminal darkness of our souls, our intentional and unintentional lies, our cheatings – all in the name of survival. We suspect and accuse others of what we ourselves should be ashamed of. Why don't we have the courage to admit that we cannot get rid of our dark side, our shadow? How can we learn to live with it, know about it, accept it in ourselves and in others? Yes, the only way is to accept it, know what we are capable of, and not project it onto others. In a world of polarities, to be in the middle is the highest achievement. From there we have to understand love, and forgive others as well as ourselves.

Why was I thinking this way? Did it have to do with my failure to tell Tatiana that our relationship was hopeless? Was it Sasha, who had mutely accused me of salvaging a senseless, empty life? Or was it my professional belief that I had to try to save people – for more suffering? Would I like that for myself?

These unanswerable questions forced upon me the pain of inner emptiness. I raised my head and looked at the moon, requesting an answer, a prescription to alleviate my sense of guilt at having prolonged Sasha's suffering. The moon looked back, indifferent.

My mood persisted throughout the next day. I did my work mechanically, aware that I just needed a spark, an idea, and things would change. Returning to my room after supper, I noticed a light burning in the back room of the pharmacy. Very often a few doctors or nurses would gather there to bake potatoes in the open fireplace and tell stories. That evening I badly needed company. Quietly I opened the door, trying not to disturb the group inside. The room was bathed in the warm light of the fire. Various people sat on pillows on the floor, their faces turned towards Bashat Asiatovitch, whom I had replaced as acting surgeon in Sossva. He was telling a story. The right half of his face glowed in the firelight; the green of his eyes changed to deep magenta and his silvery white hair was tinged with red. Bashat loved telling stories of imagination and horror, and tonight he was in his element, engrossed in a story by Rustavelli, the great Persian.

Suspense was Bashat's specialty, and just as I entered the room, he held his right hand up high, looking at his listeners, who held their breath, transfixed. Suddenly he delivered the punchline. His audience sighed in relief while Bashat laughed his high-pitched, triumphant laugh. He loved these abrupt changes of mood, this deflation of the tension he had so artfully built up. He was one of the greatest storytellers I have ever heard. He also had a sense of humour that endeared him to the people of Sossva, free and imprisoned, springing as it did from his great wisdom.

Bashat kept his private life stricly secret and thus evaded gossip, despite his beautiful face and wonderful smile; he was the hand-somest of men. And while to some extent he envied my reputation as a surgeon, he was a trustworthy friend.

When the gathering broke up I invited Bashat for a nightcap, telling him that I needed his advice and help. I had good reason to solicit Bashat's counsel. During the last few weeks Sara's behaviour had started to change. Every morning, as a rule, she would bring some special food that she had prepared for me, reminding me that I still bore traces of the malnutrition I had suffered in prison. She stressed her experience in these matters and insisted that I, who came from the affluent West, did not understand. It was clear that Sara was becoming dangerously infatuated with me. Since I was not attracted to her, I found myself in a very uncomfortable situation.

I unburdened myself to Bashat. I also told him about Sasha, the boy I had saved from suicide, and my concern that I might not have done the right thing. Bashat took his time before responding.

"The problem with Sasha is easy. You did everything that you should have done for him. If I could, I would have done the same. The only thing this fellow needs is something to reconnect him to life. He needs somebody to love. He needs a substitute parent. Why don't you ask the authorities – you have good contacts – to attach him to the hospital personnel and later make him your personal attendant? Once you become his benefactor you will give him the greatest gift, somebody to serve and to love. This is all he needs, an aim in his life."

The situation with Sara Abramovna was, in his view, much more delicate and difficult. While he had heard no gossip about her special feelings towards me, I should be careful. The safest solution would be for me to get transferred, for example, to the Central Hospital in Stupino. There would be more of a professional challenge for me in such a place. Stupino already had a surgeon, one Dr Deminski, but in Bashat's view, he was not in the same class as I. "The bosses are aware of it," he concluded, "but they want you here and they will not let you go, unless there is the threat of a real scandal. And I think even then they would cover it up. They like to have you close."

"Let me think," he said. "If only there were some political reason for a transfer, but I can't see how political issues could be brought into this. Only the NKVD could get the administration to do such a thing with no questions asked. But you know as well as I do that it won't happen. In the meantime, I advise the utmost caution. Let me ponder the problem a bit more. I will get back to you if I think of something." Bashat hugged me and left my room. I did not sleep well. I tossed and turned. Attacked by subconscious anxiety, I slept badly. But I was coming to expect sudden strange reverses, and I knew that I could not afford to let myself be consumed by fears about things that had not even happened yet.

It was still dark when Misha woke me up, telling me that David Aronovitch Resnik's sleigh was waiting for me. There was an emergency at his home. I was certain that Sara had invented an emergency to make me come to her. I could see a sleepless night ahead of me, but again I resolved to be calm and handle the

situation like any other. After all, there was no personal involvement, at least not where I was concerned. But I feared being
involved in or accused of something I was not guilty of.

When we arrived at the Resniks' home, Sara was lying on a sofa
in their living-room, dressed in an attractive nightgown. Her face
was contorted with pain. David held her hand and bent over her
in tears. I asked him to leave us alone. Once he'd gone Sara
grabbed my hand and began to sob. It was as if some enormous
emotional barrier had suddenly broken and all the feelings so
long held in check could find free expression. I let her weep like
this for a while and then tried to piece together the story of her
sudden affliction.

"Where does it hurt, Sara Abramovna? Please tell me." I looked
into her eyes for an answer. She understood immediately that I
had come to handle an emergency. I hoped she was reading my
thoughts, which urged her to have mercy on her husband who
loved her so much, and to remember that that was her primary
obligation.

This wordless dialogue lasted only a few seconds. Then she
indicated with her hand the spot on her belly where she supposedly suffered pain. I acknowledged by a look that I understood
everything she wanted to tell me. I knew her life was not easy.
She was the wife of a very highly placed Party member who had
fallen into disgrace during the Kirov purges, and many sleepless
nights they both must have spent in fear and uncertainty. They
had no children; David, an *apparatchik*, a mere pawn in the Communist Party game, had no time for family life. Though warmhearted by nature, he was neither poetic nor intellectual. He loved
Sara in his own way, but he did not know how to express it or
show her any affection.

I explained that she needed some drugs for the pain and something to soothe her nerves. She stopped crying and calmed down
a bit. I called David in and told him that we were not certain about
the diagnosis, but it looked like a biliary attack. I gave her a small
intravenous dose of morphine and she fell asleep right away.
David was very grateful.

This sudden call to Sarah's house showed me that the problem
I had discussed with Bashat had become urgent. I needed time
and wanted to rest from thinking about my position in Sossva,
which was becoming ever more precarious.

The next day after breakfast, I asked for Sasha to come to my room. The boy greeted me with a look of expectation. His whole appearance conveyed a different message from the last time I had seen him, and it looked as though he would now be more receptive to the offer of a better future and some meaningful content in his life.

After a few introductory questions I found out that he could read and write and that he liked nature, walking into the forest whenever he could. He was especially fond of animals. "Listen, Sasha," I began. "I have a serious proposal for you, but before we start I want you to tell me why you were sentenced for murder. You know I can get these details through the official channels, but I'd rather hear it from you." He answered readily.

"That's quite simple – I've got nothing to hide. It was this bastard of a guard in the lager for young offenders. You know I was with the *bezprizornyie* [children without parental care or supervision], sentenced for theft. This guard didn't like me, I don't know why. He made my life a misery. One time when I was going out to work, he kept me in the guardhouse and started to beat me with a *nahaika* [leather whip]. I couldn't lie on my back for a whole week. I was totally helpless, I couldn't defend myself. The only thing I could do was cry and cry again, ashamed of my helplessness. My wounds had not even healed when he took me back into the guardhouse and beat the daylights out of me again. I knew I couldn't complain because nobody would believe me and he might well even kill me."

"One evening when I was crying in the darkness on my bunkbed, Vasili, an older boy from our barrack who slept close by, asked me what the matter was. I told him everything, crying and showing him my bloody back. He thought for a while and then explained that this guard was probably a degenerate sexual sadist, and that he would keep on beating me until I got sick and died. It was not that he hated me but rather that he chose this strange way to express his love for me. Vasili's face turned serious and he said there was no other way – I would have to kill the fellow or he would eventually kill me. He spoke of a similar case in another lager for *bezprizornyie*. That boy finally died and nothing happened to the guard, as nobody even cared."

I listened closely to the tumble of words as Sasha continued. "Vasili helped me make a plan. The guard was short-sighted and had to wear thick glasses and bend down over his papers to read.

Vasili's plan was that in the morning, when we went out to work, he would go in front of me and hand the guard his factory pass. When the guard put on his glasses and bent down over the small table at the guardhouse, Vasili would step aside and I would come forward and drive an axe through his neck with all my might."

"Everybody liked Vasili. He was a good boy and often helped other boys when they were tired or having trouble. He was right that nobody would believe me if I complained and that I'd only be hastening my end. We all knew that nobody cared. A boy prisoner means nothing. And the weak ones who couldn't do enough labour would eventually die of starvation anyway. That was the reality and it seemed there was no other choice for me. As Vasili said, it was me or the guard.

"For the next two weeks Vasili trained me in the forest until I could sever a heavy branch with one blow from a sharp axe. He then told me I was ready. The hardest part of the plan was to smuggle an axe into our barrack and keep it there until the bastard came on duty." Sasha was immersed in his terrible story. But he watched me as he spoke, trying to read my responses.

"One day when some repairs were being done to another barrack, Vasili was able to hide an axe there without anybody noticing. Before the day we had chosen, Vasili offered to kill the guard himself but said that I'd get a lighter sentence, being younger. He also warned me not to tell anyone why I did it and to be very firm about it. To tell the truth would be to accuse the establishment of employing a pervert, and that would end in disaster for me. Nobody ever accuses the NKVD of making mistakes without regretting it. Vasili said that if I didn't tell the truth, they would just consider me mentally unbalanced, and I'd get an even lighter sentence.

"It is now almost exactly a year since it happened," Sasha concluded. "I did my job. My clothes were soaked in blood and I almost fainted. Everyone was screaming, and I was taken away by the guards and arrested. I was sent to this Sevurallag and four months ago my sentence was handed down: five years' hard labour. The difference is one year. I got four years for stealing, which I never did, and now for this murder I get one more year. Vasili was right. The murder, which I call an execution, saved my life. It also helped me to understand that we live in such times and places that there is no protection if you don't have the courage to save your own life."

Sasha had once told his story to an old religious man in our barrack, asking him whether he was a great sinner in the eyes of God. The old man thought for a while and told Sasha that if he had told the story out of remorse, it was really a confession and God would forgive him. Sasha felt much better and never told the story again, until now. "You asked me," he said. "I don't know why I told you everything, except that I feel that you are my friend."

The gruesome story told by this seventeen-year-old boy put me into a state of helpless rebellion against the ruthless regime that drove innocent youngsters, abandoned children, to murder. Sasha was still waiting for my reaction; I told him what I thought. "It is okay, Sasha. It was self-defence, not murder. In any civilized country this wouldn't happen, but if it did, it would be judged by any court of law as manslaughter in self-defence, and you would be freed." Sasha's face lit up. Not only had I not condemned him – I had justified his action. After a silence, I explained why I had called him in. "I wanted to ask if you would like to work in the hospital as an orderly. I'll tell the nurses to train you. If we're satisfied with your behaviour and performance, I'll take you on as a personal assistant." I had never seen such a look on Sasha's face before: his entire countenance announced his delight at finally belonging to somebody who would care. He was not alone any more. He did not say a word. It seemed that he could not. He just came close, grabbed my hand, and kissed it. I gestured at him to go. I could not speak either.

My spirits remained subdued. I was oppressed by the need to obtain a transfer, the difficulty of accomplishing this, and the realization that I would have to give up my friends in Sossva. But Kuragin's warnings were much in my mind, and I felt an inner compulsion to break out of my torpor, quicken my reactions, so that I could answer questions promptly if need be and not let myself get caught out.

A nurse came to tell me that one of the NKVD bosses wanted to see me. It was Major Efimov, the one Kuragin had mentioned some time ago. Upon reaching his building I was taken by a soldier to his office. A corpulent man in his late fifties, he remained seated and did not lift his head from his papers when I entered. He was trying to intimidate me with this behaviour, though he had responded to the soldier's knock with a shrill "Come in." The tactic reminded me of my last interrogator, attesting to the routine methods of the dreaded NKVD. Only this time I knew what to do. Inwardly I ridiculed his professional training. Kuragin had cautioned me to be prepared for the unpleasant and unexpected. But I knew now how to deal with this type of adversary – you had to stand up to them, paralyse them with your courage, especially when you were in a commanding position, just as I had stood up to Kuragin when I was to operate on his wife.

The silence lasted a long while. Finally Efimov lifted his head and, looking at me seriously, said that he needed my professional help. I sat down without invitation, fulfilling my role as a doctor whose services he required.

"I suffer from terrible headaches that keep me from doing my usual work. The doctors say it is a result of high blood pressure. Can you help?"

I examined him. His blood pressure was 220 over 170, his pulse 110, and he had the widened blood vessels on his fleshy nose typical of an alcoholic.

"Citizen *Natchalnik*, there is no miracle drug for your condition. The cause of your suffering is the way you live." I told him that he was tense and overweight, that he ought to go on a salt-free diet, abstain from alcoholic beverages, and break up his sedentary occupation with daily long walks. "I will write down my recommendations, but it is up to you to follow them. If the improvement is slow we may add some medication. I know it is hard and it will take some time, but I strongly advise you to adhere to this regime if you want to prevent serious complications."

Efimov seemed flabbergasted. His concern was visible. It looked as though nobody had ever told him before what was wrong with his health. On top of that, my succinct advice, pronounced with definite authority, was not something he was used to, but he could not fight it because, where his health was concerned, I was in command.

"What will happen if I do not follow your advice?"

"Maybe nothing. Just the same, you are incapacitated by your horrible migraines and it is quite possible that such a condition, if not attended to, could lead to a stroke, leaving you crippled for the rest of you life. I know that to follow my regime is difficult but there is no alternative. If you have any reservations about my recommendations, you should consult with one of the fine professors in Moscow."

"No, this is impossible now, because of the war. I think, judging from your reputation here in Sossva, I will try to follow your advice. But you have to help me."

"Very well. Whenever you call me I will be at your disposal. Or, even better, you can come to the hospital weekly and we will follow the progress of your condition."

I was almost certain that he would not ask me to become an informer, as doing so might compromise my professional standing. But I was mistaken. Efimov said, "I accept your proposal. Now, you can do something for me that is also very important. As you know, we are in a mortal struggle with fascist criminal Germany and we have to paralyse any enemies inside our country. There are many enemies here, everywhere, among doctors, nurses, and even the highly placed administrative people in our lager. You know them well, and they trust you as a doctor. You yourself know what atrocities are going on in Europe and I want you to help us. I want you to listen and to bring to our attention any stories or agitation you may hear against our state. We will talk about the details later. You can serve us in a much wider capacity than that of a doctor. A doctor saves the lives of a few. By paralysing our enemies, we can save millions."

He was not only a scoundrel but a stupid one at that, not realizing that he could hurt somebody who had to preserve his professional authority and integrity. "I know," I replied. "I am more interested than anybody in helping to destroy Hitler, but this is impossible and it was made impossible by your own boss." Here I told him the story Kuragin had given me, about how we had become friendly after his wife's operation and how he came to our hospital and walked arm in arm with me, how people already thought I was working for the NKVD and were afraid of me, not trusting me and limiting their conversation with me to professional matters or unimportant things like food, the weather, and so on. Efimov's face assumed a strange look; he could hardly control his reaction to my story. His eyes expressed helpless rage as he struggled in vain to calm himself after this unexpected setback. He closed his eyes.

"Okay, Doctor. You can go. I will be in touch next week about my treatment and to get the details concerning my diet." When I left his eyes were still closed.

I returned to the hospital, elated at my victory. I went straight to my room and fell into a deep sleep. But I was awakened at 1:00 A.M. by the phone. It was Tatiana Osipovna. I was convinced it was an emergency. She had never phoned me before; you could never be certain there wasn't somebody recording your conversation. But Tatiana had thrown caution to the winds.

"*Dushenka*, I am so lonely without you."

I tried to remind her of the risk she was taking. "You probably have a wrong number."

"No, no, I have the right number, I recognize your voice and I don't care what happens to me. Please come over to my place now."

"It is the middle of the night and you know I cannot. I can come tomorrow to check on your health." I desperately tried to correct the impression such a conversation might make on the wire tappers. Tatiana made no reply, but suddenly I heard the sounds of a heart-rending Russian melody, sad and passionate, from her violin. For a moment I forgot about being careful; the faint music evoked a half-forgotten place and experience, mixing memory with desire. Images of Tatiana shifted in my mind.

"Can you hear how my violin is crying for you." Something in Tatiana's voice made me fearful that something bad might happen if I did not see her tonight. I told her that I would try to come right away to see what was wrong with her health and began to think how I could go there that night. I was allowed to leave the confines of the lager only during the day. It was too late to get permission from an official for a night visit. I woke Misha and told him to come with me to the guardhouse. On the way I explained what was going on. "I have to visit a sick doctor right away. Will you note down in your book the time I am leaving?" Turning to the guard, I could hardly believe how commanding I sounded. "I have to make an emergency visit to a sick doctor. Dr Kurovitch will look after things in my absence. If you have any doubts please call Colonel Kuragin immediately, but I doubt whether he will be happy to be wakened at this time of night. We doctors are used to these night calls."

A slight shiver went through the guard when I mentioned the dreaded Kuragin. Looking at me with fear and admiration, he said, "I am putting down the time as 2.10 A.M."

About an hour later, short of breath, I entered Tatiana's house. I had not even started the speech I had rehearsed on the way over when she took me in a wild embrace, wetting my face with her tears. From time to time her body shook with sobs. She was outside of herself; not a single cell of her body belonged to her. I was deeply moved, aware of the need for total passivity on my part. I responded to her embrace, falling in with her deep breathing. After a long while she said in a faint voice, "I feel it, I know it, but I cannot accept it. I am in love with you, and there is nothing for us in the future. I don't see any hope. We are both so helpless – everything is against us. This is not a transient feeling or an infatuation: I have never loved anybody so much. Before, in Moscow, when the whole world was smiling on me and there were so many contenders to choose from, I wasn't attracted to any of them; there wasn't a spark of feeling on my part, when all of them were crazy for me. How ironic! Now, in these inhuman circumstances, I have all of you in the deepest recesses of my heart, yet I know that it will lead nowhere, that it promises nothing, not even the tiniest possibility of a solution."

I felt hollow inside, full of the bitter knowledge of our situation. I could find no words. Tears began to flow as I shared with Tatiana the truth of what she said. Passion wouldn't help; only tenderness could dress the raw wounds of the soul. We continued our embrace, longing for a future. Finally, Tatiana raised her head and looked at me.

"*Dushenka*, you know all my thoughts. You knew that I was praying for both of us, for your peace and mine."

I felt then, for the first time, that I had something to say: "Who knows what tomorrow will bring? If the bad could come so unexpectedly, then why not believe that there will be a better tomorrow for both of us? You have only to believe in us very strongly. Faith will bring fulfilment."

After a while Tatiana gained her equilibrium. She got up. Looking at me with an expression of hope, she said she had been behaving like a spoiled child. "Now please go back quickly, and forgive me for being so impulsive. I would never have believed myself capable of acting in such a manner under these circumstances."

"Don't worry," I assured her. "I arranged everything according to the rules. If anybody asks, you were very sick. But next time please don't wait until you are desperate." Our parting embrace expressed total belonging. Then I was outside in the cold.

As I walked back I realized that Tatiana simply refused to grasp the situation we were in and had lost all sense of the danger of our affair. She was a free citizen, under suspicion. I was a prisoner. How could she forget this? I loved Tatiana. But the situation with Sara was also becoming explosive and if I did not leave Sossva soon I would suffer the consequences. It had become clear to me why I had been arrested. No one really believed that I had poisoned those people in the hospital at Asbest. They knew from the laboratory data that it was food poisoning, and the NKVD could easily have found another scapegoat to appease the wounded officers in the Asbest hospital instead of depriving the place of its best surgeon. But I understood that my amorous affair with Natalia Petrovna, the wife of a Soviet cabinet minister, was an intolerable situation that had to be surgically resolved. The hostile behaviour of Litvinov, the investigator in Asbest and formerly my friend, was understandable; he had been morally outraged. Here was a foreigner disturbing the peace of a high-ranking civil servant who had to spent his life in beleaguered Moscow busy with affairs of state.

I understood now that the only intimate relationship permissible in my situation was with another prisoner. Meanwhile, to prevent any new catastrophe, I would have to try to get a transfer to somewhere else, probably to Stupino. Maybe I could ask Kuragin, who seemed genuinely to like me.

It may seem strange, in retrospect, that after urging Tatiana to take joy in the present, I began to think of being transferred. The truth was, I had given much thought to the changeability of human affairs. Wars and revolutions, earthquakes and floods, joys and sorrows all come and go. Given the grotesque turns of destiny, anything was possible, even the end of the war and some form of mutual understanding between states of different social structure. Perhaps after the war, I might be able to meet Tatiana again and pick up our love affair where it left off – provided we kept ourselves alive to do so.

In the meantime, the trick was to remember the mountaintops and quickly forget the valleys. I reached the hospital at 5:30 A.M. and checked in with the guard who had let me out to visit a sick doctor. Emotionally drained. I poured myself a glass of vodka in my room and drained it in a gulp. I do not know when I fell asleep.

It was Misha who woke me, with the news that Major Efimov would be waiting for me in his office when I'd finished my rounds. I went immediately, leaving everything in Misha's hands as usual. Efimov's manner this time was completely different. It was possible that he had talked with Kuragin, but I doubted it. More likely, he knew that I had a special relation with his boss that was off limits to him. As a person trained in the frightening atmosphere of the NKVD, he knew better than to ask any questions. For all he knew, I might be working for Kuragin himself; all the more reason to treat me with respect.

He had arranged this visit not only to get further medical advice but also to try to rectify his previous behaviour, which might have displeased his superior. The door of his office was still open and Kuragin himself came in. Seeing me, he said, "Igor Morovitch, when you have finished with Major Efimov, please stop by my office." This unexpected invitation must have confirmed Efimov's assumptions about my relationship with the big boss of the NKVD of the Sevurallag. I spent almost an hour in Efimov's office writing out the details of his dietary regime and medication. He treated me like a special guest, offering the best cigarettes and exquisite tea. When I left he bade farewell as if I were a friend whom he also feared.

Kuragin was in an excellent mood, and, apart from the gratitude that he showed whenever we met, I felt that he really liked me as a person. I was somebody he could trust; he did not fear the dangers of a friendship between two people of unequal status. Perhaps he was not totally without moral fibre.

"Igor Morovitch," he began, "We both know why I've called you in here. You see, I know your movements, every day and every night. I know where you go. I know what people say about you and even what they feel about you. This information is brought to me daily, and not only about your relations with the members of the lager administration. For security reasons I have to know, for my own sake and especially for yours, what the prisoners think and feel about you. I promised that you would be under my care and I will keep that promise. So please don't be surprised that I know more about you than you know about yourself. You are aware of what you are doing, but I also know what people think and say about your behaviour. It is important. You don't realize how jealous people are. Anonymous letters keep landing on my desk from people you wouldn't suspect. It's easy for me to see what is true and what is just an attempt to hurt you. Someday, when you leave the Sevurallag, I will present you with these letters; I hope they won't make you bitter or cynical. Such is life, especially in our circumstances.

"In the meantime, and this is the reason I wanted to talk to you, I have thought carefully about your problem with Dr Sara Resnik. I feel that the time is ripe for you to be transferred."

I was astonished. Although I had not breathed a word of my predicament to Kuragin, he knew everything about it and had even anticipated my asking for his help.

"I will miss you," he continued. "Despite my position, there is no one with whom I dare to talk openly as I can with you. I have a special feeling for you – a luxury rare for someone who as a rule can't afford to trust another human being. It is not only a privilege but it has brightened up my life considerably. I think the best place for you will be Stupino. It is a huge hospital and you will be happy there; you'll have more work and greater professional interest. As for me, I will come there quite often, whenever I feel like seeing you. I shall still protect you, and I will still know all your movements.

"The problem of Tatiana Osipovna is altogether different. I know you are in love, and she is a very fine person. I sympathize, but I can't change things at present. I know that Dr Itkin is after her. I promise you I will keep him away from her. I will also arrange for the two of you to correspond in such a way that nobody knows about it. I'm convinced that when the war is over you'll be free and your relationship with Tatiana Osipovna can come out into the open. I hope you will settle in Swerdlowsk, where I know you will be offered a chair in surgery at the university. In the meantime I will prepare the ground, especially with Colonel Dolochov. He won't be happy to lose you. I have to convince him that Stupino is not far away and that if we need you badly we can get you here quickly in an emergency. I will not call you again. The order for the transfer will be sudden and unexpected. As I mentioned to you at my home, I have to be careful and limit our visits only to what is necessary, even if they are a treat for me."

Here Kuragin stopped for a moment, checking my reaction. I was totally overwhelmed, not only by the fact that he knew every detail of my life in Sossva but also by the care he invested in our relationship. He showed the openness of heart, goodness, and hospitality that I had found in many Russians. He was the only man around who could, under the circumstances, afford to show his friendship in deeds. After a short silence, I thanked him for his friendship, which I not only dearly appreciated but also returned. He had opened my eyes to an understanding of the structure and reality of human relations in these sad times. But there was something else I wanted from him.

"Andrei Petrovitch," I said, using the familiar form of address, "there is one minor thing I would like to ask you. You probably know about the young lad, Sasha, who attempted suicide. I have been able to convince him that life is worth living after all, but for a long time he will still need some semiparental guidance, which he has never had. He has to have some attachment, somebody to serve and love. I have found a way to reconnect him to the world and to his feelings, and I wonder if it would be possible to transfer him to Stupino so that he can be with me." Without hesitation Kuragin replied, "No problem, he will follow you a few days after your departure." These were the last words he spoke to me. Mutely, we each swallowed and accepted our sense of loss. He hugged me and then turned to the window as I was leaving.

The next few days were taken up with routine work in the hospital. I was very busy bringing all the patients' case histories up to date. Misha and I spent long hours in the operating room performing elective procedures, as well as in the examining areas changing dressings, replacing plaster casts, and so on. I had the impression that Misha suspected something was going on but did not dare to ask what. He knew that I would tell him as much as I could.

One morning about two weeks after my visit to her home, Sara Abramovna appeared at the hospital. She seemed in a cheerful mood and showed no trace of her recent ailment. I felt that she wanted to forget the whole incident. She did not mention why she hadn't called me all this time, nor did she say anything about her recovery. But it was evident from her demeanour that she had gone through a thorough change of attitude. She attempted, not quite successfully, to be more formal and for once brought no food with her. She was abrasive and at times impolite, a behaviour that divulged her struggle to control her feelings. I knew she would not long remain in this state and would regain her equilibrium once I was gone. I tried to busy myself with patients and stay away from the office as much as possible so that she woudn't have to see me.

It was Monday. The day passed uneventfully and I retired to my room late in the afternoon, tired and bored after the long hours of routine. Then to my surprise, my literary friend Iacov Mironovitch knocked on my door.

"It is good to see you, Igor Morovitch. I took the liberty of dropping in on you unexpectedly. You are probably wondering what I am doing in Sossva. Very simple: I was called back to my previous post to take over the Verhoturie district again. They did not fulfil last year's plan. You know that the compounds of that district are full of inferior human material – the very old, the very young, and all the people from Poland, Latvia, Estonia, etc.; it is the garbage bag of the Sevurallag. The only place that runs properly is the central hospital in Stupino. But sick inmates don't help to fulfil the Gulag's yearly plan." Though I found his ethnic slurs and his reference to "inferior human material" offensive, I was glad for my own reasons that Iacov Mironovitch would run the Verhoturie district. The books he gave me introduced me to new literary talent, despite the government restrictions on literary freedom, and gave me a sense of what people were thinking in this oppressed nation.

"Igor Morovitch," he continued, "I've heard so much about you at headquarters. You've really become a celebrity in the eyes of the administration." I didn't quite know how to answer this. "I was just doing my job and showing a bit of the human side of my profession." The work of a surgeon often produces fast and dramatic results, leading people to glorify their work. From the

surgeon's point of view such results are no more than the fulfilment of one's training and obligations. In my opinion, surgery
(except for traumatology, the repair of injuries) is just an admission of the failure of medical science to understand the origin and
mechanics of many ailments and thus to treat their causes. Iacov
listened to my views, but I got the impression that he still thought
of me as a miracle worker. I offered him a drink, which he refused,
but he accepted my invitation for supper. I sensed that he wanted
to tell me something but did not know why he hesitated. I knew
that soon in Stupino we would be able to spent lots of time
together. I thanked him for the books as he left. It had been good
to see him. Iacov represented another type of friend: highly intelligent, very sensitive and discreet, someone with whom I could
share my innermost feelings without fear either of being betrayed
or misunderstood.

Two more weeks went by without news of my transfer. I knew
I had to be patient. I called Tatiana twice during this time and she
seemed to be in a strange mood, hovering somewhere between
broken dreams and the distant hope of a miracle. She sounded
calmer. How she got along when she was alone I neither knew
nor asked, sensing that it would be painful for her to voice her
feelings. She appreciated my enforced equanimity. It was easier
for me; I knew the affair was ending and that it was for the best.
Acceptance of the inevitable would heal the wound faster, and it
was frustrating that I could not share with her the secret of my
imminent departure.

By Easter Sunday, the days had lengthened, though the snow
had not yet started to melt. On its surface abstract shapes fasioned
by the wind left strange shadows. I went for a walk in the taiga,
captivated by the peace of the forest. Huge pines reached towards
the light, and I too was uplifted. Neither tired nor cold, I walked
aimlessly for what seemed like hours, until in the dusk I returned
to the barracks, refreshed.

Early next morning Misha entered my room, his eyes swollen
with tears. "Igor Morovitch, my dear friend, they are taking you
away from us! There is an order for you to be transferred to
Stupino. A personal messenger from Colonel Dolochov will assist
you on the trip. Sasha is going with you. I will help you to pack.
They are waiting."

Outside the hospital, everyone had gathered to say goodbye. Many were in tears. Profoundly moved, I hugged Misha for a long while, both of us aware that we would never see each other again. Turning abruptly to the waiting sleighs, I gave him my last orders: "Give my love to Tatiana Osipovna and Sara Abramovna."

The horses got up a fast trot, churning up a cloud of snow that fell lightly on the people waving goodbye. Soon the buildings of the Sossva hospital had disappeared. I felt uneasy to be leaving behind, in this strange place, so much love.

Stupino

For me Stupino, although a real place, is also a state of mind. I witnessed there some of the most horrifying tyranny of our times, the memory of which I have carried for half a century. Often, my soul speaks to me in my dreams, reawakening my conscience, reminding me to redress old errors and old wrongs I may have done to others. So, haunted by the need to live my personal myth, I face the inhabitants of my nightly visions, whose chromacolour images awaken the heroes of my bygone youth, adding a fourth dimension of time, and a fifth one of magic, spirit, and beauty. I am not just remembering the past and reconstructing it but also re-evaluating it, seeing it through the prism of experience and the wisdom gained by trial, error, and failure.

I try now to recreate all those people in words, injecting life into them on the stage of my memory. Now I understand them better. They each had drives, instincts, and feelings; they were vulnerable, even during moments of cruelty. But it is only now that I can forgive.

Stupino was a small compound that served as the central hospital of the entire Sevurallag. It occupied a flat surface cleared of trees, approximately a quarter of a mile square. It was surrounded by a fence about ten feet high secured with barbed wire at the top. On each corner stood an elevated wooden booth equipped with machine guns and reflectors for the guards. The entrance was on the northeast corner, where one guard was stationed in a larger structure; two guards were sometimes necessary, especially early in the morning and late in the afternoon when the inmates left for or returned from work in the forest.

Inside the entrance along the north side of the fence were eight barracks for newcomers to Stupino who were in quarantine, and convalescent inmates who had been discharged from the hospital and were awaiting new assignments. The basic workforce of Stupino was about five hundred inmates, who were taken daily to the forest. Beyond the barracks stood the *bania* (bathhouse) with its showers and small steam sauna. The kitchen and bread-distribution facility was further away.

Along the whole west side, as well as on part of the south side, were six long barracks holding about two hundred beds – the hospital proper. A smaller structure housing the pharmacy and laboratory had been built between two barracks against the mid-west side. Closer to the entrance on the south side was the administration building. On the northwest corner were the medical administration offices, which also housed the chief doctor and the head nurse. Narrow, elevated wooden sidewalks ran between the various buildings.

Upon my arrival, I was greeted by the chief administrator of Stupino, Lieutenant Nikolai Andrevitch Denisov. They had been waiting three days for me, he said; it appeared the orders from the Sossva headquarters greatly preceded my departure. Lieutenant Denisov was a man in his middle forties with innocent-looking blue eyes. "We're glad to have you here," he said, "although our surgeon, Dr Deminski, is heartbroken about leaving us." He introduced me to Dr Yuri Petrovitch Deminski, a short chubby man in his late thirties with a round face and slight air of sadness. Deminski said, "You're coming to a nice place. I'm sure you'll enjoy the peace after that rather tense post in Sossva. Over there, most of your patients were administration officials and their families rather than prisoners. I understand that you gained quite a high rating among the powers-that-be at headquarters. I don't see why they transferred you to this place. Although this is the *Centralni San Gorodok* [central medical village], I doubt whether they sent you here because of their sensitivity, humanity, and desire to help the imprisoned souls." The pain was evident in his cynical remarks, along with a slight implication that I wanted to take his place.

I replied that I was quite happy there, aware that they liked me, and in the dark as to why I was transferred. "Any transfer is disruptive: you settle down and get used to a place, and then suddenly you leave. But what choice do we have? We're all in the same boat; therefore, I won't even apologize for inconveniencing you." Then I tried to appease him. "I don't know, Dr Deminski. Maybe they were dissatisfied – with my personality, or even with my work – but didn't tell me. I never had the opportunity to test their sincerity. Or maybe," and here came my counterstrike, "professionally, your ways will be more acceptable to them. After all, you were a Soviet citizen before your arrest."

At that moment, Lieutenant Denisov excused himself, leaving us alone. Although Dr Deminski knew his aggression had been unwarranted, he didn't change his manner. I felt sorry for him; there seemed to be more important reasons for his unwillingness to budge than there were in my case, and I thought I had better leave him alone to overcome his frame of mind.

"Thank you, Doctor, for your kind reception," I said. "I'll see you at some point. I hope you will have enough time to transfer all the medical matters to me." I stepped out of his office but didn't know where to go; this was a new place and all the people around me were strangers. For a moment I pondered my next move when a woman's voice greeted me.

"You must be the new surgeon. I'm Anna Antonovna Poderite, the head nurse of the hospital and chief nurse of the operating room." She was in her mid-twenties, slender in her white uniform. She wore her brown hair long. Her eyes were green and sad. Her smooth, high cheekbones looked as if they had been frozen in the cold wind.

"It is good to meet you," I said. "Dr Deminski wasn't in the mood to show me around and introduce me to people; so I'd be lost if it weren't for you." Anna invited me to her room for coffee. "You rest," she suggested, "while I fill you in on some details about this place." In spite of its austerity, her room was neat, warm, and welcoming, with a bed on the left side, bookshelves on the right, a small table, and two chairs. She made the coffee, then sat on the bed, her graceful legs dangling above the floor.

"You see, Igor Morovitch," she explained, "Dr Deminski is a homosexual; this transfer was a catastrophe for him because he will have to leave his partner in Stupino. His beloved is a young boy named Ian who abused his position as protégé. It became very difficult to work, under the circumstances. Now you probably understand Dr Deminski's behaviour. If you want to forgive him, that's up to you." Her green eyes were enigmatic, but I saw in them the possibility of intimacy. I was lonely and needed someone to be close to and trust, but I didn't want to rush into another relationship. The risks were too high and the partings too painful. I was unwilling to get involved, yet I feared that she had captivated me already.

At that moment, a young man entered the room without knocking. In his early twenties, he was tall and well built, with blond hair, blue eyes, and regular features.

"My doctor, Yuri Petrovitch Deminski, would like to see you now," he said. "He is waiting in his room." I realized that this must be the unfortunate surgeon's beloved and the cause of his sorrows. "Okay, young man," I replied. "But next time, please announce yourself by knocking. If you don't get permission to enter, don't try to force your presence on me. Now close the door from the other side. Go to your doctor and tell him that he will see me in due course." My stern tone made him obedient at once and produced a faint smile on Anna's face.

"I see you will get along well around here," she commented. "I like the way you put him in his place. I strongly believe in not delaying the expression of what you feel."

"It depends on the quality and intensity of those feelings." With that ambiguous reply, I thanked her for the coffee and left for Dr Deminski's office. I found the surgeon lying on his bed with a compress on his head. His face showed pain and worry.

"Igor Morovitch, I must beg your forgiveness. I haven't treated you at all as a guest and colleague, and I am sorry. There are other matters involved, far beyond the simple fact of my transfer."

"I understand. No hard feelings. Everybody's behaviour changes at times for personal reasons, especially when they're facing a major change." Deminski's face lit up. I had relieved him of the need for further explanation. He knew that I knew, and that was enough for him to return, more or less, to his normal self.

"At present, there are no serious cases of a surgical nature," he told me. "People are dying of irreversible malnutrition-related diseases; in these circumstances, they are beyond the point of no return. You will be able to take over the patients without me and make the rounds with Dr Petrenko and the three nurses. There is another problem with which you may be able to help," he continued. "You see, I'm leaving my friend Ian here, the boy I sent to you. Could you help to get him transferred to Sossva? I know that many of the high-ranking officers there were your patients, so you may have the opportunity to do something on my behalf. Will you remember? I would be forever grateful to you."

"Yes, I'll remember," I assured him, "and maybe you can return the favour. There is a lady doctor in Sossva named Tatiana Osipovna whom you'll meet for sure. I am unable to send her any news because as a prisoner I can't write to a free citizen. From time to time, therefore, you could intercept the letters and hand them to her."

He accepted my request with great enthusiasm – it was a mutual exchange of favours. We said goodbye to each other, and I never saw him again. As it turned out, I found no opportunity to request Ian's transfer to Sossva; I don't know what became of him. And as for sending letters to Tatiana, I soon abandoned the idea. In that prison, in that environment, in those days, it was futile to dream of a lasting relationship; the future was too uncertain.

Two nurses were waiting at the first barrack, along with Dr Petrenko, to take me on my first rounds. Laryssa Josipovna Bankauskini, a Lithuanian by birth, was an attractive blonde in her early thirties. Her smiling grey eyes and cheerful face stood out in that grim setting. *Carpe diem* (seize the day) seemed to be her governing principle. Her optimistic nature saved her from second thoughts or remorse – but at a price: spiritually and intellectually she was a pauper. The other nurse, Barbara Nikolaevna Karseladze, was a tall, plump, pleasant-faced Georgian girl in her twenties with large violet-blue eyes. She walked with dignity. Her uncle was the notorious Lavrenti Pavlovitch Beria, head of the NKVD and personal friend of Stalin's. Beria had had her entire family arrested, including his own sister, Barbara's mother, solely to avoid charges of nepotism. Barbara had been sentenced to twenty-five years in the Gulag.

Together we visited the two barracks occupied by terminally ill patients. At the time, there were about two hundred patients in the six barracks of the hospital. Approximately eighty were seriously ill, many of them about to die. I was accustomed to medical emergencies and mass casualties on the front lines or at field hospitals. But I couldn't assimilate this mass of innocent people dying slow, senseless deaths because of the cruelty of others. A doctor must try to leave his work behind him when he leaves the hospital, try to be objective about the suffering he encounters; otherwise he is in danger of going mad or giving up in despair. It was hard to be objective under these circumstances. I felt utterly helpless.

I wanted to be alone. Once outside again, I thanked the nurses and the doctor for their help and told them that I would be busy with administrative work for the next two days and they would have to look after the patients by themselves.

Even nature had lost its soothing quality. The huge sun set behind the clouds, staining the horizon red. In my helpless fury I went and hid behind the southern wall of the administration office so that I wouldn't be disturbed. Where was God's understanding, His clemency, His leniency? Didn't He create human beings in the likeness of angels, close to His own image? Why had He abandoned us in this agony, so that we couldn't even leave His world praising His name? In spite of the seasonal warmth, I was bathed in a cold sweat. Why this reaction? Surely after living with it for two years I'd be immune to such cruelty. Stalin trumpeted the glories of his prison camps whose convicts, instead of rotting in cells, were allowed freedom, fresh air, and the dignity of work. But the demonic truth was that the convicts, without proper nourishment, burned up their own bodily tissues to get the energy to continue working. The only mercy was that they soon died and went to heaven. Perhaps it was not as cynical as extracting the gold teeth from the victims of the gas chambers as the Nazis did, but it was certainly more sophisticated.

Anna's voice caught me unawares.

"Why don't you go for dinner? It's late and Sasha didn't know where you were. I've been looking everywhere for you." I hadn't wanted to be disturbed in this frame of mind. Thinking that I must look weak, I tried to pull myself together. Then I thought that if she was interested in me, she might as well see me as I was. She walked me back to my room. I thanked her and said that I wasn't hungry and would go straight to bed. She did not insist that I join her for a meal. It was a terrible night, my sleep filled with dreams of torture and strange ghosts.

The light of the early dawn slipped into my room. I got up and fell to my knees, praying to the Almighty to forgive me for my weakness and doubt. His ways and means were unknown to us; we could only accept His purpose. I harboured a painful regret that I had abandoned the Spirit within, which is accessible only through humility and prayer. I asked for forgiveness to re-establish the dignity and independence of this entity within myself. I couldn't allow it to become part of my shadow side. If it did the Light would disappear, the deep trust in goodness, and the unknown power of help that brings salvation in the midst of the most hopeless situations in life.

The hopeless situation that had unnerved me the previous day could be seen at its worst in Barrack No. 4, where the prisoners were ill from malnutrition and overwork. Those sentenced to hard labour had to meet a quota of lumber production, measured in cubic feet, or their rations would be cut. From the first day, the prisoners usually fell short of the quota by two to three cubic feet. Immediately they entered a vicious cycle, never able to catch up, progressively losing weight, strength, and the will to live.

Associated with the malnutrition was pellagra, caused by deprivation of vitamins. The deficiency led to swollen legs with cracked, oozing skin, and dry, swollen tongues. The disease is called alimentary dystrophy. It progressed through three stages. In the second stage, the victims' gastrointestinal tracts were so thin that they could not retain any type of food. Diarrhoea meant that they lost the few calories they had ingested in the crude hospital rations. In its final stages the disease led to the atrophy of all muscles, especially marked in the buttocks, and protrusion of the anus. A patient who had reached that stage was called *dochodiaga*, or "approacher to death." In certain cases that were not far advanced, the malnutrition could be reversed if chemically purified sterile food were given intravenously, but none was available.

Barrack No. 4 had thirty-two beds, all filled with patients in the third stage of the illness. They survived only two to three weeks. No one ever left there alive. They were segregated so as not to depress the patients in the earlier stages of the disease, who had a slim chance of recovery.

In the days and weeks that followed, I would walk alone on the narrow paths of the zone, trying to think of some way to save them. I kept telling myself that it was impossible, that I could do nothing. But at least I could be with them and try to comfort them in the last moments of their lives.

One morning when it was still dark outside, I left my room and quietly made my way to Barrack No. 4. In the foyer of the barrack there were two barrels containing an opalescent fluid made of pine needles soaked in water. The administration claimed that it held some traces of Vitamin C and could help the patients. Trying to remain unnoticed, I found a little stool in a corner near the first bed.

Since taking over my medical duties, I had assigned an attendant from the less-sick barrack to help in this one. The majority of the patients here were so weak that they could not go out to the latrine and had to be helped with a bedpan. Some, almost unconscious, would pass their liquid stool involuntarily and, before I arrived at Stupino, died bathed in excrement. With another attendant, we could at least keep them dry and clean.

Some of the patients, when transferred to Barrack No. 4, knew it was their last stop in life. This segregation seemed cruel to me and I made numerous futile attempts to change the system. "We know why we do it," said the administrators. "Better to spare the feelings of those who might still survive. Many of the patients in the last stages are semiconscious anyway." This seemed out of keeping with the Hippocratic oath, but there wasn't much I could do. After sitting there for a while, I noticed that the patient near me had turned his head in my direction. His eyes had an anxious look, as if to say, "Who are you to come here, and what do you want? Why are you disturbing my last moment?"

Silently I begged his forgiveness. I hoped my presence might help to alleviate his loneliness. All I wanted was permission to be with them, to hold a hand. Eventually his expression changed; an almost imperceptible smile appeared on his face. He accepted my goodwill.

In the past I had often been with dying patients during their last moments, but this encounter was unique. I felt like an intruder who had been granted a passport into a region reserved for absolute solitude, when the soul is at an end. In a faint whisper the man asked, "Why did you come here? Who are you?"

"I am the new doctor taking over from Dr Deminski."

"So why are you here? We see only nurses here."

"I just wanted to be with you for a while. Maybe I can help in some way – mail a letter to someone close to you, for instance. Or maybe you want to talk to somebody. Or maybe you want to share some time, even in silence. It must be quite lonely here. Everyone likes to be with someone who cares."

Large tears ran in two narrow streams down his pale cheeks. Then after clearing his dry throat with an effort, he said, "I feel my end is close." He closed his eyes. "Your being here makes me feel I'm not completely forgotten. Look at me … a shadow of what I was. Before, I was a real person, recognized and respected." I sat down on the edge of the bed, took out the small bottle of milk I had brought with me, and pressed it to his lips.

"This is milk. Where did you get it?"

"Just drink it and don't ask. It's not important."

After drinking the milk his voice became less hoarse. He rested for a while and then told me his story. His name was Alexei Petrovich Afanaseev. He was thirty-nine and had been a commander of a tank division with the rank of lieutenant colonel. "I received the medals of Lenin, the highest distinction in the Soviet Union, and many others for the heroic actions of my units. In the bulletins to the front I was thanked by Chief Commander Comrade Stalin." He dreamed of the gratitude he'd be shown after the war and the good life that was in store for his family. Then one day, the NKVD came and arrested him for spreading "defeatist propaganda" by allegedly predicting that the Soviet forces could not defend Stalingrad. Following interrogation and a year of imprisonment, he had been sent to Ural Lag to work in the forests. "After double pneumonia I couldn't do my share of the work anymore and deteriorated to the state I'm in now. I know I'll never see my wife and my two little boys again. They don't even know that I'm dying, and they never will know."

Alexei started to weep and could speak no longer. I leaned over and whispered in his ear, "I will be here tomorrow at the same time and will take down any letter you want to dictate. I'll see to it that your family gets it. For the time being, goodbye, and wait for me."

I walked back to my room through wet snow. The wooden walks were dirty, covered with brown mud. The heavy fog tainted the sky a greyish hue.

The following evening I returned to Barrack No. 4. Alexei was not there any more; another man was in his bed. The night orderly said that Alexei had died shortly after midnight, but he had left an envelope behind. I took it and left the death barrack. It contained a note to his wife and a message for me: "Never in my life had I so much to thank someone, for being with me when so little time is left. I feel I will die soon. If I deserve heaven, I will pray for you there."

For a few days I was acutely depressed and unable to perform my duties. Even so, I went back to Barrack No. 4 twice a week, taking milk, the only food the emaciated patients could swallow. I continued visiting the barrack throughout the winter and talked with many dying men. One was Yuri Nikolaevich. He was only nineteen and had been a mechanic at a tank factory in Siberia. He had been sentenced to twenty years for attempting to improve the firing power of the tanks. "The Soviet tanks are the best in the world and do not require any modification," his interrogator said. In Sevurallag he had been doing well in the forests until he sprained his right shoulder joint and could not fulfil his quota. With slowly decreasing rations his health ran down and he was sent finally to Stupino.

Now he was a skeleton with sunken eyes and grey skin, hardly able to move or lift his head. His will to live was enormous, and I fed him milk for twelve days. It did not change his appearance, but I was hoping nonetheless that he would survive; he was so young. Then one Thursday morning, on my fourteenth visit, I found another patient in his bed.

Yuri did not leave a message or note. He was not forgotten, though; for a long time, his sad eyes haunted me. He was the longest of my survivors, and when he died I shed my illusions, no longer hoping against hope. What was my work for? I witnessed death after death and watched helplessly, trying to prove that I was doing something. I was of no real benefit to the patients, and for me, there was bitterness and a loss of faith in humanity. All talk about a loving God and good people seemed like nonsense.

But inside I knew that being with these people meant something – meant a lot, as Alexei had said, when the end was so near. Dying alone is awful.

It took me a long time to get used to this role of "Being With." Listening to the tragic stories of the wretched and abandoned became my existence and filled me with compassion. I was also depressed and for weeks on end could not shake my mood. Life became difficult, as sluggish and laborious as moving about in tar.

The deceased had to have autopsies no matter what the cause of death, and the final diagnosis was always given as "Adynamia musculi cordis – weakness of the heart muscles." In truth, the authorities wanted to get as much work as they could from the prisoners without feeding them. Sustained by the calories obtained from their own fatty and muscle tissues, the victims were left to die once the tissue had disappeared. It was an evil policy and the true cause of the deaths in that barrack.

Early the next morning, Vasili Alexandrovitch Tchechladze, the cook, came into my room with Sasha, who served me breakfast and dinner. Tchechladze had been chief cook at the Kremlin before being sentenced, during the frenzy of mass arrests after Kirov's death, to twenty years in the Gulag for telling an anti-Soviet joke. He had an idea that a man of position such as a doctor should not eat alone but should partake of his meals with friends or colleagues. To this end he supplied me with for too much food – *piroshki* filled with meat and mushrooms, steaming coffee, and other treats. On that morning, Sasha laid my breakfast on a white tablecloth with good bone-china plates and sterling-silver cutlery. Overwhelmed, I asked him where he got all these luxuries. He responded to my curiosity the same way he always did: "Don't ask me, Igor Morovitch. In the Gulag you don't ask where things come from." Sasha behaved like a major-domo in an English stately home. He always stood at my door during meals so that nobody could come in or disturb me. When I was through eating, he collected the dishes, washed them, and put them away in a special wooden box made by our cabinetmaker.

Twice a week, late in the evening, he arranged a bath for me in our *bania*. He took two helpers to scrub the floor and walls of the steamroom, and I was able to wash in privacy and relax in the steam. For the convicts, however, bathing was an unspeakable ordeal. When the tired convicts returned from the forest and before the evening kasha, they were driven to the *bania*. Divided into large groups of sixty to eighty men, they were taken into an another room where they had to undress and hand over their clothes for fumigation. The place was small, allowing hardly any room to undress. The screams and curses of the inmates as they jammed into this room were unbelievable. When rats are taken from their normal cages and placed in very cramped spaces, they become wild, aggressive, and cannibalistic. The effect of the changing room on the inmates was similar.

After undressing, the naked inmates were taken to the showers, which were rarely lukewarm and usually cold. Ther was no soap. They were given barely enough time to wet their bodies, let alone wash off their sweat, before they were ordered back to the cramped dressing space. There were no towels. Their clothes were stacked in the corner in a heap. Some were burned, some were still cold and full of lice; the heat treatment that was used for delousing clearly didn't work very well.

Fights often started as the prisoners scrambled desperately in the heap for their clothes. Rarely did an inmate get all his clothes back, and many inherited somebody else's lice.

It was a shocking scene, and I added the bathhouse to the list of changes I was resolved to make at Stupino.

The day before, I had asked Sasha to find among the convalescents a dozen good workers, men who would be discreet and ask no questions. I had also asked him to find a carpenter, an electrician, a bricklayer, and a metal worker, skilled men who would help me bring the hospital into working order. Back in my office, I told Sasha to fetch the four tradesmen.

The carpenter was a tall lean man with a long grey beard. Before the war he had worked as a foreman in a furniture factory in Tchelabinsk. He had been sentenced to fifteen years in the Gulag because he was an elder who regularly attended church. Worse, during lunch breaks he had told his co-workers stories about the Immaculate Conception, the life of Christ, and the symbolic meaning of the church rituals.

I explained the type of furniture we would need. He knew how to construct the special desks and filing cabinets in my office so that they could be closed by rolling down wooden shutters. Calling them American furniture, he said he only needed proper tools and a supply of hardwood.

To the bricklayer, I explained that the stoves in all the barracks had to be reconstructed. The electrician was a good-looking, smart young fellow from Tbilisi, Georgia, who, when he was a sergeant in the army, had been arrested for noting that they had better food in the German army. He was sentenced to fifteen years. His job was to install electricity throughout the hospital, starting with the operating room.

Sasha had also brought a young Chinese fellow from Charbin, Manchuria, who knew how to build a greenhouse for growing vegetables in the winter. All he needed were bricks to construct a broad flat chimney a foot underground; above it, he would build a wooden frame structure for the glazing.

The men were to work under Sasha, who was also responsible for procuring the necessary materials. Sasha and his workers carried out their tasks admirably. It wasn't long before all the stoves had been reconstructed, though I couldn't imagine where the materials had come from.

Late one evening when I couldn't sleep, I went for a walk. It was already quite dark. Suddenly, the silence was broken by loud commanding voices, and long beams of light like the legs of a giant insect cut the darkness into strange geometrical shapes. Then, just as suddenly, the light disappeared and silence resumed. A voice reached me in the darkness.

"You're probably surprised at what is going on." It was Anna Antonovna. "At this time of night, I often walk around here. There is always some commotion when the train from the lumber mill stops in Stupino to get water and firewood for the engine. I myself didn't know about it until I noticed one morning that part of a roof had been covered with new boards. It seems that someone takes boards from the train and transfers them onto the roofs the same night."

Though surprised by Anna's keen observations, I refrained from comment and returned to my room. When I asked Sasha about it the next day, he explained that there was a secret entrance to the hospital grounds from the railway tracks. He couldn't divulge its whereabouts, he said, which in any case I didn't need to know. The most important thing was that the work was progressing as planned and everything would be finished on schedule.

At noon I visited the pharmacy, which consisted of a front room with shelves full of bottles and jars, and another two rooms in the back for storage and preparation. Anton Pavlovitch Shevelov was in charge of the pharmacy. Before his imprisonment, Anton had

been one of the deputy ministers of the Soviet Union's pharma-
ceutical industry. Boris Shimkin, the pharmacist at Kasalmanka,
had been his friend and co-worker and was arrested at the same
time. He got fifteen years, but Anton was sentenced to twenty-
five.

While telling me the story of his arrest, Anton Pavlovitch
moved to one of the shelves and poured something from a large
flask into two small glasses. "Let's drink to your good health and
successful stay here in Stupino." The golden liquid had the
exquisite taste of a fine old brandy. He explained that they
obtained two hectolitres of pure alcohol every year for the needs
of the hospital and used half of this supply to produce good
drinks that he deemed "absolutely necessary" for running the
place. "Colonel Dolochov often invites the commissars from
Moscow to check on our fulfilment of the five-year plan. The
reason he selected this place is that we have the best chef in all
of the Sevurallag. Quite often ten or fifteen people come; naturally,
we have to give them dinner and serve drinks. And do they know
how to drink! The more alcohol they consume, the better their
opinion of our work in the Sevurallag. We use the remaining
hundred litres of alcohol for medicinal purposes; if we're short,
we substitute chloramine."

Now I began to understand the mechanics of bribery in the
Soviet system. It was like influence peddling in the capitalist
system, where almost everything is bought with money. No government system can ever be perfect as long as human beings
themselves are corrupt, devious, and treacherous. It is impossible
to get economic equality without improving the human soul. In
theory, the communist system is based on the principle "from each
according to his abilities, to each according to his needs." At the
time, however, the Soviet system lacked the means to function on
this basis and described itself as a transitional social system in
which everybody was supposedly paid according to the quality
and quantity of their output. In practice, it didn't work that way.
Many achievements were stifled because private property was not
allowed; without the ownership of land, without the accumulation of goods resulting from their work, the peasants had no
interest in working for the government. They were promised that
the future would bring a just system, a true communism wherein
everybody would be equal and happy.

Unfortunately such a system was impossible to achieve; therefore, everything had to be enforced. There were spies everywhere
– friends spied on friends, children on parents, and parents on
children. The ugly aspects of human nature were maximized,
further undermining the chance of achieving the "true" communism based on the principle of human goodness and understanding. The only benefit, if any, was the elimination of envy from the
system: nobody had anything that others could envy. But incen-
tive for any voluntary act was lost. Values were distorted, quality
deteriorated, and life assumed a greyness beyond imagination
surmounted by a fear that even this limited freedom would be
lost.

The last place I visited was the hospital laboratory. The man in
charge there was Anton Ianovitch Biernacki, a tall, heavily built
man in his early sixties with mean grey eyes. He had been arrested
because he was a wealthy businessman before the war. He had
only recently acquired any knowledge of laboratory work. His
sentence was comparatively short, only seven years. "It's too
bad," he began, "that Dr Deminski had to be transferred, but
people tell me that you are also a good surgeon. I hope we will
get used to you. You know, I am a liberal man; some of my best
friends are Jews." That comment, with its anti-Semitic overtones,
told me exactly what kind of relationship I could expect to have
with this man. Still, I tried not to prejudge. Later, Anna
Antonovna told me that everybody was afraid of Biernacki
because he was an informer. He didn't even try to explain his
work.

It was already mid-August. The large green bushes of potatoes in
the hospital's southern field announced that summer had almost
come to an end. The crop would have to be collected over the next
few days and stored in a huge hole in the ground to protect it
against the winter frost. All the hospital personnel would be
employed in the harvest. It was an important task because potatoes were the main source of carbohydrates and, unlike bread,
were not rationed.

The work around the hospital had been completed. The barrack
roofs were new; the inner and outer walls of the buildings were
newly painted; all the stoves had been reconstructed; my office

had new furniture; and the electrical wiring of the hospital had been completed. It was unbelievable that, in only two months, all this work had been accomplished without official requests for materials or any other help from the authorities. Everybody could see the changes, but interestingly enough, nobody asked how and when they were achieved. Additional allies of this enormous undertaking were the long bright days of the short summer. As I went with Sasha to inspect the work, he saw the admiration on my face. I didn't ask questions either; I only looked at him with gratitude.

But Sasha's face wore a frown. "Igor Morovitch, I don't know whether I should tell you, but somebody has to." He explained that in Stupino there was a new rule to the effect that the men and women prisoners must be separated. For a while, it had been all right, but the month before, the women had demanded a return to the previous state; they wanted to have the men with them. The new rule was not reversed. "Last night," Sasha told me, "Nikolai Andrevitch Denisov [the head of Stupino] went to inspect the barracks and listen to the grievances of the women. There was apparently a dead silence, as if nobody was there. Suddenly, a bunch of them caught Nikolai Andrevitch. Eight women tied him up and undressed him, and each one of them raped him." Nikolai Andrevitch was now at home, communicating with no one. Most of the prisoners regretted what had happened because he was, in general, a good enough administrator. They were now afraid that the authorities would send somebody far worse to replace him.

As I listened to Sasha, I noticed Anna Antonovna waiting for me with an air of impatience. Thinking that there was perhaps an emergency, I thanked Sasha for his information and approached Anna.

"Igor Morovitch, there is something I have to tell you. Nikolai –"

"Yes, I know," I interrupted her. "Sasha just told me that he was raped last night."

"I figured as much when I saw him telling you something and looking around to ensure that nobody was eavesdropping. I've just come from Nikolai's place. I was called to attend to the lacerations on his arms and legs. He's all bruised and looks awful. He's beyond depression, doesn't communicate, and looks like a zombie. His wife cries all the time. She was too ashamed to call you."

Anna felt that we ought not to leave the situation to mend itself, because it probably wouldn't. "Apart from the fact that he is a relatively good man, I feel sorry for him as a human being. If we don't do something now to pull him out of this state, he'll most likely end up in a mental asylum. If anybody can help, it's you, Igor Morovitch. You can salvage this man from self-destruction."

"I don't know, Anna Antonovna." I hesitated. "I'm not a psychiatrist. How do I approach him? I need some time to think it over. I'll see."

I spent almost an hour in my room trying to figure out the best way to get out of this impasse. It was important to prevent the news from spreading any further, so as to eliminate the need for the authorities to handle the problem. If they did, there would be awful consequences for the female prisoners, guilty or not, as well as for Nikolai Andrevitch. The rest of the hospital personnel would also have to suffer with some new NKVD tyrant. I knew that I had to act fast and decisively. I went straight to Nikolai's house.

Nikolai Andrevitch Denisov lay in his bed, his face bruised, his sunken eyes gazing into space. His wife Anastasia Petrovna had swollen eyes from crying so much. Assuring her that everything would be all right, I approached her husband's bed.

"Nikolai Andrevitch," I began, "You don't know me well, but I'm very stubborn when it comes to saving a human life. Under normal circumstances, it is during an operation, and I have to cut open the body. This time, I have to open your soul. Usually my patients can't help me with their own recovery as you can. Now, listen." I was talking so loudly that it probably hurt his ears. "Your future is in your hands: your life and that of your family. Time is of the essence. We have to close this affair before the authorities find out. You didn't suffer any major physical damage; the pain is all in your heart, and it will pass. I know it's difficult, but get up. Get up. Get up." Repeating these words, I lifted him into a sitting position, encouraging his wife to help me. He didn't resist. We put on his clothes and brought him to a chair. I pulled out a small bottle of the brandy-like drink I had brought from Shevelov and poured it into three small glasses standing on the table.

After the second glass, tears flowed from his eyes. I knew then that the barrier had been broken. He had returned from denial to the painful but welcome world of feelings and visible emotions.

So fast a recovery could never take place in normal life. Only here, in this harsh world, could one reach for life with such astonishing speed and cling so tenaciously to the precipice. I poured a third glass of brandy for all of us.

"You have to act as if nothing had happened," I told him. "Nobody except Sasha, Anna Antonovna, the guard who helped you home, and your wife know what really happened, and none of them will breathe a word of it. I'm sure of that. Tomorrow, Iakov Mironovitch is coming, and I will settle the problem with him. It will never reach Sossva. The guilty women will be transferred and the whole affair will be forgotten in no time. Trust me." Nikolai brightened. Both he and his wife embraced me and wet my face with their tears.

By helping Nikolai pull himself together and resume his duties, I had restored the "devil that we knew," so to speak. For while his departure could have brought us a harsher administrator, I was not oblivious to the suffering of the prisoners under his administration. In September, for example, four hundred Estonian prisoners were sent to Stupino. Most were intellectuals, unused to hard labour. Within the first few days, they had already started to fail in their performance and were consequently put on a reduced bread ration. Gradually, they sold their belongings – clothes, blankets, watches, etc. – for bread, until there was nothing left to barter. When November came, not one of them was alive. At the time, the soil, deeply frozen, was hard as rock; they could not be buried. They were placed in two rows like logs of wood in the least visible place, the southwest corner of the zone behind the last barrack, to wait until the soil was soft enough to make a common grave. I will never forget some of their faces.

One was a philosophy professor, a wonderful person, handsome and intelligent. From time to time when he came to the outpatient room, I would give him some bread, secretly so that nobody could see, but it didn't help in the end. When he was hospitalized later, his condition was already irreversible. I felt terribly guilty about having proper food when all around me people were dying like flies. I felt completely helpless but told myself that if I stopped eating in defiance, it would not change the situation.

Another person who made an impression on me was a Greek Orthodox priest, Grigori Sergevitch Altanov. He was emaciated, always hungry, but always smiling. In his mid-thirties, tall and handsome, he was a graduate of the divinity school at the Sorbonne in Paris. After university, he had travelled a lot. He told me once that all his life, he had dreamed of visiting a famous monastery of holy monks high on a mountain in Greece. After spending the whole day climbing and thinking about all the unanswered questions he would be able to put to the monks, he finally reached the top of the mountain where the monastery was located. The monks were on the lawn, praying in the setting sun. Feverishly, he asked questions of the brother on the left, then the one on the right, but he got no answer from them; they were deeply immersed in prayer. Suddenly, he realized that this was a convent of silent monks. He stayed a little longer at the top and, like them, fell into deep prayer; all his questions were answered.

One afternoon, I met him at his barrack. His eyes closed and it looked as if he were praying. I invited him to my room for supper, but he refused to accept any food. Begging my pardon, he reached into his pocket and took out a piece of bread. He accepted some tea, but didn't even take the little lump of sugar that I offered him.

The Russians drink tea by putting a lump of sugar into their mouth and sipping the tea through it. This way of drinking tea is called *na prikusku* in Russian. When sugar was scarce during the war, a rumour was circulating that a lump of sugar was hung from the ceiling above the table, and allowed to swing like a pendulum, people licking the piece when it was in reach of their tongue. That way of drinking tea was called *na prilizku* (the licking method). Then, when sugar was very hard to obtain, one could only admire the swinging lump, and this was called *na prigliadku* (the looking method). Finally when sugar was completely unavailable, people could only think about it. That way of drinking tea was called *na pridumku* – the sweet taste was only in your thoughts.

The young priest and I sometimes talked until late at night about history, philosophy, and religion, about holy places, the immortality of the soul, and everyday miracles as the manifestation of the Almighty. Normally, it was too late for him to return to the barrack, so I would offer him a bed in the other room. In the mornings, when I woke, he would be waiting to thank me for our evening. He always slept on the floor; he couldn't sleep on a bed while his brothers slept on hard bunks. Soon his body lay among the cadavers awaiting burial at a warmer time. Remembering his sacrifices, I pondered the enormous gulf between his ethical code and mine.

Shortly after my visit to Nikolai, Iakov Mironovitch came to see me. I wanted to confide in him about the rape and get his cooperation in hushing up the matter. But as he greeted me with some books by contemporary Russian writers, I sensed that he wanted to confide in me too. I was right. He wanted to unburden himself of a secret that had been choking him for a long time – the story of his arrest, which he had never shared with anyone before.

An aviation engineer specializing in unsteady aerodynamics, he had been head of the Department of Missiles at the Soviet Union's Ministry of National Defence. Before the war, he spent about a year in Germany on a mission to familiarize himself with their experience in missile technology and performance. Right after his return, he was arrested and accused of having been recruited by the Gestapo as a secret agent. "I denied the accusations," he told me. "They interrogated me, using every method of torture imaginable. After days of burning my heels with hot irons and pulling out my nails, they tried a different method. They hung me by my hands and beat me with heavy bamboo sticks. They returned me to my cell unconscious. I woke up in a hospital in Gorki. A nurse explained that the doctors had had to remove one kidney and patch up the other one, which was bleeding. She said that I still had bloody urine, but they hoped everything would be all right."

"After two months of convalescence I still hadn't been accused of any crimes, and was posted to the Sevurallag in the capacity of supervisor of production. Originally I was assigned to Stupino because of my frail condition, but I was later transferred to Sossva for a more demanding job. Because of my medical history, Colonel Dolochov sent me here again, to be close to the hospital. "That's all I have to tell you," he finished. "Please heal my physical problems, and, if at all possible, my suffering soul. I don't know where my family is; I have no right to inquire about their whereabouts until the war is over."

Iakov's now-pale face, contorted by an inner pain, had probably been different in his days of glory. Although trained in the sciences and mathematics, he was spiritually inclined, basing his

decisions on intuition and feelings. I said, "It's no use returning
to the past. It doesn't exist any more; it's gone. What goes on is
beyond our control. The future is so uncertain." Citing my own
situation, I told him that horrific things were probably happening
under the Nazis in Poland where I had left my own family. "I try
not to think about my helplessness. If I survive, I may have more
horrors to face. Neither you nor I can afford to speculate about
things out of our control." I spoke of the law of survival that
allows us to overcome tragedies beyond imagination and orders
us to keep living, even if we don't know why; no matter how
often we ask why, there is no answer. In this universe, chaos is
the driving force behind events that seem haphazard, without
cause or effect, without reason. Yet the benefits of those events
often manifest themselves long before the pain is healed. Nature
abhors symmetry and geometrical order; look at the haphazard
shape of the mountains, the rivers, the waterfalls. Chaos sur-
rounds us throughout life. Our linear consciousness longs for
order. Only through experience and wisdom can we bridge the
polarities and attain peace of mind.

After a while I stopped lecturing. Iakov, who had listened attentively, said, "I sense a lot of truth in what you are saying, but it is
so difficult to see in these dark nights. At least you are here; at
least I can turn to you."

Time was flying, and Iacov had things to attend to. He put his
nightmare away and changed the subject, asking if he could help
with my repairs and renovations. I pointed out that we had no
electricity. "Can you imagine dealing with an emergency in the
operating room by candlelight? Sometimes it can't wait until
morning; I just don't know where to turn for help."

Iacov thought for a moment. Then he told me that he had one
generator in the sawmill that was beyond repair as some parts
were missing. He promised to send it to me in the hope that my
workmen could improvise something. "If the generator is
repaired, don't advertise the fact," he told me, "because then we
will have to take it back from you."

"There is another problem," I said, and told him about the rape
of Denisov.

"I've already given orders to transfer the offenders," he told me.
"I've also warned all the other women to forget the incident or
be transferred. As for the guard, he will get some free time to visit

his family, and then he will be sent to another lager. Thank you for helping Denisov. We need him here." With that, Iakov left. It was noon.

I arrived late at the operating room. Three patients had complicated and infected fractures and I had advised Anna Antonovna that I would check on them every day. Many of the patients had been neglected; with their lowered nutritional status, they could hardly be expected to recover. A debridement – cleaning the wounds of dead bone and frequently changing the dressings – would speed up the healing process in certain cases. Some patients got food parcels from their homes; this had the greatest effect.

I liked working with Anna. Her presence, charm, and fascinating beauty were like an invisible drug, tranquillizing, strengthening, and improving my mood. Silently, she took it upon herself to care for me. At first I objected; I did not want to lose my independence. But later, I accepted her care with gratitude. I tried not to see how this was changing our relationship. I didn't ask about her background, or why she was a prisoner here. Yet I didn't fight my sense of loneliness without her, or my efforts, perhaps unconscious, to find excuses to be with her. I didn't even notice the tension that grew out of my increased need for her in our calm and innocent togetherness.

At times, seeing this beautiful young woman every day, I regretted the anaemia of our relationship. I couldn't understand why I wasn't longing for something more. Only later could I explain it. Our relationship was not threatened by sudden separation. We were stuck in this place together, so the fear of loss was absent. A subconscious process was going on, preparing us for a serious involvement. We didn't have to rush into anything.

Late in the afternoon when I returned home, I found another guest waiting for me, a tall handsome man in his mid-forties.

"I am Mikhail Osipovitch Varnadze, medical chief of the Stupino central hospital. *Zdrastwuite*, Igor Morovitch. It is good to meet you." He had a high forehead, large dark brown eyes, and a nose like the beak of an eagle. His skin was the light olive typical of Georgians; his black hair was already flecked with silver at the temples. His posture was straight as an arrow.

We shook hands. "I have heard a lot about you," he continued.
"I was impressed by your stand in several cases that required
determination and sacrifice. These lagers are strange places; news
travels fast." Thanking him, I said that I had always liked Georgians. "You can trust them. The only Georgian I detest is Iosif
Visarionovitch Dzugashvili, Stalin himself. May my remarks be
proof of my total trust in you."

"Don't be too trusting," Mikhail warned. "Beria is Georgian too.
Not all Georgians are good. You can't be too careful. Hunger and
suffering don't breed noble feelings around here."

I invited my new guest for dinner. After our second drink, he
told me his story. He was head of the Forensic Medicine Institute
at the University of Leningrad. Late one night he was called to
the institute, where nine cadavers had been brought in by three
NKVD officers. They had all been shot at the base of head a few
hours before. It looked like a professional job; the bullets had been
aimed at the brain stem, resulting in instant death. By their uniforms and distinctions, it was obvious that the dead were NKVD
officers. The victims had probably come under suspicion of
involvement in a plot against the state.

One of the three men who had brought in the bodies explained
to Mikhail Osipovitch that he would have to perform an extensive
autopsy on all of the deceased. He would then have to sign an
official report early the next morning stating that the officers died
as result of multiple injuries caused by an unfortunate explosion
purposely ignited by an enemy of the Soviet Union. Without
hesitation, Mikhail announced that he would perform no autopsies, that the real cause of death was as clear to him as it was to
those who had coldbloodedly shot them. He left abruptly, leaving
the officers with the dead cadavers in the institute. When he got
home he told his wife to pack a few things, and they left that same
night for his parents' home in Tbilisi, Georgia. Two weeks later,
he returned to his post to find that he had already been replaced.
He was arrested and taken to the notorious Lubianka prison in
Moscow.

After eight months of interrogation and terrible beatings,
during which he had to be operated on twice because of internal
bleeding, he was sentenced to five years. He was sent first to the
Vorkuta lager and then, because of his skills in the field of health
administration, to the Sevurallag, where he had been in charge of

Stupino for the last two years. His wife was also an MD and ran the health clinic in Verchoturje, a village close to Stupino, where they lived in a small house.

"That's my story, Igor Morovitch. I hope yours isn't so bad. We are just pawns in the national tragedy. Fear pervades the land – the fear of losing your so-called freedom and being incarcerated or executed. The most privileged people in the highest government positions, if they show the slightest deviation in political philosophy, are marked for extinction. Such are the intricacies of this police state. After the assassination of Kirov, all who had participated were themselves killed, and *their* killers as well. In the process, so were many others. Motivated by fear, people were willing to become "witnesses" and accuse even their friends and family to save their own skins. But their safety was ephemeral: every "witness" to true or false crimes is eventually accused and executed or banished to Siberia. In the highest echelons of the Bolshevik party, imprisonment is always followed by execution – such is Stalin's policy."

Mikhail told me that, after the death of Kirov, the architects of the revolution, Lenin's comrades, were put on trial; under physical and psychological torture they admitted their guilt in exchange for the promise that they and their families would be spared. But the promise was rarely kept and about thirty thousand NKVD officers were killed, often along with their families. In the waves of terror that followed, some three million died while three times that number were imprisoned. Thus, the murder of one man, a top Communist offical, was the tip of an iceberg that claimed millions of lives. Once sated, Stalin published a little booklet entitled *Golovokruzenje od uspiecha (Vertigo from Success)* and stopped the bloodbath.

As Mikhail pointed out, it was only the criminal classes – frauds, thieves, murderers – who were immune to the prevailing fear since, no matter how numerous their victims, they posed no threat to the political regime. Such immunity was good for life. Partially immune were those already imprisoned in the Gulags who served some purpose for the administration – office staff, cooks, bread cutters, medical personnel – and were thus protected from physical exhaustion and starvation. But even in the Gulag the NKVD had its web of informers. They knew everything, every thought, word, and deed of the people around them.

It was late when Mikhail Osipovitch stopped talking. He seemed exhausted, as if he had just relived the horror of his imprisonment. He took his leave, expressing the hope that we might talk again, of other things. When he was gone I stepped outside. It was a warm night. A gentle breeze from the north moved the tall firs and pines, bending their crowns in a graceful dance. A sadness and longing for a past that had disappeared ate at my heart. The imagery of human closeness and openness, of forgiveness and love, was losing its contours. The warmth of the past slowly faded into oblivion, squeezed out of memory by an ugly present.

Then I saw Anna Antonovna, out on one of her nightly walks. "Good evening, Doctor. I have been following you for a while. You seem to be absorbed in another world. We all do the same at first. With time, however, you stop thinking about what was and start to concentrate on what is." She had read my mind. "Even in the worst moments God can provide goodness and even magic."

"I know," I said. "Let's just walk and enjoy the silence."

It was very dark. A thin crescent moon gave off silver rays that barely illuminated the shapes of objects close by. As we moved along the narrow wooden walk, our arms would touch from time to time. Again, I was not impatient for anything more. Destiny had thrown us together, and perhaps in time we would find a way to convert pain into joy.

When I awoke the next morning, the world had turned white. Winter had suddenly arrived. The mounds of snow shone pink and gold in the rising sun. The northern wind stirred the treetops and blew the dry snow crystals into misty circles of sparkling dust. Nature was full of an indescribable harmony and splendour.

I got up early for a brisk walk along the cleared paths, pleased to see the smoke rising from the chimneys all at once, ensuring even temperatures in the hospital rooms; clearly, Sasha had followed my orders to the letter. The underground ducts for heating the future greenhouse had been laid. Above ground, covering the area for the prepared vegetable beds, a frame had been erected using the outside windows of the barracks, which could be removed at the end of winter.

That morning, I asked Dr Petrenko to replace me in my usual duties; I had decided to visit the Stupino Home for Children. The home was outside the hospital zone because the children, the offspring of prisoners, were considered free citizens. The inmate mothers who worked there were allowed beyond the fence of the lager. They were referred to as *bezkonvoine*, as I was, since they were trusted to work within an established territory outside the fence. Like the barracks, the nursery was constructed from logs and covered with stucco. Inside, on both sides of the long corridor, were rooms for the children, who were grouped according to age: infants, toddlers, and a few older children up to the age of eight or nine. The older ones belonged to mothers who had long sentences and no family to claim their children.

The manager of the home was a plump, kind-looking woman in her late forties. She had been a midwife in Moscow before the mass arrests. Having completed a five-year sentence in the Kurganda coal mines, she had been appointed to run the nursery at Stupino. "I have been expecting you to visit for quite a long time," she said, after a pleasant greeting. "We don't have any problems at the moment, just some minor things that I can handle myself. Please let me show you around the place." At the time there were about ninety children in the building. There was a special room where, under guard, the mothers came to wash themselves after work and breastfeed their children. There was also a room for the nurse and doctor to examine and, if necessary, treat the infants.

I had come during breakfast. The older children were sitting together in the dining area. They were given some crude cereal made of corn and rye with a tiny bit of milk diluted with water. There was no sugar or fat available. In spite of the meagre meal, all the kids smiled and eagerly consumed their food.

Our cook, Tchechladze, had loaded my pockets with tiny cookies and candies for the sweet-deprived children. They surrounded me in a tight circle, kissing my hands again and again as I gave out the treats. "*Dorogoi Diadia* [Dear Uncle]," they clamoured, "come see us more often."

It was a heart-warming and very moving scene. I never imagined that the children of hardship would behave so well.

On the way back to my quarters I met Nurse Laryssa Petrovna Bankauskini. She had been waiting to invite me to an evening of

Russian songs with some of the hospital staff. It was to be held
after supper, though we would be served potatoes baked in the
fireplace. I thanked her for the invitation and promised to be
there. At the appointed time I went to the large room close to the
steambath that was usually reserved for gatherings of the staff
and administration. On one wall a kerosine lamp gave off a faint
light; the whole room was basically illuminated by the glow from
the large fireplace in the corner. People sat against the walls on
small pillows or folded coats. All the nurses and orderlies were
there, along with our pharmacist, Shevelov. Sasha had already set
aside a place for me close to Anna Antonovna.

I was introduced to the troubadour, Vasili Ivanovitch Bulgakov,
a tall man in his late forties whose large blue eyes showed curiosity when he found out that I was from the West, the land of
freedom. A civil engineer by profession, he was in charge of the
department that built highways and bridges in the eastern part
of the country. He was unhappy in his work because he was
forced to use substandard materials. A righteous and rebellious
man, he constantly protested to no avail. One day, very upset, he
went to the ministry and, as a sign of defiance, threw his Party
ticket on the superior's desk. For his refusal to remain a Party
member he was sentenced, without court proceedings, to twenty-
five years in the Gulag camps. Here in Stupino he worked in the
accounting office of the administration. His prisoner's garb was
immaculate, his wrinkled, emaciated face clean shaven, and his
hands and nails well groomed. His exterior and manners showed
an aesthetically sensitive person suffering the inner devastation
caused by a permanent discrepancy between his own standards
and a far shabbier reality. Vasili Ivanovitch looked like a man who
could accept no compromises; a sick man forcing himself to exist.
His survival in the Gulag seemed precarious.

Barbara Nikolaevna, the evening's organizer, asked for our
attention while she made an announcement: "Last week I asked
our NKVD boss, Lieutenant Shishkin, for permission to have this
social gathering. I took the liberty of inviting him to take part in
this evening of baked potatoes and song. Guess how he replied:
'No thank you, I'm very busy. Besides, I doubt you love me so
much that you crave my presence. On the other hand, if this
invitation is to make sure that you're not accused of having any
political agenda there, don't worry. Out of the twenty guests

invited, eighteen are informers working for us.' Dear friends, I hope this won't spoil our good time this evening."

There was a long pause. Then, a soprano voice of superb purity and strength broke the silence with a song about a great love that happens only once in a lifetime, a love mixed with special pain of intense emotion.

Great feelings are best conveyed through music. Collective states of the soul shared by most sensitive people, heroic, conquering, and of inner rebellion, are assimilated by outstanding compositions from the genius who has the urgent need to express them. Then the God-given gift allows them to present the whole truth with a disciplined sensitivity in the framework of harmony and elegance. Such creativity results in immortal works that join the souls of all human beings and enable them to achieve the supreme heights of the human spirit.

On the other hand, emotions of an intimate nature, of personal suffering, of crying souls, require a special sensitivity to express them. The Russian people have a gift for expressing these feelings and do so most ingeniously in the Russian romances, of which this song was one. The singer was Ludmila Ivanovna, presently a nurse's aide and previously a soprano in the Leningrad Opera. Her voice was accompanied by the melancholy sounds of Vasili Ivanovitch's guitar. We were still absorbing the beauty of the song when Bulgakov began another, *Jamshtchik poganiaj loshadei* ("Coachman, speed up the horses"), the story of a coachman who falls hopelessly in love with his master's wife. While driving his master somewhere in a blizzard, he urges the horses to run faster and faster in a futile attempt to relieve his pain. The profound sadness of his hopeless infatuation was eloquently expressed in Vasili Ivanovitch's baritone.

Many beautiful romances followed, romances of longing that displayed the loving nature of the Russian people in their vast land full of rivers, lakes, endless fields, and steppes. The evening left us all with a warm feeling. I wanted to share something with someone; I didn't want to be alone or go to sleep. Once again, Anna Antonovna read my mind.

"Igor Morovitch, you're not going to bed yet." Her voice was so captivating that even if I had wanted to be alone, I would have found it hard to resist her. "Now it is time to be with someone else. Come and have coffee with me. I've got some goodies from

home." Of all the people I would have liked to be with at that
time, Anna was the first.

The moon penetrated the darkness of her room, drawing amaz-
ing shapes on the wall. The atmosphere between us was one of
tension and sweet expectation. For a moment we were motionless,
as if trying to verify what we had both understood from our first
encounter. When they came, her kisses burst like oxygen bubbles
in my impatient blood. Slowly, she freed me of my clothes. My
skin enjoyed the freedom; all my senses hungered for contact. I
felt her embracing me. As one we fell onto the bed, she pulling
me down on top of her. Firmly holding her legs together, her lips
caressed my face, begging for an interlude of exploration as she
moved her breasts and thighs from side to side. Her hands wandered slowly, exploring the geography of my body and sealing in
her memory the areas of differing sensitivity. When finally I left,
I took with me the feel of her arms and legs, holding me firmly.

The next morning brought a visit from Dr Vala Romanovna Leshkevitch, assistant to Mikhail Osipovitch, Stupino's medical chief.
An obese woman in her early fifties, she looked like someone you
had to watch out for and keep away from, especially in this place.
She had been a good friend of Dr Deminski and very close to our
laboratory head, Anton Biernacki. Their trio had been broken
when Deminski left, and, as I later found out, Dr Leshkevitch
blamed me for the transfer of her buddy. Good relations, let alone
a friendship, seemed out of the question with her, and I knew I
would have to be businesslike and cautious.

"Good morning, Igor Morovitch. I see you are already well established in your new place. I wish you success in your position."

"Thank you. What brings you to Stupino so early in the
morning?"

"I have a very important matter to discuss with you, Igor
Morovitch. I'm sure you are aware of the large numbers of people
we are losing because they can't digest their food and have constant diarrhoea until they die. We must do something about this.
I have sent a letter to headquarters asking for some sugar. The
patients can't eat, but we can certainly sterilize the solution and
inject it intravenously. This way we can keep them nourished so
that the diarrhoea stops and they can eat again. Today we received

a shipment of three hundred pounds. It will last for quite a while, even if we put them all on the intravenous sugar drip for a long time."

I was surprised at her ignorance of basic medical data. Her proposal was dangerous.

"Vala Romanovna, it's not that easy. First of all, this is not glucose but a complex sugar that isn't absorbed as well as simple sugar. More importantly, before intravenous use, glucose has to be chemically treated to remove pyrogen bodies that can cause shock when injected."

"I don't want any excuses, Igor Morovitch. This is an order."

"I'm sorry, Vala Romanovna," I insisted, "but I flatly refuse to obey it. I don't accept orders to kill people, even from the most important person in the land. If you would like me to repeat this in the presence of witnesses, please invite them."

"In that case," she retorted angrily, "I will have to do it myself. We'll settle our accounts later."

Without further discussion, I ran straight to the home of Nikolai Andrevitch Denisov, the Stupino administrator. He was in my debt, not only because of the matter of the rape but also because, with the help of my fellow prisoners the storekeeper and the accountant, I sometimes augmented Denisov's meagre family food rations with a few extra bags of flour from the store or alcohol from the pharmacy. In this way I was assured of his goodwill.

"Nikolai Andrevitch, I need your phone," I began. "I have to make a couple of calls to different people in our section, and maybe a call to Sossva."

"Go ahead," he said, without hesitation.

"No, you will have to connect me with them. First with Varnadze, then, if necessary, with Iakov Mironovitch and Kuragin in Sossva."

"I see, you're reaching high up the system. But you know best, so I'll do what you tell me." Varnadze was away. I reached Iakov Mironovitch, who didn't know anything about medicine. However, he said that if Vala Romanovna's intentions could result in death, it would be better to report the matter directly to an NKVD officer. Officially I should have called Mikhail Osipovitch Varnadze or, in his absence, Lieutenant Shishkin, who looked after Stupino. But I decided to call Kuragin since I knew him so well.

Denisov turned pale at the thought of phoning Kuragin but got him anyway, and said in an uncertain voice that I wanted to talk to him.

"Good morning, *Grazhdanin Natchalnik* [Citizen Chief]," I began. "Sorry to bother you, but this is important." I told Kuragin all about Vala Romanovna's proposed treatment and the fact that I had refused to obey her orders.

"Why are you calling so late, and only now when you have a problem? I expected to hear from you within the first few days of your transfer to Stupino. How are you doing there?" With some impatience I told him that all was well, except for Vala's brain-wave.

"Everybody misses you here in Sossva. I'll probably come visit within the next few weeks. We're very busy here. About this matter: since Varnadze is away, I'll call Shishkin and tell him to settle the whole misunderstanding. I have to handle it with caution because Vala is a member of the Party. Don't worry, I'll be coming soon. In the meantime, all the best." Denisov couldn't believe that I had spoken to the dreaded Kuragin like a good friend.

When I returned home, Vala Romanovna was gone. Anna came in with some coffee and cookies from Tchechladze. I told her about my meeting with Vala Romanovna and the order that I had refused to obey. "She is a dangerous and unpleasant person," Anna warned me. "We all suffer because of her; everybody is afraid of her, even Varnadze." She embraced me. "I am so sorry that our beautiful flower blooms in this swamp of human suffering. Nevertheless, it is lovely." She kissed me gently and left.

The next morning, Dr Petrenko called me to see some very sick patients among those suffering from malnutrition and diarrhoea. I encountered a hellish scene. The pale, emaciated, severely ill people were shaking in their beds as if they had suffered a brutal attack of malaria. They were all unconscious, their pupils dilated and oblivious to light. Their bodies were cold to the touch, but they were running fevers of approximately 105 degrees Fahrenheit. Their pulses were in the range of a hundred to a hundred and ten beats per minute. Petrenko said, "Igor Morovitch, I believe this is a reaction to the intravenous sugar solution that I gave the patients according to Vala Romanovna's orders. I got the sterilized fluids from the pharmacy just this morning."

"Dr Petrenko, these patients are in shock. They won't survive; it's too late to do anything now with the means we have at our disposal."

When Lieutenant Shishkin arrived early that afternoon with the message from Sossva to stop the injections, it was already too late. Shiskin's right cheek and nose were pulled to the right side of the face, a deformity resulting from Bell's paralysis of his left facial nerve. The deformity interfered with his speech, making him gasp for breath as he spoke. When I told him what had happened, he said, "I guess now you'll be very busy. I wanted to talk to you about a few things, but I'll see you the next time I come to Stupino."

Early next morning I was awakened by Dr Petrenko, who looked very frightened. Eight of the injected patients had died during the night and two were in a coma. I was angry. "Did you expect anything else, Sergei Pavlovitch? Did you honestly believe that you would save their lives? You weren't there when I refused to obey Vala Romanovna's orders, so you couldn't have known of my opinion. But if you were aware of the danger, you yourself should have taken a stand." There was no way of knowing whether he had administered the injections out of fear or merely out of ignorance. I decided to give him the benefit of the doubt. "Don't worry," I said. "Nothing will happen to you for obeying the orders of your superior, a free doctor and Party member. Yesterday I called Sossva. An order was given to stop this sugar injection, but it was too late; you had already done it. Perhaps I'm morally responsible since I didn't warn you to wait until we had an answer from headquarters, but I didn't know Vala Romanovna would give the order to you. I know those patients might have died of their diseases within a month, but it's just not acceptable to me, as a doctor, to hasten their demise when we are taught to relieve pain and reinstate health." With bitter sarcasm I added, "Just start their autopsies and write down the usual cause of death: insufficiency of the heart muscle."

Later that morning while I was having breakfast, Mikhail Osipovitch Varnadze stepped into my room. He had heard the news about the injections. "Next time I go anywhere, I will leave my address so you know where to contact me. You did very well in informing headquarters. I didn't know that the big boss of the NKVD was such a good friend of yours."

Suddenly Anna Antonovna burst in, announcing that Major Efimov's wife was on her way to us. She had apparently been sick for the last two days, suffering from severe cramps and running a temperature of 102° (39.2° C).

"We have become the central hospital," remarked Mikhail Osipovitch. "Stupino has never received any patients from Sossva; now, even the top brass is using our facilities. Why didn't they ask Dr Deminski? He was right there and he's a competent surgeon. It's Kuragin's influence. He probably told Efimov, 'Igor Morovitch saved my wife's life, so don't use anyone else.'"

"I don't think I can operate in the dark," I said, "certainly not on the wife of the second in command to the NKVD boss. They took back the generator. Before I came to Stupino, emergency operations at night were performed with lighting from a kerosene lamp. Nobody cared because all the patients were prisoners. Now that we have become a regular hospital for free civilians, somebody has to look after our facilities."

"I'll get the generator back right now," he assured me, rising to go to the phone. "How long will it take to fix it? Have the people ready."

When the patient arrived three hours later, Denisov came to tell me that the locomobile (a steam engine that can drive an electric generator) had also arrived. Sasha, an electrician, and some other people were assembling the generator, which would be ready in about an hour. I excused myself and followed Anna Antonovna to the room in which we prepared the patients.

Catherina Stepanovna was in her mid-forties, slightly obese, with fair skin and a kind pleasant face. Her cheeks were reddened from fever, and drops of perspiration were visible on her forehead.

"*Zdrastwuite*. I know your husband. He once asked me to examine him for his headaches. How is he doing now?"

"Oh, he's much better. Your advice was very helpful." Upon examination, I could see that the patient's belly was distended. There was a scar on her stomach from a previous procedure for the removal of her left ovary. The left part of her abdomen was very tender; her bowel sounds were loud and metallic in character. This was a typical case of mechanical bowel obstruction.

We gave her two bottles of intravenous drip for her dehydration. Then, after Dr Petrenko had put her under anaesthetic, we opened her belly and noticed a very distended small-intestine

loop caught in an adhesion, most likely from the previous operation. The loop was gangrenous and would have to be removed.
We cut it out and anastomosed (reconnected) the small bowel.
After the procedure was completed, I asked Anna Antonovna to
stay with the patient for the night so she could watch the intravenous fluid running. The second night, Laryssa or Barbara
would replace Anna.

The short late December day had passed by imperceptibly, and
when I left the operating room it was already pitch dark. I went
to Denisov's home and called Major Efimov in Sossva, informing
him of the procedure and telling him his wife was in good condition. He thanked me. "Colonel Kuragin was right to recommend
you. I wanted to take my wife to Swerdlowsk, but he asked why
I needed to look for someone untried and untested when there
was already someone proven to be competent closer to home.
Anyhow, I should be there in about five days to take her back to
Sossva." He sounded much friendlier than when he had tried to
enlist my services as a spy.

"From what I can see, Igor Morovitch, they should let you go
free," remarked Denisov naively when I had finished my conversation with Major Efimov. "There is no reason to keep you here
as a prisoner when you are so respected by the powerful people
in the Sevurallag."

"It's nice of you to say so, Nikolai Andrevitch, but either you're
naive, or you've forgotten about the reality in which we live." I
took my leave.

On the way back to my room, Anna Antonovna invited me for
a cup of coffee. "I wonder what is happening on the front," I said
as we sat sipping Anna's good coffee. "I noticed that in the kitchen
Tchechladze has some *swinnaia tushonka* (pork stew) in a large can
made in the US. This means that they are our allies, and maybe
there is already a second front. We don't know yet what has
happened at Stalingrad. When will this war end? If neither side
wins, there will be chaos everywhere and no means of communication. How will we ever get back home?"

"That's strange," said Anna. "I was thinking the same thing,
and have already made a plan. We could easily get a horse and
buggy and load it with instruments, sanitary materials, and medication. We could take Shevelov as well as some nurses with us
and slowly move west. We would provide medical assistance to

the farmers and general population in small places and, in return, get food and board. I've even started to prepare some preserves in jars that can keep for a long time. It really is too bad that we are in the dark about what is happening in the world."

The idea of going away with Anna was appealing, but her contingency plan was not something we would try unless the Germans took over the area in which we were living. It wasn't something two prisoners would dare to try under the regime as it was. I was exhausted, physically and emotionally, from the strain of dealing with members of the top brass and from the uncertainty of my life. I reminded Anna to look after the special patient, then excused myself and went to my room to get some rest.

I woke up to a clear winter morning. The icicles had melted on my windows, creating bizarre patterns. I felt rested, much better after the tension of the day before. I went to see Catherina Stepanovna and found that she was doing well. According to Anna, she had spent a quiet night. I told her that in two to three days, she would feel some discomfort as the bowels recovered and started to move. When I left Catherina's room, Sasha told me that Lieutenant Shishkin wanted to see me in the administration office.

"*Zdrastwuite*, Igor Morovitch. It seems you have made yourself known all over the Sevurallag by operating on my boss's wife. They must have a lot of confidence in you, sending her to Stupino instead of leaving her with Dr Deminski in Sossva, or transporting her to the university clinic in Swerdlowsk." Without commenting I took a chair at his desk.

"For quite a while I've wanted to talk to you about something of great importance," he continued. "As you may know, our mother country is engaged in a terrible war with the German aggressors and requires every assistance at home in fighting our internal enemies —"

"Yes, yes," I interrupted him, watching his surprise. "I know what you want. Some time ago, I was approached by Major Efimov, who asked me to do the same, but I explained to him that it was impossible. Since it is privileged information, I shouldn't repeat it; you'll have to ask Major Efimov about it when you're in Sossva." This reply sounded extremely secretive, just what the NKVD loved. Shishkin immediately changed the subject and asked how the new patient was doing. He tried to act as though he weren't upset by the unexpected turn in the conversation and his failure to recruit an important spy. His expression, however, betrayed great disappointment. He asked me to stay so he could show me something. I wasn't sure whether he wanted to display his power over other areas, or whether he just wished to punish me in some way for exerting my independence.

"I think you'd find it interesting to see what happens to those who try to escape from the Sevurallag. I got a phone call telling me that four people have been caught trying to escape from Stupino; they'll be brought here shortly."

I rose, asking him to let me to go and make my rounds of the sick. I promised to be back soon. I ran into Sasha in the barrack where the injected people had died the day before and asked him right away if he knew anything about an escape attempt. Checking to make sure nobody was listening, he said, "I've known for a long time. It was four of the *bezkonvoine*. They were supposed to bring supplies from Verchoturie to Stupino. They were planning to escape. I told them it was crazy to try it in the cold of winter where every step could be traced in the snow. I tried to make them see that they were the least confined of all the inmates, that they could move around freely. And they were always doing some business, smuggling stolen goods in small amounts. They should have been the last prisoners to run. Obviously, they didn't listen. I didn't want to tell you; I didn't want anyone to think that you were involved in helping them in any way. I knew that they were going to certain death. If they are kept alive, there will be a serious investigation to find out who else was involved." As he spoke I saw the inmates coming in from work. They were placed in rows at the front of the administration building; it was going to be a public show. We stepped out of the barrack, and I went back to Shishkin.

Half an hour later, six NKVD soldiers with rifles came through the gate, pulling a cart laden with bodies. The bodies were dumped in the middle of the yard on the snow, facing the gathering of prisoners so that their faces were visible. The first thing that struck me was that the cadavers were awfully short. Then I saw why: their legs had been cut off above the knees. What was the reason for this mutilation? Was it because they were too tall to fit into the cart, or was it to illustrate the folly of trying to escape the Gulag?

I was appalled. Were we really living in the twentieth century? Was this really the people who gave the world Pushkin, Tolstoy, Dostoyevsky, Chekhov, Tchaikovski, Mussorgski, and so many others? Is this what Lenin had in mind, or was it just Stalin, the Great Father? I tried hard not to betray my emotions; I didn't want anyone to see my state of inner mutiny. Shishkin stepped forward.

"To all prisoners gathered here today," he announced in a thunderous voice, "this is the end that awaits those who try to escape from the Sevurallag. We are patient with you. We give you clothing and food in exchange for the work that you do for your socialist fatherland. When you complete your sentences, you will go home. There is no other way. We can always break you if you oppose the will of the people of our Soviet homeland."

The corpses were taken to the mortuary – the busiest place in Stupino – where the autopsies were done. I accompanied Dr Petrenko to get a better look at the mutilated bodies. They had been shot from behind; each had about a dozen bullet holes in the back and some in the neck. The bullet entries were close to each other, and some were in a line, indicating that they had been killed by machine gun. Their legs had been cut off above the knees with an axe; the soft-tissue wounds had uneven scalloped edges, and small bone fragments were still stuck to their thigh bones.

"Listen, Sergei Pavlovitch," I said. "I don't want to perform an autopsy on these bodies, nor do I want to see your signature on the documents. How, for God's sake, can you put down that they died from a weakness of the heart muscle? How can you hide the bullet holes and the mutilations and still sleep at night? Let me see what I can do. In the meantime, we do nothing." By then the prisoners had gone back to work and Shishkin had left. I went back to Denisov's home to use the phone. I called Mikhail Osipovitch Varnadze to tell him about the public show, asking what to do about the autopsies.

"Yesterday I got an order from Sossva to transfer Vala Romanovna to the headquarters in Swerdlowsk," he said. "I'm not sure what the reason is, but I do know that I won't miss her. I haven't told her yet. I'll advise her that, as a free employee of the NKVD and a Party member, it is important that she perform these autopsies personally. Since the documentation in these cases of escape has a special medicolegal importance, the job will be entrusted to her." Mikhail Osipovitch had been removed from the

Party and sent to work in the Sevurallag because he didn't want to conceal a mass murder by the NKVD and refused to perform a phoney autopsy. For him, it was a triumph to "entrust" such an important task to a devoted member of the Party. Once again, life had arranged itself in an unexpected way. I began to believe in the Russian proverb *Ne imiei sto rublei no imiei sto druziei* (Don't have a hundred rubles; have a hundred friends instead). In these precarious circumstances, the proverb proved especially true. Had Vala Romanovna been transferred by Kuragin because she was my enemy?

The next day, 31 December, began with heavy clouds hanging ominously above the white surface of the land. A violent snowstorm raged outside and the wind blew snowdrifts above the window sills. The stoves, loaded to capacity, could barely heat the large rooms of the barracks. Early in the afternoon, the wind finally subsided and the sky started to clear, allowing the inmates to go outside to remove the snow from the paths.

As prisoners in the Gulag our lives were such that our emotions could turn quickly from sorrow, pain, and sadness to tranquillity and even the prospect of joy. It was a way of surviving. Thus, I was able to forget the horrible events of the day before as Tchechladze came to ask what he should prepare for the New Year's Eve party, and what kinds of gifts we should send to the nurses. I asked him to contact Nurse Laryssa instead, as she was in charge of the preparations. Meanwhile, the hospital had assumed its normal routine. Major Efimov came to my room after a short visit with his wife. He was pleased that Catherina was in good condition, but he wanted to know the consequences of removing fifteen inches of her bowel. I told him that she would be perfectly well. He wondered how he could ever repay me for saving her. I said, "You don't owe me anything. There is a superior power, in which you are not allowed to believe, that rewards me. I work in my profession, and I have food and board. People are good to me and grateful, and I'm not afraid that I'll be arrested." I don't think he noticed the irony in my reply.

When Efimov left, it was time to prepare for the party. The small hall had been decorated with drawings and paper cut-outs. Thanks to the recently installed electrical lighting, the place was discreetly lit by two bulbs. The guests sat against the walls on small pillows or bundles of winter clothes. The air was pleasantly warm from the huge fireplace. In one corner a table was covered with food. The punch that was to be consumed at midnight was hidden somewhere about. When everyone had their seats, Laryssa got up and addressed the guests.

"This is the first time we've celebrated the coming of the New Year here in Stupino. Until now we felt too hopeless to do anything. We didn't realize that lifting our own spirits would give us new energy to resist adversity. But now we know that any bit of creativity in our daily routine can bring happiness and expectation. For this we have Igor Morovitch to thank. Look at what he has done in the last few years for the hospital, the patients, the personnel, and even several bosses in the NKVD administration. On behalf of everyone gathered here, I wish to express our sincerest thanks to Igor Morovitch for helping us find a new sense of meaning."

In the silence that followed her words, I rose to respond. "Dear friends, I thank Laryssa for her kind words. My work is an expression of my way of life. Under any circumstances, hopeless or hilarious, I never forget Providence, in whose grace I exist. Faith has always kept me going, even at the times when I have doubted that I would survive. Love, forgiveness, and prayer are the compasses directing my endeavours. I'm sure you know that I love you all. Without your help, it would have been impossible to accomplish all that we have. I never dreamed that you would work so diligently to fulfil our plans. For all your commitment and hard work, I thank you from the bottom of my heart. This evening is to honour us all. Now, let's greet the New Year and pray that it is the year of our release from bondage."

When I sat down the man on my left turned to me. Mikhail Petrovitch Koverdin was the chief of all military academies in the Soviet Union, which were under the direct command of Stalin, and a four-star general. He had an aristocratic manner.

"Igor Morovitch, I admire your determination and your modesty. It takes courage to praise the Almighty openly and advocate love and forgiveness. That is anti-Soviet propaganda. Aren't you afraid? I'm sure that here among us are a lot of people who wish they could tell the authorities about your speech." I knew something about Koverdin's background. During the *Otechesnaia Voina*, the war for the fatherland, he had been entrusted with the special operation of transferring all the armies from the Far East to the Western Front for the decisive offensive when the Allies were to establish the second front. During the complex operation, he disagreed with the boss over certain technicalities; as a result, he was arrested and sentenced to twenty years in the Gulag. At Stupino, he performed the duties of a *chleborez* (bread cutter), an enviable profession. A *chleborez* never went hungry; when cutting the bread for a few hundred people he could always contrive to have enough "leftovers" to barter.

"Michail Petrovitch," I said, "I don't behave any differently here than when I'm with the NKVD bosses. That is my philosophy, and I believe in it. They know how I am. I can't change all of a sudden, or pretend that I've embraced atheism. That would accomplish nothing."

Koverdin looked at me for a while. "You're right. At least you're true to yourself, and that gives you inner strength, a rare commodity today."

Then Barbara Nikolaevna called everyone to the table, where Laryssa served each guest with a plate of thick kasha and, to everybody's surprise, a thin slice of real roast meat, followed by hot tea and a *pirozhok*, a white roll with potato filling. After this unbelievable feast, we returned to our seats for the formal part of the evening, featuring music and songs.

Ludmila Ivanovna, a former opera coloratura, opened the show with the "Song of the Nightingale," accompanied on the violin. It was a story of lost love and heartbreaking memories of past bliss that would never return. On the high notes Ludmila's voice was indistinguishable from the violin. It was a beautiful performance. She was followed by a talented young lyrical tenor, Ivan Andreevitch, who treated us to the famous Russian romances written and composed by Viertynski. No words can convey the spirit, the longing, or the *Leidenshaft* (melancholy) of the tormented Russian soul lost in the wasteland of hopeless love.

It was close to midnight when Vasili Ivanovitch Bulgakov concluded the musical evening with the aria from "Boris Godunov." His rich baritone filled the hall with the powerful solemn notes of this mighty opus. I remembered his telling me a story once about being in the famous cathedral of St Petersburg. The mighty walls resonated with sound as Fiodor Shaliapin sang Ave Maria.

Outside on the streets, people listened in awe to the titanic bass of this unique maestro. Shaliapin had always been Vasili's idol, and as he told me the story he was close to tears.

At the end of the finale the old year was counted out as small glasses of punch were passed around. At a sign from Tchechladze, we all wished each other a happy New Year, not very loudly or convincingly, and raised our glasses hesitantly. People started to hug each other; then the hurt and the tears began to show.

Anna came over and embraced me as she wept. "I know, my dear," she said, "that tomorrow won't bring anything secure. I know that fate will separate us at some point and we won't be able to do anything about it. I love you very much. May this New Year allow us to be together as long as possible and give each other all that we can, so that when we part we will never forget each other." I returned her embrace but said nothing. The strongest feelings are often the most transient; their very strength lies in their brevity. For me to express such feelings in terms of eternity would not have rung true, though I felt as Anna did.

The guests started to leave the hall, deep in their own thoughts. Anna and I went out into the darkness, heading towards my quarters. The enchantment of the evening, the love it had built up, made everything seem new. Anna did not repeat her words but kept me in a constant state of ecstasy, until we fell asleep in each other's arms.

A New Year

The stars pierced through the grey dawn. A gentle wind was blowing and a slight haze like the thinnest silk enveloped the first day of the new year.

The sidewalks were clear as I put my head out to smell the air, trying to imagine what was in store for me this year. Outside there was total silence. I sat in my office longing for my home and my family, for a past that would never return. Although I doubted whether I'd ever see them again, I felt strangely that perhaps one or two of them were still alive. Maybe someday fate would let me see them.

Bulgakov the troubador interrupted my reverie. "Igor Morovitch, please excuse me, but all night I've been in pain, and now it's much worse."

"Why didn't you wake me? Come in, and we'll check you out." Upon examination, I could see that his belly was distended, and the upper right area of the liver was very tender. His bloodwork indicated a parasitical condition rather than an inflammatory process. It was a rare condition that he had had for quite some time – probably, without symptoms, since childhood, when he might have picked it up through contract with dogs. I suggested that he have an operation.

Three days later, when we opened up his belly, the left lobe of his liver was distended like a balloon, and through its thin paper-like surface I could see different-sized spheres full of liquid. I had been right about the diagnosis: he was infected with a parasite called echinococcus that is spread by dogs. We removed the left lobe of the liver very carefully so as not to spill any of the parasitical spheres and then closed up his belly. Within eight days, Bulgakov was released from the hospital in satisfactory condition.

A few days later, we admitted another patient with a rare and complex condition. Vania Fiodorovitch Kulikin, a forester from Verchoturje, had gone deep into the taiga one day with his ten-year-old boy. To his misfortune, he was confronted by a female grizzly bear with three young offspring. Defending her cubs, the frightened mother bear tore the rifle from Vania's hand, kicked him to the ground, and crushed him with all her weight. Vania's little son took aim with his light gun and frightened the bear away. The boy then rushed to the nearest phone and called for help.

It was clear that Vania was in shock. His left eyeball was missing and the right one hung from its optic nerve; both had been pulled out by the bear's claws. He had eight broken ribs and multiple wounds all over his head and body. I didn't believe that I could save him.

After giving him transfusions of blood from two of his friends (soldiers sent home as invalids who were type O donors), we started an operation that lasted almost eight hours. I cleaned and repaired both eye sockets, reconstructed his crushed bone palate, and stabilized his broken ribs by a traction of his breastbone up through a pulley over an installed frame above the bed. Dr Petrenko attended to the small lacerations after I left the operating room.

Two weeks later, six of Vania's friends, all good hunters, went deep into the taiga in search of the grizzly bear. They finally hunted her down and shot her. They sent us one of her paws, its claws the length of a large man's fingers, along with a piece of excellent bear sausage.

Vania improved very quickly and was discharged from the hospital within less than four weeks. Due to his blindness, the authorities asked Varnadze to keep him on at the hospital indefinitely. Vania retained his *joie de vivre*; he recognized all the hospital staff by their voices, and in nice weather he would sit at the entrance to his barrack, singing and playing the harmonica.

In late February it was still very cold. That year we had a rough winter. The snow, compacted by the driving winds, was hard enough to stand on. Two colours prevailed: the pale blue of the sky and the endless white of the land. We often saw the northern lights, which always reminded me of Misha. I missed him a lot.

One day Denisov told me that Colonel Dolochov had asked him to hold a reception for eight members of a commission coming from Moscow. "This meeting is very important to our boss," he explained. "The commission is going to assess the completion of the plan for the Sevurallag; a lot depends on the goodwill of these guys from Moscow. From my experience I can say that if you give them a good time and an excellent dinner, their opinion will be quite favourable."

I sent for Tchechladze, the cook, and told him to prepare a dinner for fifteen that would include the eight guests from Moscow and any others Dolochov might invite. Tchechladze pulled a piece of paper from his pocket. "Let me check my reserves in storage." He used to stockpile food, which he obtained in various ways. From the inmates who got parcels from Georgia and the Crimea he bought all kinds of wine, dried dates, figs, and raisins. Once in a while, he got sausage, caviar, and smoked beluga from them. He also obtained chickens, ducks, and geese from neighbouring farms in exchange for bread and flour, which were prized because of the shortages.

Before my arrival at Stupino, there had been nowhere to keep all these treasures. Then, while the barracks were being repaired and a new one built near the kitchen, we also erected a small log cabin that was ideal for storing food. It was protected against burglary by iron sheets obtained from disassembled machines in the sawmill. Inside there were various shelves and a wine storage, all according to Tchechladze's plans. The items were properly camouflaged by pharmacy products such as cotton bandages, bottles, empty cartons, etc. The room was not heated; the low winter temperatures acted as a deep freeze, preserving the food supplies for long periods.

After examining his inventory list, Tchechladze thought for a moment and then pronounced. "Since we haven't had any major events lately, we are pretty well supplied. I can offer the following menu for our guests: to start with, we can serve smoked beluga, smoked eel, caviar, hot *piroshki* made from French dough with mushrooms, a good French salad – my own recipe – and white rolls with fresh butter. Of course, the whole meal should be swimming in chilled vodka; Shevelov should take responsibility for that part. For the second course, I will serve arctic char in a lemon aspic, and for the main course we'll have baked goose and a baked piglet with a special sauce. I will serve the meal with white and red wine that I have saved over the last year. For dessert, we'll have *blinchiki* [crêpes] and assorted French pastries. I have most of the products. I'll have enough time to get a few fresh items from my farmers. I hope this menu is satisfactory."

I couldn't believe such things existed here. The juxtaposition of lavish abundance with meagre rations and starvation was difficult to grasp. While the inmates turned into animals, demoralized by hunger, cold, and humiliation, their oppressors enjoyed luxury even in the Gulag. And in Moscow, the killers at the top swam in champagne, comfort, and profligacy.

Which side was I on? Did I lick the bones they threw in my direction? Should I refuse to take part? If I did, I would end up like Grigori, the monk who still lay in the mountain of corpses, waiting for spring and eternal rest in a common grave. On the other hand, I could opt for survival and perhaps one day go back to my home. Why was I assuming the role of moralist? Self-sacrifice was mere stupidity. I shouldn't invite trouble; it would come by itself if it was meant to.

Tchechladze and Denisov waited for my opinion. "If all that food is possible," I said, "then we should more than satisfy Colonel Dolochov."

In the next few days I checked with Shevelov about the drinks. He assured me that he had enough alcohol to get everyone satisfactorily drunk. On 9 February, Tchechladze asked me to view his preparations before the reception. I could see why he had been head chef at the Kremlin. The table decorations outdid those at the best restaurants in Paris. The dinnerware was exquisite; I had no idea where Tchechladze had got it from. The huge arctic chars in their shimmering aspic were a masterpiece of culinary art, as were the well- browned ducks, geese, and piglets.

At exactly 7:00 P.M., the party of ten arrived. Laryssa, Barbara, and Sasha were serving, having been trained well in advance by Tchechladze. When at 12:30 the dinner was over, my Georgian accountant entered the hall and, on a fine plate, served the guest officers their bills for the meal. The charge was the same for everyone: two and a half rubles. You couldn't buy a match in Moscow for that amount of money. The purpose of billing was to prove that the guests had not been bribed. I regretted not having a camera; without photographs, who would ever believe that such things could happen in a prison compound in Northern Ural?

One morning in March 1948, I woke up early and looked out of the window. Nothing had changed; it was the same space, the same barracks, and the same fence with its four watchtowers. I had spent so many years in these surroundings that I didn't know if I would ever leave.

The severe Ural winter still reigned and temperatures dipped to about minus sixty degrees Fahrenheit. Breathing was difficult on such days. Outside you could not inhale straight into your mouth. The whole face had to be covered, except for the eyes. After some time outside, the lashes would be covered with icicles.

Mikhail Osipovitch Varnadze kept me up to date on the news. We were aware that the war had turned around in favour of the Allied powers. In the Soviet Union, the Red Army had forced the Germans to withdraw at the battle of Kursk. In mid-January 1944 the 890-day seige of Leningrad had been lifted, and by mid-July the Red Army had pushed deep into Poland. I knew of the Allied invasion of Normandy on 6 June 1944 and of the surrender of Germany in May 1945, followed by the bombing of Hiroshima and Nagasaki and the surrender of the Japanese.

So many had died. People my age and younger had perished. What about my family, my brothers and sisters and their children? Were some of them alive. If so, how had they been saved, and where had they gone? I told myself that I had been saved, here in this monotonous security, for reasons I couldn't know. I shouldn't complain and sin by being unhappy. Maybe this was the best that fate could offer me.

The days were filled with work, worry, uncertainty, and the fight for survival. Although we had enough food in caloric terms, we didn't have enough vegetables, and we had no fruit at all. Years had passed since my arrest, but I still had signs of alimentary dystrophy: my legs were swollen, and my tongue was still

not completely covered with mucosal lining. Anna had once
brought me a lemon from an inmate who received parcels from
Georgia. When I put a slice of it in my mouth, I experienced an
intense burning sensation as if I had put a hot iron on my tongue.
I gulped down a few glasses of water, but the burning lasted for
quite some time. It appeared that if I was ever to be able to eat
fruit, I would have to start with sweeter ones. I went without
vitamin C for years.

The days passed slowly, the years imperceptibly.

One day I was sitting with Mikhail Osipovitch in the pharmacy.
Located in the central part of the large barrack, it was the most
insulated and therefore the warmest place in Stupino. We were
discussing the huge number of frostbite cases in Stupino and the
ones that other compounds had sent us that winter. We must have
performed almost two hundred amputations of gangrenous toes,
whole feet, and even some parts of the lower leg. The patients
were already in poor condition with advanced malnutrition, and
more than three-quarters of them eventually died. There was
nothing we could do about it.

"Mikhail Osipovitch, you bring me all the news," I said. "The
war is over. Japan has capitulated and there is no more military
activity. They promised that I would be sent home as soon as
the war was over. It has been three years already, and nothing
is happening. The German prisoners of war were sent back last
summer. There were a few Polish citizens whom they separated
into other camps, and as I've found out, they were repatriated.
What about me? It looks hopeless. Do you think they consider
me a Soviet citizen just because they gave me this phoney
Soviet passport and converted eastern Poland into western
Ukraine?"

He looked at me steadily. "Dear Igor Morovitch, as I told you
before, you will stay with us until your sentence ends in February
1950. You have another two years to go. They will probably leave
you in the Sevurallag because they need you here. They will never
trust you – they have no confidence in their own citizens. The
whole state is driven by paranoia. Nobody trusts anyone. Conditions will improve in a few years; there will be more food; you
will be able to travel the way I do; and life won't be so bad. Just
don't make yourself miserable by believing what they promised.
They will never let you become a professor at a Soviet university.

With your Western ideals, you will influence the young students even if you try to be cautious.

"That's their way of doing business, that's what they've done with all of us: with me, with Resnik, and with all other *nieblago-nadiozhnye* [the untrustworthy]. It is easiest for them to keep you in the Sevurallag where they can watch your every move. Don't worry, you'll have a family here, and your life will be quite good."

Have a family here?

"I left my whole family in Poland," I told him. "I don't know what happened to them, or even if they're alive, but I have to find out. When I'm free, let's say in two years, they can't keep me separated from my brother and sisters and their children."

"So you think, my dear Igor Morovitch," he said sadly. "After all these years you still don't understand our reality."

There was a knot in my throat. I knew I was going to cry and didn't want anyone to see me. I jumped to my feet and started running. Outside it was awfully cold. Once again, the fury of the North Pole ridiculed my despair. My legs were drowning in the high snowdrifts, and I couldn't see a yard ahead of me. The snowstorm had been raging for two days. The paths could not be cleared; if we tried they would just be buried again within a few minutes. Nobody was outside.

I didn't care. For the first time, I didn't want to fight anymore. A thought went through my mind: why don't I stay outside? How long would it take to stop feeling? I didn't move. I tried to look at the sky through the snow that was driven into my eyes. It was almost completely dark; nothing could be seen. Holding my arms up, I was slowly becoming a snowdrift.

Suddenly, somebody caught my hand and pulled me strongly. I couldn't see anyone, but I heard a voice screaming into the wind: "What's going on? Are you hurt?"

I didn't know that Anna could be so strong. With enormous force she pulled me out of the snow heaping around me. Within minutes I found myself back in my room. Varnadze and Shevelov were there. They had run after me when I left the pharmacy. When they couldn't find me they went to Anna, who ran back and forth from my room to the pharmacy a few times, until she found me in the snowdrift.

"You just don't meditate in this weather. Sometimes you have to stay where you are and not try to go home when it's like this outside." Mikhail Osipovitch reprimanded me in a loud voice. Anna was sobbing, her face turned away. I felt like a child in the presence of loving parents.

"I feel cold and very strange. Get me a drink, please, something strong." I strove for self-control. The straight alcohol felt good. As I drank the room started to spin and I passed out. I woke up with a burning sensation in my feet; it came from the hot bottles Anna had put there.

"How are you? You gave us quite a scare, you know. But your pulse and blood pressure are all right. I told your friends to leave us alone; I said that I would look after you and call them if necessary. They are both in the pharmacy; Mikhail Osipovitch didn't go home. The weather is still terrible."

"Anna, please tell my friends in the pharmacy that everything is fine, and let them go home whenever the weather allows them to. You yourself can go to your room. I'm fine, and I'd like to be alone for a while." Anna looked at me pensively, put on a smile, and left.

I thought about my reaction to the hopeless future that Mikhail Osipovitch had outlined for me. But why should I believe him? He spoke out of bitter experience, thinking that everyone would be treated the way he had been. No, I wouldn't believe him. My life would be different. I knew it, I could feel it. My prayers would be answered. After this autotherapy, something changed within me. Hope returned. I was just tired of the monotony.

The blizzard had lost its fury and the heavy clouds had broken up, admitting light as they dispersed. The pines at the edge of the taiga were still. As I admired the view in this strange place, I saw someone running towards my quarters. As the figure approached I could see that it was Barbara Nikolaevna, the nurse, all bundled up so that only her eyes were visible. She knocked at my door, entered the room, and unbundled herself.

"It isn't that cold outside," she panted apologetically, "but I ran because I didn't want anyone to see me, and I wasn't sure if you'd be up yet – it's not an emergency and I didn't want to wake you. However, I am lucky that you are up. Perhaps I'm being overly cautious, but I've been burned so many times that I'm careful now. I try to avoid any dealings with people like my uncle; may he never see daylight again." Barbara paused to catch her breath before telling me why she had come.

"Laryssa's room is close to mine," she began. "We share a small space with a primus for heating things up or making tea. Anyway, throughout the last year, I noticed that whenever that ugly Shishkin comes to Stupino, Laryssa is usually called to go there, and she spends quite some time with him. I'm sure that people have already told you who the informer is in Stupino. Although Laryssa is a very nice person – and I've always felt that she was trustworthy – I'm completely lost now and I don't know what to think. I can't see why else she is always called at night. I'm scared because I don't remember all the things I've told her. You know my story. I always spit when I talk about my uncle, Beria. I'm afraid and I don't know what to do, so I've come to you. They'll send me to Kalyma. It's awful that your best friend can sell you out. Please help me if you can."

Barbara was really shaken up and I assured her that I would look into the matter. Although I liked Laryssa, I might be able to pull some strings and have her transferred. First, though, before the morning rounds, I asked Sasha to call Laryssa into my room. After greeting her, I looked into her eyes for a long while without saying a word.

Laryssa started to smile. I tried to look neutral but friendly, slowly adding an element of curiosity to my expression. It must have been trying for her. She gradually became serious, then tears formed in her eyes. We rarely think about how much we can tell one another without speaking. What frightened her was that I usually looked friendly and always smiled at her when we met.

"What is it?" She broke the oppressive silence. "What did I do wrong? You never look at me this way. Your knife isn't in your hand but in your eyes."

"What have you been doing all those nights with Shishkin in his office? I'd be very unhappy to hear that it's what some people think it is."

Laryssa's face turned crimson. Then after a silence she started to laugh uncontrollably. "I know what people think, but you are all so wrong. Listen, I can be many things, maybe even a whore, but I would never sell out innocent people. Not I. What right do you have to interrogate me as if you were one of them? You are not my father confessor, or an NKVD officer. What I did there with

Shishkin is my personal affair. No one will be harmed by his visits. Why are you subjecting me to this inquisition?"

"Listen, Laryssa," I said. "I love and respect you as a kind and decent human being. When I was told about your visits to Shiskin I could hardly believe it. I called you here to discuss the matter mainly for your sake, because I care for you and I want to protect you. Go back to your room and think it over and when you realize that I only want to help, come back and we'll talk."

Deep in thought, she didn't answer right away. Then, turning to leave, she said, "I know you're on my side."

She didn't go far. Within a few minutes she had returned. "This is so difficult," she began, "and my heart is heavy. I know I'll never find a better friend than you, so I'll tell you everything, although I'm afraid you'll think I have no character and that I'm not worth helping."

She told me her story. A year earlier, Shishkin had come to her room at midnight, smelling of alcohol, his eyes bloodshot. He grabbed her and threw her on the floor, forcing himself upon her. She fought back, hitting him with her fists, but he twisted her arms and started screaming that she was a whore and that he would send her to Kalyma or maybe somewhere even worse, where she would rot in starvation and die like a dog. He seized his gun and for a moment she thought he was going to shoot her, but instead, he struck her with it and she lost consciousness. When she came to she found herself stained with blood and sperm and knew that he had raped her. He was sitting there smoking. She struggled to her feet and ran to the door, but he stopped her, saying, "From now on, no more fights, unless you want to perish in one of those lagers from which no one ever returns." For a year Shishkin had been visiting her from time to time, and she had given in to him.

"I didn't want you to think I was weak or that I had no self-respect," she said.

"I wish you'd come to me sooner," I said. "We can finish this bastard off for what he is doing. Next time, tell him to go to hell. If anyone is going to rot in Kalyma, it'll be him."

Laryssa left my office looking relieved and determined. I went to Denisov right away and asked to use his phone privately. I called Kuragin and told him Laryssa's story exactly as she had described it. He made no comment. He merely asked me to have

Denisov call him as soon as he had finished with me. Then he excused himself, saying that he would be coming to Stupino very soon and that he had a lot to tell me. Before I left, I told Denisov to call Kuragin immediately.

Several days passed. Late one evening when I was working on some papers for Varnadze, Laryssa knocked at my door and entered with a smile on her face. "Listen, Igor Morovitch. Shishkin came in late tonight and called me. I made him wait until I had prepared myself." She lifted her skirt up to her neck. "You see? My stockings are sewn to my panties, and the panties to my shirt, and the neck of the shirt is closed by a heavy pullstring suture. I just wanted to show you that nothing happened tonight. When he asked me to lie down on the floor as usual, I refused and told him that never again would he force me to do anything like that. I told him exactly what you, Igor Morovitch, advised me to say. He was shocked, screaming at me to leave the room, saying he would send me to a place I'd never get out of alive. But still, I walked out of there smiling."

I congratulated her but warned that she must never tell anyone about the incident or about our conversations.

Next morning, Sasha came into my room with breakfast and told me that a shipment of Japanese and Chinese prisoners had come to Stupino. Dr Petrenko had been told to examine them and wanted my opinion.

"Igor Morovitch, I have to write case histories for each of the eighty inmates; most of them are Japanese and a few are Chinese. They're from Manchuria, where they were arrested before being sent here. There are a few Japanese officers whom I'd like you to see. Their complaints indicate that there may be some surgical problems."

While I was examining the Manchurian inmates, Mikhail Osipovitch came in, smiling. He told me that Denisov had been called to Sossva with Shishkin. Denisov had asked him to look after affairs in Stupino during his absence. "It's strange to see those two together. They've never liked each other. Denisov looked quite relaxed, but Shishkin was in a sombre mood. Something unusual has definitely happened, but we'll probably never find out what."

I didn't say anything, but I felt sure that Kuragin's phone conversation with Denisov had something to do with this turn of events. Perhaps Shishkin was finally getting his just desserts. Meanwhile, Mikhail Osipovitch had something else on his mind.

"Let's go to the laboratory. Lately I've noticed that the results don't come in on time, and Biernacki complains that he doesn't have enough paper to record the results of the analyses. I really can't think why else he might want the paper, and he barely needs a quarter of a sheet for his results."

We found Biernacki bent over some papers on his desk. Since the affair of the intravenous murders and the departure of his protector Vala Romanovna, he had tended to remain shut up in his office. "*Zdrastwuite*, Anton Janovitch," said Mikhail Osipovitch. "I've come to find out why you don't have enough paper. What happened to your usual supply?"

"Lately the paper has been disappearing. Maybe someone is stealing it."

"Nobody is stealing it. Nobody is hungry for your paper; it's not bread. If you need to use the paper for other purposes, let the people to whom you're writing supply you with it; they have lots." The allusion to "people" was so obvious that I was surprised Mikhail Osipovitch had the audacity to accuse Biernacki, albeit by inference, of doing the dirty work of an informer. As if to confirm his suspicions, Biernacki made no reply and dropped the matter.

It was unpleasant to witness this confrontation. Although Biernacki seemed to be aware that people thought he was a spy, he showed no fear. Maybe he enjoyed the fact that other inmates were afraid of him. Then again, since no one would confide in him, his effectiveness as a spy was questionable.

Mikhail Osipovitch said nothing more but looked at Biernacki with an expression of disgust and loathing that made my blood run cold. When we left the laboratory, Mikhail Osipovitch was fuming. "What a scoundrel! To think I have had to live with this animal for so long and can't find a way to get rid of him. I'm allergic to these beasts, but what can I do?" He took a deep breath and began to calm down. "I understand, Igor Morovitch, that you held a reception here for the members of the commission from Moscow. I heard it was successful. In Sossva, I was told that the Sevurallag was the top performer in all of the Ural Gulag. You had better watch yourself. Our boss Colonel Dolochov may never allow you to leave here."

We went to my quarters and Sasha served us a lovely dinner, accompanied by a good Georgian wine that Mikhail Osipovitch had brought. Mikhail longed to be free of his degrading job and return to his old job at the university. As he spoke of these things Denisov came in, having returned from Sossva. Seeing Varnadze in my room, he turned to him.

"It's good that you're here. I have to inform you both that Shishkin did not return; he was sent to the Special Personnel Department of the NKVD headquarters in Moscow. Colonel Kuragin asked me to inform you that he will not be returning to his usual duties in Stupino and that somebody will be sent here to replace him. In the meantime, we will look after the hospital."

I sensed that Denisov knew more than he had let on, and I also strongly suspected that Shishkin's transfer was connected to Laryssa's case. The only thing I didn't understand was Denisov's role as a NKVD officer, in the whole affair. However, I knew that he would later confide in me over a glass of vodka.

Among the inmates from Manchuria were two brothers, Fiodor and Jasha Kanilov. Both had been born in Charbin. Their father was Russian, their mother a mixture of Russian and Chinese. Before the war their father owned a large furniture factory, and they had been raised in an affluent environment. Both had become dentists at the University of Charbin. They seemed to be nice men. Fiodor had a gangrenous big toe on his right foot caused by frostbite; Jasha had an open infected fracture in one of his left forearm bones. We booked them both for surgery as soon as possible.

That evening I went to bed early, but for many hours I couldn't sleep. I was thinking about the Laryssa affair and how fast Kuragin was acting. I was intrigued by Denisov's role in this case. I decided not to tell Laryssa anything until I had all the details. As I lay there thinking, my wandering tongue found two large cavities on both my lower premolars. I understood then why I experienced sensitivity whenever I drank very cold water.

Suddenly, I had a great idea. We badly needed a dental facility in Stupino, where inmates were often released from work because of toothaches. Perhaps the administration would help. I put my suggestion to Vernadze the next day. He agreed and later that afternoon when I met with Denisov I repeated the idea, as a prelude to my greater concern – finding out whether Shishkin would ever be back to bother Laryssa again. When Denisov had had a few drinks I broached the subject. "I was the first to know of the Shishkin business and reported it," I said. "I know you took action, but Laryssa still lives in fear of the consequences of her disclosure."

Denisov told me that he had been terrified when Kuragin asked for him on the phone. "He rarely talks to me," he said, "and I've never before helped incriminate an NKVD officer. I told him I could eavesdrop from the storage room and see what was really going on between Shishkin and Laryssa, and I did, and reported that he had indeed been forcing himself upon her. Kuragin had me accompany Shishkin to Sossva, thinking up a pretext so that Shishkin wouldn't be suspicious."

I admired the way Kuragin had handled the case and was glad we could tell Laryssa that Shishkin was definitely gone. That evening, I told Barbara that she could trust Laryssa completely. But Barbara had other news for me: Anna was sick.

I had noticed that Anna wasn't at work but had been too busy to look into it. I went to her room, where I found her resting and looking very pale. She produced a tiny smile when she saw me.

"Sit down, Igor. I need to share something with you. I hate to burden you with this problem, but I feel you ought to know. I became pregnant for the first time in my life. At first I was very happy to be having your child, but after a few days I seriously began to question whether, under the circumstances and due to the insecurity of our situation, we had the right to have this baby. I wouldn't want to give the baby away to this horrible children's home. Do we know what tomorrow brings? It didn't take me long to see the foolishness of trying to go against the odds. I decided to end the pregnancy. Forgive me for not consulting you. I knew that you had the right to take part in that decision, but I wanted to spare you."

Her beautiful face showed her deep need for my acceptance of what she had done and my trust that she had done what was best for us. Not for a moment did I question her wisdom. She had acted in the way that she felt was right, in defence of something sacred in her mind and heart. She didn't want to contaminate her motherhood with a tough compromise.

"You know, Igor," she said, "if the Almighty has a future in store for us, then he will keep us together; if not, we won't question His will. We will just have to thank Him for the great gift of love that He has given us, and be content to live with our memories." I wept as Anna spoke. She kissed away my tears with the utmost subtlety. A perfect silence ensued.

It was quite dark when I returned to my room. I told Sasha that I wanted to be left alone for the rest of the evening. He put the cot before my door and slept there so that nobody could disturb me.

At around noon Denisov came into my office saying that Varnadze had called from one of the compounds of Borovka, about twelve miles north of Stupino. There was an emergency: Grigori Andreevitch Kotarin, the commandant of the lager, was very ill and in no condition to travel. His wife had been promised that help would arrive from Stupino as soon as possible.

Then Sasha came in with Lee Po, the Chinese man who had built the greenhouse. He had brought me two baskets of vegetables – tomatoes, cucumbers, radishes, and green onions. "These are the first ripe vegetables," he said. "There are a lot more, but it will take another few weeks for them to ripen, depending on how much sun we have." It was so good to look at the baskets. For such a long time we had had no fresh vegetables at this time of the year. I turned to Denisov.

"Nikolai Andrevitch, one basket is for you, and please try to deliver the other to Iakov Mironovitch with my compliments. Sasha and I will be on our way to Borovka. We should give the remainder of the vegetables that have ripened early to those patients who need them most. Perhaps it could be Barbara Nikolaevna's responsibility to distribute them, with your approval, of course."

It had been snowing since yesterday. The sky was dark and the air still. Visibility was poor when Sasha, Laryssa, and I set off in the northern direction of Borovka. Denisov had given us his beloved sleighs and three of his best horses. Sasha knew the road, which he had travelled many times before. Laryssa had prepared all the instruments and materials for anaesthesia and intravenous solutions.

We passed the tall pines at Stupino and then tried to follow the railroad. After a while, Sasha stopped to check that we were indeed following the tracks, digging them out with a shovel. When it got dark we stopped often to check the rails. It looked as though the horses were finding their way without difficulty, but Sasha would not rely on them and verified the presence of the rails again and again. We were completely covered with snow; from time to time, we would get up and shake off the thick layer from our heavy fur coats.

Time passed slowly. As we peered into the unrelieved darkness we felt an anxiety that was relieved only by the metallic sound of Sasha's shovel hitting the rails. Eventually even these audible markers lost their power to reassure. I took refuge in my authority, convincing the others of what I myself was not entirely certain. Stories from Tolstoy about people perishing in blizzards came back to me as I strove to impart courage.

"We're going in the right direction. It looks like we'll reach our destination soon."

"You're right, Igor Morovitch," replied Sasha. "Judging from my previous trips to Borovka, I'd say we should be there soon. The horses are in excellent shape, and it's not too cold." We drove on, listening to the swish of the sleighs on the soft snow. By the time we saw the lights of Borovka indifference had replaced our anxiety. Sasha stopped the horses about two hundred feet from the compound. He went out to determine how we would enter the gates and where the commandant's house was located.

The watchtower lights crawled over the fresh surface of the snow. One beam stopped before Sasha, and some distant voices could be heard. Shots from a machine gun punctured the silence and Sasha fell to the ground. Paralysed for a moment, I began shouting, but we were too far away to be heard. As I tried to leave the sleigh, Laryssa stepped out and blocked my path.

"Igor Morovitch, they will shoot you, those criminal bastards. We should never have let Sasha get out of the sleigh. Don't move. Stay in the sleigh and let the horses take us there. When people see the horses, they'll realize that the doctor has arrived."

She took the reins and drove forward, leaving me to follow her. When I arrived, a woman was waiting with some soldiers. It was Olga Nikitovna, the patient's wife. "I'm sorry about what happened. When Grigori is sick and there's nobody to help him, things happen ..." Without a word I ran to where Sasha lay. The snow around him was bloody and I could not find his pulse; he looked unconscious.

"Let me first attend to this; then we'll examine your husband." Two soldiers carried Sasha into a small room, faintly lit with a kerosene lamp. His coat was full of blood. He had no pulse. On his chest were six bullet wounds, all close to the heart and great vessels. Foamy blood bubbled from his mouth and nose as I pressed slightly on his chest. Without a doubt, he was suffering from massive bleeding around his heart and aorta, which were probably torn by the bullets. Even under the most favourable conditions, to attempt to open his chest and repair such massive damage would be futile. I remembered these traumas from the western front in my Red Army days. Sasha was dead. I tried to tell Laryssa, but I couldn't speak. We embraced tightly, and I hid my face in her shoulder to hide my tears. We remained like that for a long time. Finally I told Laryssa to make arrangements about Sasha, whom we would probably have to leave there, and went with Olga Nikitovna to their little house.

Kotarin was a lean man in his mid-forties whose ascetic appearance was accentuated by the loss of bodily fluids. His eyes were sunken and his skin was dry; his tongue was also dry and heavily coated. His pulse was quick and thin, and his belly was as firm as a board, very tender above the navel. It was a neglected case of a ruptured duodenal ulcer. The patient was feverish and at times incoherent as he answered my questions.

"Olga Nikitovna, your husband is very sick. I don't understand why he wasn't taken to Stupino the very first day, when he could still travel. The compresses that the old woman told me about are no help. We will put some fluids into him and see if he can be operated on tomorrow." Laryssa put the patient on an intravenous drip and gave him injections of prontosil, the first red-coloured penicillin that we'd got, every four hours. Olga Nikitovna accepted my prognosis with remarkable calm. It appeared that from the start she had wanted to bring her husband to Stupino, but Grigori didn't want to leave his post. They had lost two sons on the front; now she faced the possible death of her husband.

Tchechladze had prepared some food for the road. We asked for some *kipiatok* (hot water) and urged Olga Nikitovna to have some tea, a luxury she hadn't enjoyed for a long time in that wilderness.

Having no appetite, I refused supper, so Laryssa asked Olga to eat some of my food. We were put together in a little room in the Kotarins' house. From time to time, Laryssa would check on the patient, or give him an injection.

I didn't even try to sleep. I thought continually of Sasha, of saving his life, of his total devotion to me, something I had never before experienced. While he was alive, I hadn't realized the strength of my attachment to him. I would never have such a relationship again. Sasha's death was a great loss, and I mourned for a long, long time.

The next morning Kotarin was in much better shape, so we decided to operate. I told the local *feldsher* how to give the ether anaesthetic, and Laryssa assisted.

There was pus-like fluid in his belly, and on the front of the duodenum I saw the hole of the ruptured ulcer. We closed the opening in the bowel, patching it up with some tissue. After the procedure, the patient was in satisfactory condition. Shortly afterwards, I went to the administration office to arrange my departure and decide what to do with Sasha's body. I had already told Denisov over the phone what had happened. Arkadi, the *feldsher*, came into the office.

"Igor Morovitch, your nurse Laryssa told me how much Sasha meant to you. As you know, the soil is frozen now so we can't dig, but there are three graves outside the zone that Lieutenant Kotarin had already prepared. In the absence of the commandant, I went to see Olga Nikitovna and asked her permission to use one of the graves for Sasha. We will have everything ready in about an hour so you and Laryssa can see the grave."

When Olga Nikitovna came to the office I told her that Laryssa would stay in Borovka to look after her husband until he was ready to travel to Stupino. She would have all my instructions and the necessary medication and could contact me by phone if necessary. We then followed Olga Nikitovna outside the zone. Arkadi had already placed Sasha, along with his bloody coat, in the grave. The body was stiff. We watched in silence as Arkadi began to push the frozen soil into the grave. I was glad that Sasha wouldn't have to wait in the pile of corpses for the common grave at Stupino. It was my last gift to the man who had lived and died for me.

Back at the hospital life went on as usual. Denisov wanted to assign me a nice clean fellow to replace Sasha, but I refused. Once she had recovered, Anna Antonovna tried to do everything that Sasha had done. People were nice to me, giving me time to get over the loss and forget. Varnadze was unusually understanding and almost tender in the way he treated me.

Weeks passed monotonously until suddenly it was the end of June. It grew very warm under a brightening sun and a mild breeze helped to melt the snow. Summer had arrived. All the greys and bronzes turned to green. It was time to plant potatoes.

One day, Kuragin arrived unexpectedly in Stupino and made his way immediately to my quarters.

"Good to see you again, Igor Morovitch. I heard what a fantastic dinner you prepared for the commission from Moscow. Dolochov didn't tell me about it but I was glad that our guests were happy. They had a favourable opinion of us and suggested that the Sevurallag receive a commendation."

"It pleases me that we could be of help, and not only in the field of medicine," I replied.

"You know, Igor Morovitch," Kuragin resumed, "you are the only one who knows that I can be a good and affectionate friend. You understood it right away and somehow our relationship is free of suspicion. I know that I can trust you. Everyone else is afraid of me and that is the cause of my loneliness – no friends, and that's tough. By the way, here is the packet of anonymous letters I told you about from jealous people who resented you for being special. Many of these people were transferred to places where they won't find anybody to envy."

I was overwhelmed. I was glad to have been in Kuragin's good graces, able to do my job and to get some concessions, now and again, for those who worked for me. At the same time, I had agonized over my privileged status and was uncomfortable with the knowledge that he had gone beyond protecting me and despatched my enemies. He was a lonely man, likeable, but with a sinister side. When he came over and hugged me, I had such conflicting feelings that I could think of nothing to say. Kuragin spoke instead.

"We have no official order yet, but I know for sure that you soon will go home. It is common knowledge that political prisoners who are former Polish citizens are to be sent back to Poland; we will get the same order soon. It will be hard to forget you, but I am glad for your sake. Of course, they'll ask if you want to remain in our country and offer some high position commensurate with your knowledge and talent. You can stay in the Soviet Union, but I doubt if you will. You have family over there."

Kuragin looked at his watch and told me that he had things to do but would drop in afterwards to say goodbye. He hesitated for a moment, then looked at me. Coming close, he embraced me warmly, his eyes moist. Kuragin said: "You know, apart from my wife and children I have nobody. I am a very lonely man. Everybody is afraid of me, and I cannot open myself to others. You are the only one who broke through this loneliness, which was like a heavy armour enclosing my heart, and now I have you as a friend. And even when you are far from here I won't be lonely anymore." He took from his left hand a golden signet ring with a black agate stone and handed it to me. "This is the ring that my uncle gave to me. My father died young and my uncle took his place. He was my teacher and he brought me up. Please accept this ring as a token of my brotherly affection for you. Whenever you look at it you will remember me and I will feel it. Goodbye, my dear friend."

He turned and quickly left the room. I never saw him again.

Anna was trying to organize my time in such a way that I would not miss Sasha's presence. Among the recovering patients she found a nice fellow, Vanya, who was in his late twenties and very clean. Before his arrest he had been a schoolteacher in Estonia. He would bring my food from Tchechladze, take care of my quarters, and prepare the bath for me. Somehow the dreams of going home did not come to me anymore. I had accepted life the way it was, as the only life that was real and not imaginary.

Not long after my return from Borovka the equipment for the dental surgery arrived. A suitable place was selected and the two dentists began their practice. As one of their first patients, I was treated with special care. Jasha put some temporary material into my two cavities, suggesting that if gold rubles could be found he would make me wonderful fillings. After a couple of days, he told me that he had found what he needed. "When I mentioned to Tchechladze that I was looking for some gold rubles for your teeth, he asked me to wait and within a few minutes returned with six coins. I took only two, that's all we will need." A week later Jasha had put my fillings in. To this day, forty-five years later, I still have them, and they are admired by all the dentists I have visited in Canada and the US.

One morning early in July Denisov suddenly burst into my room. His face expressed the greatest joy. He pulled me out of bed, embraced me so that I could hardly breathe, and almost shouted: "Igor Morovitch, you are free, free, free! Do you understand? I just received an order from Sossva to prepare you for departure early tomorrow morning. You are going home, back to your home!"

I had been forewarned by Kuragin that this day would come, but now I was unable to comprehend the news. So soon? Tomorrow morning! How could I leave everything here? I wasn't ready. There was so little time to say goodbye, or to understand what goodbye meant; everyone around me was devoted and loving.

Suddenly I felt great anxiety. Once again, after a static and predictable life, I would face uncertainty. Despite the horrors of this place, my existence was secure, without real effort or struggle. But all unknowns create anxiety: did I feel I didn't deserve freedom? Had I lost the ability to stand on my own feet? I was not the one to decide or choose anything. A little bit longer here and I might have lost the ability to think creatively. The kindness of my friends and colleagues was a fetter that limited my courage.

Anna's voice interrupted my thoughts. "Igor, everyone already knows you are going home. I am happy for you, though I am unhappy for myself. It will be lonely without you. But even if I had the power to keep you here with me, I wouldn't. Your life belongs only to you." Not for the first time it was brought home to me how powerless I really was. During my years at the prison camp I had been in a special position because of my skills and had been able to make friends with my captors and secure certain improvements in the way the hospital was run. But I could do nothing for Anna, this woman whose background I knew nothing about, yet whom I loved. She was still a prisoner, and I couldn't change that.

"Anna, everything has happened so suddenly. I feel I can hardly speak. Everything will be empty without you." I clung to her for a long time until she turned suddenly and ran out of the room.

The mist began to lift, clearing patches in the blue sky. To the East the dawn greeted the world, announcing my freedom from bondage. Everything was prepared for me, my few personal belongings and some food from Tchechladze, his last service to me. Denisov came to take me to the train. Outside the barracks the hospital employees, nurses, and orderlies, auxiliary hospital personnel, and many of the patients – all had gathered to say farewell. Anna was with them. She did not want to be different or to show what everybody knew so well. As we walked past, people were crying "Igor Morovitch, *rodnoi otiec uiezhdzaiet*, Igor Morovitch, our own father, is leaving us."

A last embrace from Denisov, and I boarded the special wagon normally reserved for the bosses. The train started to move. Watching through the window, I cried as that ocean of human love disappeared.

Feast in the Wilderness

At Nizhny Tagil we were transferred to a train carrying many freed prisoners on their way to the West. All the privileges of my years in Stupino were gone. Once again I was a convict, treated the same as all the others – the same four hundred grams of horrible bread that contained everything but flour, a cup of *kipi-atok* (hot water), and in the evening a bluish salty hot water called soup.

I was very hungry until we reached Swerdlowsk. Then, as my stomach shrank, I got used to starvation. At various stations we would stop for long periods while wagons were changed or prisoners and soldiers brought aboard. Often we were transferred for a day or two to local prisons, crowded together in small cells. We slept on the cement floors, surrounded by the smell of tired bodies in dirty clothes.

At the station in Perm I fell ill with a bloody dysentery. Painful cramps accompanied by shivers from fever were followed by attacks of diarrhoea. In the prison in Perm I asked for medical help. I was taken to a small office where the woman doctor understood from my presentation of the symptoms that I was a colleague. She asked about my time in the Sevurallag.

"You really should be hospitalized. It is difficult to travel in your condition. On the other hand, you are on the way home and if I leave you here, who knows when you'll be attached to another transport? There are no individual papers for you. You go with all the others under a common order. We have no drugs here, nor food that would be helpful in your condition. Just have a look at what we can offer you." She took me to another cell; there on the floor were two patients, also with dysentery. Both looked moribund. After a moment of silence, she said, "Normally it would be my duty to take you off the train and keep you here. I'm forbidden to give you advice, but in your place I would take the risk and continue the journey. You have the same chance on the move as here on the cement. And you know as well as I do that hope is an important factor in recovering from illness."

I thanked her and asked if she would give me as much opium as she could spare. She hesitated but finally went to the little cabinet, took out a bottle of opium, and gave it to me. "Here you are. But be careful, there is less danger in losing some blood than in taking too much of this. You know it is poison."

Back on the train, I was very careful, taking only a few drops at a time when nobody was looking. After a day the urgency stopped and the diarrhoea abated, although I had difficulty getting up from the floor of the wagon. I was getting weaker and weaker; I knew I had to get some nourishing food; otherwise I would not reach the border alive.

The authorities knew that as free men we should get better food, but they didn't care. Formally, they had to stick to their agreement to send the released prisoners home. But apparently there were no rules about how we should be treated on our way to liberty. Whatever happened to us during this interim was just too bad.

They treated us like cattle. We were not placed in quarters for free citizens but in prisons like convicts. In the USSR and in the minds of the NKVD bosses, we were still criminals. But it was useless to think this way; I had to use some initiative to save my life. Supervising the last few wagons was a very nice young Russian soldier with whom I had talked about my home. I felt that I could trust him. I still had some money with me, including two gold coins given to me by Tchęchladze. That night the soldier came to inspect the sleeping inmates. He saw that I was awake but neither of us moved; we were waiting for something.

"Could you get some food for me? Otherwise I don't think I will make it much further."

He looked at me, and then looked around as I handed him a bunch of banknotes. Next morning he took me to a separate wagon used for NKVD guards. There on the bench was a jug of milk and a loaf of good bread. He returned whatever money he had not spent, saying: "You just eat slowly, as much as you can. I will bring you here to eat whenever I am alone."

In this way he fed me until we reached Kazan. There the guards were changed and I never saw him again.

In Kazan, a cold winter sun set lazily at the edge of the horizon amid streaks of pale pink and green. There was no wind. The air was thick and frosty. The descending darkness in the eastern sky swallowed the day, bringing forgetfulness and tranquillity. The streets of Kazan lost their contours in the dusk. A vast column of prisoners in rows of six wound its way from the railway station to the "hotel," the old Iekaterine prison, for the night. All around the column, ten steps apart, guards with loaded submachine guns and Alsatian dogs surrounded the dark mass of tired dirty flesh. I was somewhere in the eighth row.

We were ordered to stop and fall on our right knees. From their superior height the guards found it easier to observe the prisoners. We were told that the guards would shoot without warning if we made any attempt to move. They began to count us.

The road was covered with ice and snow. After a while, I lost all sensation in my right knee as the skin froze solidly to the ground. When the counting was over we were ordered to our feet again. The will to endure had left us long ago; we no longer cared. Perhaps it would come today, perhaps tomorrow – the end often seemed so close and so desirable. After more than an hour of marching, we were driven through the gates of the dark prison building.

About a hundred of us were packed into a small cell. There was no room to lie down; we could only sit on the cement floor with our knees drawn up, supporting our heads as we fell into dreamless sleep. Waking was like a knife cutting into the sweetness of nonexistence, laying bare the shabby details of reality, the dirty, scratched walls, the miserable, foul-smelling prisoners.

We were ordered to undress one by one. Our rags were sent out for delousing while we were herded naked under cold showers.

When the scorched rags were returned to us, we were allowed to
clothe ourselves before being led off for physical examination. The
doctor was a young woman, one of the new generation. The
severe lines of her face were drawn with fatigue. Her expression
revealed determination, a life of discipline, and a will to survive.

When my turn came, her first question was: "Why is your hair
so long?" I explained that as a practising doctor in the labour
camp I was allowed the privilege of keeping my hair long. She
rapped out her reply: "It is against regulations. No special favours
will be granted. You must obey orders if you want to avoid
punishment." I said that threats were unnecessary as far as I was
concerned and that I did not intend to break any regulations.
"Then go to the barber right away," she said, with an edge to her
voice.

The barber's shop was located on the east side of the large
prison building. It was a small room containing two chairs, both
of them occupied. I waited. The barber was a tall, handsome
young man with the typical features of a Georgian. His long hair
was dark, almost midnight blue, and combed to the back. His eyes
were dark brown, deep set and penetrating. There was something
peculiar and inexpressible in his features. The faint hint of cruelty
in the face was belied by the eyes, which showed a determination
to survive. He too was a prisoner, serving his term in this capacity.
I moved into a chair vacated by the last customer and explained
the doctor's order.

"Who are you and what is your name?" His voice was low
pitched and firm. Before I had time to complete my brief account
he interrupted. "Don't you know you are on your way home? I
won't cut you hair."

"Please do it," I replied. "Why complicate my return and cause
yourself trouble?"

"Get lost before I lose my temper!" he shouted. "To hell with
your medical colleague. I know her, that bitch. Get lost."

Although I did not understand the barber's behaviour, I had no
choice but to return to my cell, hair uncut. The dim cell contrasted
with the frosty outside world, which looked so clean and innocent
in last night's powdery snow. I immediately recoiled from the
stagnant air and the stench of sticky, malodorous rags saturated
with sweat. Around me were the tired, pale, yellow grey faces of

my fellow prisoners waiting for their next meagre meal with sickening expectation.

Prisoners in transit are quite unlike those who are living out their sentences together in a prison cell. Friendships, feelings of solidarity, likes and dislikes, develop among this "family" in a life ordered by meals, outdoor walks, etc. It does not take long before various functions, privileges, and obligations are assumed by each prisoner. A routine evolves independent of orders from above. One prisoner becomes a storyteller, another cleans the cell, another distributes the rations of bread and *kipiatok* and soup, still another sets the schedule for use of the wooden barrels that serve as a toilet.

But prisoners in transit are a collection of strangers, each preoccupied with his own fate and with what the next day will bring. Communication is kept to the minimum, so quarrels rarely take place. Basically, the prison cell sleeps – everyone is lost in his own thoughts.

It was the second half of April, but the only sign of spring was the lengthening days. Late in the afternoons a fragile light still filtered into the cell through the narrow part of the barred window above the metal cover. After the evening's watery kasha and *kipiatok*, night came quickly. My head dropped onto my knees, weighted by the emotions of the long day. One night my sleep was interrupted by a voice screaming my name; the guard must have shouted several times before I realized that the doors had been opened with a squeak of rusty hinges.

My first thought was, why me? Was there something wrong with my papers? Would I somehow be prevented from returning home? Was there some other worse complication? I moved towards the voice; stumbling in the flickering light of two candles, trying to avoid the mass of the legs and arms. I followed the guard in silence. It was no use asking him what was going on: the guard is never told. He has his orders and must carry them out, no questions asked.

We walked down corridors that must have been underground since we had descended many flights of stairs to get to them. Here and there in the unending passageways a candle or lamp shed enough light to enable one to walk but not enough to discern any details of the cement walls or floor. After a while, the guard stopped at a half-opened door and told me to enter. I found myself in a sort of anteroom. There was no light.

The guard then knocked at another door and I was taken into a lighted room of moderate size. A bed stood in the far corner. On a small table shone a kerosene lamp. There were some hangers with clothes and a few shelves with books and household items. The walls were clean. Opposite the bed was a small barred basement window completely screened with metal.

A man stood in the middle of the room. He gave me time to recover from the anxiety of my summons, and then I recognized him. He was the barber who had refused to cut my hair. Now his eyes had a completely different look, a mixture of joy and empathy. After a moment, he said: "I am a Jew from Buchara. Tonight is the feast of Passover and the first seder night." He knew that I was Jewish. He told me that he spoke Hebrew but not Yiddish. Did I know the language? he asked. I answered in Hebrew, "Yes, fluently." He was glad to know that. He was sorry that it was so late, 11:30 at night, but he could not have arranged to get me out of the cell earlier. In a few short sentences, he told me all I needed to know about himself, about his life in prison, and how well he had managed to survive, how he made small business deals with the prison personnel and even with higher officials and guards, how they treated him as a confidante. He did not tell me why he had been imprisoned. He said it would be a great honour, pleasure, and "mitzva" (good deed) to have me as his guest for the seder; if his old father could see that his son was not reciting the "Hagadah," the Passover story, alone, he would be moved to tears.

He pushed open another door and we entered a smaller room, better lighted. A small stove with an iron top stood in the corner. On it were a few pots, and its pleasant warmth revived me. The greatest surprise was a table in the middle of the room, covered with a white cloth and set for two. On it were the traditional candles in two brass holders and a platter with traditional symbolic food such as matza, bitter herbs, haroset, or cut apples with nuts sweetened with honey, and peeled, hard-boiled eggs as a side dish. Beside each dish was the opened Hagada with a picture of the enslaved Jews in Egypt under which the first line read: "We have been slaves in the land of Pharaohs."

I wept. The traditional meal and reciting and singing of the Hagada lasted about three hours. There was no hurry; we surrendered ourselves completely to the spirit of the biblical events, to the mystical union with God, the comforting ties of the covenant with His chosen people and the never-failing conviction among believers in His might, mercy, and miracles. We were deeply moved by our joining together, two strangers in this holy night, two bodies in one heart, one soul.

The ceremonial supper was over. My host rose and advised me that the guard would soon come. He reached into his pocket, withdrew a heavy envelope, and handed it to me. "Here is some money; take it, you will need it." When I protested he said, "Don't hurt me by refusing. My joy in this mitzva would be not complete if you refused."

Supreme moments of elation are all too short. Their brevity is a part of the mystical impact preceding separation. But there is always something left, more than memory, something inexpressible, after a vivid experience. The "I and Thou" disappear but the newborn "It" remains with you forever, kindling in one's deepest awareness an eternal light like a ray of hope and faith in goodness.

The guard took me back to the cell. I crawled in the dark over half-asleep bodies to my spot on the cement floor. I closed my senses to the heavy breathing and stench, trying to forget my surroundings and retain for as long as I could the warmth and gratitude of the night I had passed. I prayed: "Thank you Almighty, for your everlasting might that fills the universe, thank you for your mercy towards the lost ones and the miracles of joy that you give them." Then I fell into a deep sleep, as sweet as the taste of the Georgian wine.

Epilogue

Early next morning we were taken to the railway station and herded onto cattle trucks. My hair was still long. The barber had been right: I hadn't seen the woman doctor again. The train stopped briefly in Moscow, then moved west, towards Poland. At Biala Podlaska, on the border, we received temporary identification cards, stating our return from the Soviet Union. Special committees were there to greet us.

Since Lwow was now the capital of Western Ukraine, annexed to the USSR, there was no way I could go there. Instead I went to Warsaw and then to Walbrzych, where I stayed for around six months. I made inquiries about my brother and sisters but nobody knew what had happened to them, only that none of them were on the list of survivors of the Holocaust.

Thirty-two family members – my brother, four of my sisters, and all their children – had been murdered by the Nazis in the concentration camps. I learned that my youngest sister and her boy had survived, having somehow procured Aryan documentation in Warsaw. A few months before my arrival in Poland they had emigrated to Canada.

When I learned of her survival, I tried to write a letter to my sister. It seemed an impossible task; I was paralysed by emotions of grief and joy. Finally, after four days of unsuccessful effort, I started with the following sentence: "I thank the Almighty who in His infinite mercy preserved each of us, so that we are not alone in this world." I did not see her until, two years later, I went to Canada.

While in Warsaw, I met a high-school friend, George Sawicki, who was then a law professor at Warsaw University and attorney general of Poland. He had represented the Polish government in the proceedings against the Nazi war criminals at Nuremberg. In a small café we embraced in tears, recalling the days of our youth and the horrors of war. Of all our schoolmates, we were the only survivors of the Holocaust.

George tried to convince me to stay in Poland. "Just select for yourself a chair of surgery at any university," he said, "and I will help you to become all that you can be, and all that you ought to have been." It was tempting. As I listened, though, I could not help but remember what another friend – a Mr Landes, a childhood friend of my father's – had told me since my return. "Only last week there was a pogrom in Kielce and many Jews were killed. The Nazi influence is still there. This is an anti-Semitic country, and it is soaked with our innocent blood. Don't add to it with your own. Go to Israel." The next day I went to the office of the Hagana, the armed forces of Israel, and told them, "I want to go to the land of my forefathers as soon as possible."

Two weeks later, travelling with a phoney Polish passport to Colombia and no visa, I left for Israel with 1,200 other volunteers. From Gdynia we sailed to Le Havre and from there travelled by train in sealed wagons to Marseilles. On 9 November, we left Marseilles for Haifa. The feeling on the boat was unique. Never before had I been in a large group of people of one mind, willing to fight and die for their freedom, the freedom of an ancient people whom God abandoned for a while, then forgave for their sins, and now led to the land of their forefathers.

A few hours before landing I convinced the French captain of the ship to give us a few sheets for a flag. When the Star of David was hauled up the mast I could not stop crying.

"Hear, O Israel, the Lord our God is the only One."

My sobs were drowned out by the "Hatikwa," the national anthem of the reborn Israel, as the coast of Haifa came into view in the afternoon sun.

Almost half a century has passed since I left the Soviet Union, now the Confederation of Independent States. After spending years in that vast and distant land that I had never really intended to visit, I cannot forget it: the endless landscape, the incredible beauty, the unforgettable sky with its northern lights, and the infinite taiga, where, in many places, no one had ever trod.

And above all, the people. Never before had I suffered for so long, been so cold, hungry, humiliated, and degraded as I was under the police regime of Stalin. Yet even the worst oppression could not destroy the profound humanity of the Russians. I have forgotten the cruelty, but I still carry the memory of their decency, goodness, and love like a gift from the inhabitants of that distant land. I left a major part of my heart there, and I will never be able to reclaim it.

The people, the language, the poetry and the music. Since that time I have travelled widely and been with many people. But nowhere have I met with so much kindness as in the snows of the Urals. Where are all these people whom I loved and who loved me? Could I meet them and see them, at least for a short while? Might they have changed? Or am I just longing for the years of my youth?

Years ago, it was impossible to get in touch with them. Just sending a letter might get the recipient into trouble in those dark days under Stalin. Now perhaps I could try; but would they still be alive?

I wrote this book because I wanted to show the evil of Stalin's regime in Russia and the longing of the people for the freedom to believe and worship as they saw fit.

But I also wanted to show the power of love, which can heal even in times of horror. At the apex of despair when suffering is at its most intense, when the only thing left is prayer, a miracle can happen and a way out can be found. Wounds heal, and you can become whole again, a little stronger and more human than before.